# A SEARCH IN SECRET EGYPT

# A SEARCH IN SECRET EGYPT

## DR. PAUL BRUNTON

SAMUEL WEISER, INC.

York Beach, Maine

First American paperback edition published in 1973 by
Samuel Weiser, Inc.
Box 612
York Beach, ME 03910-0612
www.weiserbooks.com

Revised edition published in 1977
Second Revised edition published in 1984

08 07 06 05 04 03 02 01 00 99
14 13 12 11 10 9 8 7 6 5

First American edition published in 1936
by E. P. Dutton & Co., Inc., New York

Library of Congress Catalog Card Number: 83-50399

ISBN 0-87728-603-5
MG

Cover photograph by Owen Franken/Stock, Boston
Reproduced by permission

Printed in the United States of America

The paper used in this publication meets the minimum requirements of the
American National Standard for Permanence of Paper for Printed Library
Materials Z39.48-1984.

## Dedication to
## His Highness Prince Ismail Daoud

*Three men drove out of Cairo one beautiful spring night and chatted for an hour near the Great Pyramid.   One of them was Your Highness, another was the Ambassador of a certain Oriental Power, while the third was the Scribe of these notes of travel and thought. Your Highness made the remark that it would be difficult to find in present-day Egypt any traces of the unusual spirituality or strange magic which lure me from land to land in their quest. On several other occasions you repeated the same opinion.*

*Despite that, I persisted with my search and found a few things which I deemed likely to interest the people of the West. If I offer them to your Highness also, it is because I venture to hope that you will glean from them a further glimpse of the faith that holds me, and perhaps understand a little better why I hold it. And I offer the dedication of this record, too, as an insignificant token of my pleasure in that personal regard which subsists, irrespective of intellectual differences, between us.*

*Finally, let these pages stand as a tribute to Egypt, the country whose modern face you know so well and whose ancient fanes attract me so much. If I may be permitted to revise the old Roman phrase, I should add: "He who has once drunk Nile water, must ever be a friend to those who dwell on that mighty river's banks."*

# A PERSONAL NOTE

Dr. Paul Brunton died July 27, 1981, in Vevey, Switzerland. Born in London in 1898, he authored thirteen books from *A Search in Secret India* published in 1935 to *The Spiritual Crisis of Man,* in 1952. Dr. Brunton is generally recognized as having introduced yoga and meditation to the West, and for presenting their philosophical background in non-technical language.

His mode of writing was to jot down paragraphs as inspiration occurred. Often these were penned on the backs of envelopes or along margins of newspapers as he strolled amid the flower gardens bordering Lac Leman. They later were typed and classified by subject. He then would edit and meld these paragraphs into a coherent narrative.

Paul Brunton had lived in Switzerland for twenty years. He liked the mild climate and majestic mountain scenery. Visitors and correspondence came from all over the world. He played an important role in the lives of many.

"P.B.", as he is known to his followers, was a gentle man. An aura of kindliness emanated from him. His scholarly learning was forged in the crucible of life. His spirituality shone forth like a beacon. But he discouraged attempts to form a cult around him: "You must find your own P.B. within yourselves," he used to say.

K T H

# Contents

7

# *Illustrations*

(*Between pages* 160–161)

SNAKE "ASLEEP" WITH MAGIC TALISMAN PLACED UPON ITS HEAD
"RA-MAK-HOTEP"—HIS EYES
ROCK-CUT ENTRANCE TO A TOMB
THE VALLEY OF THE TOMBS OF THE KINGS

IN THE TEXT

# CHAPTER I

THE last hungry tourist had gone; the last black-robed guide had repeated, for the thousandth time, his smattering of superficial lore for the benefit of alien visitors to his ancient land; and a group of tired donkeys and weary, snarling camels had hastened homewards with their last riders for the day.

The fall of dusk upon the Egyptian scene is an unforgettable event, an event of unearthly beauty. Everything is transformed in colour and the most vivid contrasts come into being between sky and earth.

I sat alone on the yielding yellow sand before the stately, regal figure of the crouching Sphinx, a little to one side, watching with fascinated eyes the wonderful play of ethereal colours which swiftly appear and as swiftly pass when the dying sun no longer covers Egypt with golden glory. For who can receive the sacred message which is given him by the beautiful, mysterious afterglow of an African sunset, without being taken into a temporary paradise? So long as men are not entirely coarse and spiritually dead, so long will they continue to love the Father of Life, the sun, which makes these things possible by its unique sorceries. They were not fools, those ancients, who revered Ra, the great light, and took it into their hearts as a god.

First it had rested low in the sky, magnificently flaming all heaven a glistening red, a red like that of glowing embers. Then the colouring toned down and a soft rosy coral flush spread across the horizon. Softer yet it became until, like a rainbow, a half-dozen different hues, from rose-pink to green and gold, made a fitful bid for life. Finally it moved to a greyish opalescence as twilight crept quickly over the scene. The breath-taking tints disappeared together with the great round dying light.

And against the opal background I saw the Sphinx begin to take on the colour of night; no longer did the last red rays shine vividly across its featureless face.

Out of the omnipresent sands it emerged, this giant face with recumbent body that inspires superstitious Bedouins with such fear that they name it "The Father of Terror," and sceptical travellers with such wonder that in every age its colossal figure has raised questions upon the lips of those who gapingly behold it for the first time. The mystery of this unnatural combination, this lion with a human head, has vaguely attracted an age-old procession of visitors. It is an enigma for the Egyptians themselves and a puzzle for the entire world. No one knows who carved it or when; the most expert Egyptologists can but guess blindly at its meaning and history.

In the final glimpse which the vanishing light permitted me to receive, my own eyes came to rest on the stone eyes of the Sphinx, which, still and quiet, had watched myriads come, one by one, to look at it questioningly, and then depart perplexed: which, unmoved, had seen the dark men of a now-lost world, the Atlanteans, engulfed under millions of tons of water: which, half-smiling, had witnessed Mena, the first of the Pharaohs, turn yonder Nile, Egypt's beloved river, from its course and force it to flow through a new bed: which, silently regretful, had seen the grave saturnine face of Moses bowed in a last farewell: which, mutely, sorrow-stricken, had viewed the sufferings of its ruined and ravaged land after fierce Cambyses burst over Egypt from Persia: which, charmed yet contemptuous, had seen the haughty, silken-tressed Cleopatra land from a vessel with gilded stern, purple sails and silver oars: which, delighted, had welcomed the young wandering Jesus as he sought the Eastern wisdom, preparing for the appointed hour of his public mission, when his Father would send him forth with a divine message of love and pity: which, secretly pleased, had blessed a brave, generous and learned young noble, one Saladin, so that he rode away, his crescent-inscribed, green-pennoned lance in the air, to become one day the Sultan of Egypt: which, warningly, had greeted Napoleon as an instrument of Europe's fate, that fate which would set his name so high as to eclipse all other names and then force him to stand with gloomy brow upon the smooth planks of the *Bellerophon:* which, slightly melancholy, had seen the attention of the whole world fixed upon its country when the tomb of one of its proud Pharaohs was opened, his mummified carcase and regal ornaments becoming the prey of modern curiosity.

Those stone eyes of the Sphinx had seen all this and more, and now, disdainful of men who fret themselves over trivial and transient activities, indifferent to the endless cavalcade of human joy and suffering which passes across the Egyptian valley, knowing that the great events of time are destined and inescapable, they gaze out of their large sockets into eternity. Yes, one felt powerfully that, themselves changeless, they look across the shifts of time into the beginnings of the world, into the darkness of the unknown.

And then the Sphinx turned soot black and the sky lost its silver-grey opalescence, the while darkness, complete, all-absorbing, conquered the desert.

But the Sphinx still held me, still gripped my attention as with powerful magnetism. For now, I felt, with the approach of night it was coming into its own. The background of darkness was its appropriate setting, and in the mystic quality of an African night it would breathe a fitting atmosphere. Ra and Horus, Isis and Osiris, and all the vanished gods of Egypt come creeping back at night, too. So I determined to wait until moon and star should combine to reveal the true Sphinx once more. I sat alone, and yet, despite the profound desolation of the desert, I did not, nay, I could not, feel lonely.

¶

The nights of Egypt are strangely different from the nights of Europe. Here they are soft-footed, mysteriously palpitant with a host of unseen lives, shaded to an indigo blue whose effect upon sensitive minds is magical; there they are somewhat hard, brutally matter-of-fact, and definitely black.

I perceived this for the hundredth time, when the first evening stars joyously reappeared, twinkling as close and bright as they can never be in Europe; when a seductive slip of a moon revealed her presence; and when the sky became a canopy of blue velvet.

And now I began to see the Sphinx that tourists seldom see: first the bold dark outline, cut from the living rock, as high as a four-storeyed London house, lying quietly in its desert hollow; then, as ray after ray began to light up its detail, the silvered face and outstretched paws of the old familiar figure. Now it became for me the striking symbol of that Egypt whose mysterious origin mounts to immemorial antiquity. Couched like a lonely watch-dog, keeping eternal vigil over prehistoric secrets, brooding over Atlantean worlds whose very names are lost to the frail memory of mankind, this colossal stone creature will outlive every civilization which the race has spawned up to-day and still maintain its inner life intact. That grave and grandiose face betrays nothing, those silent stone lips are pledged to everlasting silence, and if there is any hidden message which the Sphinx holds for man and that it has passed down through the centuries to the privileged penetrative few, then it will be whispered only as the Masonic "Master's Word" is whispered in the candidate's ear "at low breath." What wonder that Roman Pliny wrote of the Sphinx that it was "a wondrous object of art upon which silence has been observed, as it is looked upon as a divinity by the people of the neighbourhood."

Night provides a perfect frame for the Sphinx. Behind and on either side of it there stretched the so-called "City of the Dead," a region which literally teems with tombs. All around the rocky plateau which juts out of the sand south, west and north of the Sphinx, tomb after tomb has been hollowed out to take the sarcophagi of royal flesh, mummified aristocrats and priestly dignitaries.

For six years the Egyptians themselves, following the lead of Western pioneers, have been making a systematic and thorough effort to unearth the entire central portion of this vast necropolis. They have shifted thousands of tons of the great sand-drift which formerly covered the site, revealing narrow passages, cut like trenches in the rock, which cross and criss-cross from one tomb to another, and paved paths connecting the pyramids with their temples. I have traversed this ground from end to end, visiting the burial chambers, private shrines, priests' rooms and mortuary chapels which honeycomb it. Truly is it worthy of its name, "City of the Dead," for, separated by several yards in space and nearly three thousand years in time, two great burial-grounds lie superimposed on each other within its confines. Those old Egyptians dug deep when they wanted to hide their dead, one chamber being no less than one hundred and ninety feet below the surface of the famous causeway. I have entered Fourth Dynasty burial rooms wherein the five-thousand-year-old stone effigies, perfect representations of the deceased, were still standing, their features clear and recognizable, though their reputed services to the spirits were more questionable.

Yet, scarcely a tomb can be entered without finding its heavy sarcophagus lid moved to one side and everything of value gone, every bit of jewelled treasure vanished, just as the excavators found it. Only the canopic jars, containing the internal organs of the mummified bodies, and the stone statuettes had been left behind. Even ancient Egypt had its tomb-riflers and when the common people rose against declining and degenerating ruling castes, they turned for loot and revenge upon this vast cemetery, where high dignitaries had been given the honour of reposing near the mummies of the kings whom they had served during life.

The few whose mummies eluded the early robbers of their own race, slept in peace for awhile until Greek, Roman and Arab in turn awakened them. Those who passed safely through these ordeals were given a long rest again until the early part of last century, when the modern archæologists began to sieve the under-soil of Egypt and search for what the robbers had missed. Let us pity these embalmed Pharaohs and poor princes, for their tombs are desecrated and their treasures pillaged. And even where their mummies were not hacked to pieces by thieves in quest of jewels, they are doomed to have no kindlier resting-places than museums, there to be stared at and commented on by the crowd.

In such a dismal region, once packed with long-buried corpses, stands the lonely Sphinx. It has watched yonder vaults in the "City of the Dead" plundered by rebel Egyptian and rifled by invading Arab. Who can wonder that Wallis Budge, the famed Keeper of the Egyptian Collection in the British Museum, came at last to the conclusions that "the Sphinx was made to keep away evil spirits from the tombs which were round about"? Who can wonder that King Thothmes IV caused to be inscribed on the fourteen feet high stone slab which he raised against the Sphinx's breast, three thousand four hundred years ago, words like the following: *"A magical mystery has reigned in these parts from the beginning of time, since the form of the Sphinx is an emblem of Khepera (god of immortality), the greatest among the spirits, the venerable being that rests there. The inhabitants of Memphis and of all the district raise their hands to him to pray before his countenance."*    Who can wonder that the Bedouins who live in the nearby village of Gizeh have plentiful traditions of spirits and ghosts flitting at night across the area around the Sphinx, which they regard as the most haunted spot on earth? For an ancient burial ground of this kind is like no modern one on earth, and in embalming the bodies of their best men, the Egyptians deliberately protracted the contact of these spirits with our world for an abnormal number of years.

Yes, night is the most appropriate time in which to view the Sphinx, for then, even to the dullest of us, the spirit world seems closer, our minds become more sensitive to previously unfelt sensations, while in the regnant darkness even the hard shapes of the environing material world assume ghostly outlines. The night sky was now purple-indigo, a mystic colour that suited my enterprise well.

¶

The stars had increased in number till they domed the darkened world by the score. The moon, too, made its strengthened contribution to light up the silent spectral scene around me.

The long recumbent lion's body stretched itself out more visibly still upon the oblong platform of rock. The enigmatic head held itself up a little more clearly. Beyond and behind me, the small plateau vaguely joined the desert, which spread away until it disappeared, swallowed up by the surrounding darkness.

I gazed at the graceful lappets of the wide-flowing, wig-like headdress, whose outlines were now faintly discernible. The royal headdress gives the Sphinx majestic grandeur and complete distinction; qualities which are capped by the kingly cobra that rests upon the forehead and rears its upraised hood, by this uraeus-symbol of sovereignty and power over worlds temporal and spiritual alike, by this emblem of both divine and human sovereignty. The figure of the Sphinx often appears in hieroglyphic writing as indicating the Lord of the Land, the mighty Pharaoh, and one old tradition even declares that the statue encloses the tomb of a monarch called Armais. Mariette, the French archæologist and director of the Egyptian Museum at Cairo, took this tradition so seriously that he decided to explore the rocky foundations below the Sphinx. "It is not impossible," he said at a meeting of a learned society, "that inside some part of the monster's body there exists a crypt, a cave, a subterranean chapel which might be a tomb." But not long after he made this plan, death called at his door and he was, himself, enclosed in a tomb. Since then no one has tried to penetrate the stone floor that surrounds the Sphinx, nor the rocky platform upon which it rests. When I raised this matter with Professor Selim Hassan, whom the Egyptian authorities have put in charge of the "City of the Dead" excavations, and asked about the possibility of undiscovered chambers beneath the Sphinx, he pushed the point aside with an emphatic and final reply:

"The Sphinx itself is carved out of the solid rock. There can be nothing but solid rock underneath it!"

I listened with the respect that the Professor fully deserved, but could bring my mind neither to accept nor to reject his statement: I preferred the open mind. The name Armais closely resembles that of Harmachis, the Sun god, whom another legend said that the Sphinx personified. Quite likely, there is no tomb beneath it at all and the two traditions have got somewhat mixed during the slow course of time. But rock chambers can be cut for other purposes also and the early Egyptians were not above doing this on occasions; witness their subterranean crypts wherein guarded and exclusive religious functions were performed. There are old and persistent traditions in Chaldean, Greek, Roman and even Arab sources that tell of an underground passage and chamber through which priests conveyed themselves from the Great Pyramid to the Sphinx. In the main these traditions may be baseless, but there is no smoke without a little fire also, and with a people like the early Egyptians, who were so fond of hewing passage after passage through solid rock, and who loved to hide the entrances to these passages, no Egyptian can safely point to the ground on which he stands to-day and declare that no human moles ever burrowed their way through it. The ancient artists who cut the granite stele of Thothmes that lies between the fore-legs, show the Sphinx as resting on a cubical plinth, which is itself a building with a great central doorway and recessed decoration. Was there some ancestral, now-lost legend upon which they based their picture? Was there a plinth-like temple cut out of the rocky hill, with the Sphinx resting like a giant upon its very roof? One day we shall know.

And the fact even stands that the Sphinx is not carved out wholly of rock. The sculptors found the size of the living rock insufficient to carry out the design which had been given them, and so they were forced to build up part of the rounded back and the fifty-feet-long forepaws with specially baked bricks and hewn stones in order to complete their tremendous task. This added casing has yielded in parts to the attacks of men and years, so that a few bricks have become dislodged and some stones have disappeared.

Then came Colonel Howard Vyse, a hundred years ago, homeward-bound from army service in India. At Suez he had to leave his ship and take to the post-coach, which was maintained by the old East India Company to bring its officers to Cairo and then to the Mediterranean for further embarkation. He dallied awhile in Cairo, attracted by the pyramids and Sphinx, to which he made several visits. Hearing of the old legends and determined to test them, he procured long iron boring-rods, mounted with chisels at the ends, and had the Sphinx's shoulder pierced through to ascertain whether or not it was hollow, but with disappointing result. He penetrated twenty-seven feet into solid rock, and the holes left by his efforts still scar it. But, unfortunately, in Vyse's time nothing but the face and head were visible, the body being entombed under an enormous mass of sand. So his work left three-quarters of the statue untouched, while never even approaching its base.

¶

The night crept surreptitiously on, quiet and silent as a panther, save for the ghastly, semi-human whinings of some desert jackals which marked the passage of the hours. We sat there, the Sphinx and I, under the clear African starlight, strengthening the invisible tie which had brought us together, turning acquaintance into friendship, and perhaps gaining some fresh understanding of each other.

When I first came to him, several years ago, he had looked away in calm disdain. To this giant I was then but one more pigmy mortal, one more hurrying creature peregrinating on two legs and compounded of vain self-sufficiency, fickle desires and foolish thoughts. To me he had seemed to be a gloomy emblem of that Truth which man would never find, a gigantic idol dedicated to the Unknown before whom all prayers fell, unanswered, to the pale sands, and all questions fell, unheard, into the void. I had turned away, more cynical and more sceptical than before, world-weary and embittered.

But the years did not pass in vain. Life is another name for spiritual education and the Unseen Schoolmaster had taught me one or two things that mattered.

I learnt that our whirling globe does not whirl through space for nothing.

I returned to the Sphinx in a brighter mood. As we companioned each other in the darkness, he crouching in his hollow on the edge of the Libyan Desert and I squatting with crossed legs upon the sand, I speculated anew on the mysterious significance of this Colossus.

The entire world knows the photograph of the Sphinx and can recognize its mutilated visage. What the world does not know is why and when it was excavated out of the solid calcareous stone which emerges from the sand, nor whose hands transformed this solitary rock into a statue of such gigantic proportions.

Archæology is silent, hanging its head in secret shame, for it has had to withdraw those guesses dressed up as theories which, even up to a few years ago, it put forward so confidently. It does no longer utter a definite name, nor venture to offer a precise date. It may no longer assign the Sphinx either to King Khafra or King Khufu, for it now realizes that the discovered inscriptions merely indicate the statue's existence during their reigns.

Beyond the Eighteenth Dynasty there is, in the discovered papyri, practically no reference to the existence of the Sphinx, and beyond the Fourth Dynasty no lettered stone records it. Excavators, seeking for ancient spoil, have found an inscription which speaks of the Sphinx as a monument whose origin is lost in time and as one which had been rediscovered by chance, after having been buried under the desert sands and completely forgotten. This inscription belongs to the period of the Fourth Dynasty, a line of Pharaohs who lived and reigned in Egypt nearly six thousand years ago. *Yet to those ancient kings the Sphinx was already unutterably aged.*

¶

Sleep comes with the night, but I had resolutely thrust it aside from hour to hour. Nevertheless, at this point in my nocturnal pondering my eye-lids began to droop in involuntary revolt and my mind became a little drowsy. Two forces were now contesting for supremacy within me. The first was an ardent desire to spend a night's vigil and watch the world with the Sphinx; the second was a growing inclination to yield flesh and thought unto the soothing soporific caress of the environing darkness. Finally I made peace between them and signed a treaty whereby I kept my eyes scarcely open, narrow unseeing slits they were, and my mind scarcely awake, and I let my thoughts slip away into a reverie of colours passing in procession.

And I rested a while in the serene languor which comes when thought is suspended. How long I remained thus I do not know, but a moment arrived when the colours disappeared from my vision and a great open landscape took their place. It was weirdly lit up with a silvery light, as a landscape might be lit up under a full moon.

And all around me there moved throngs of dark figures, hastening to and fro, some carrying loads in baskets set upon their heads and others climbing up and down frail poled scaffoldings fixed against a huge rock. Overseers there were among them, issuing orders to the labourers or carefully watching the efforts of men who worked with hammer and chisel upon the rock, the while they chipped into pre-designed pattern. The air rang with the sounds of their repeated blows.

The faces of all these men were long and hard, the skins tinted reddish brown, or greyish yellow, and the upper lips, also, were noticeably long.

And when their work was done, lo! the outcropping rocky escarpment had turned into a gigantic human head set upon a huge lion body, the whole figure resting in a great artificial hollow cut out of the plateau. A broad and deep magnificent stairway led down to the hollow. And upon the top of the figure's curious headdress, whose wide folds stood out behind the ears, there was set a disk of solid gold.

*The Sphinx!*

And the people disappeared and the landscape became as

quiet as a deserted grave. Then I noticed a vast sea which stretched its waters over the whole country on my left, its shore-line being less than a league away. There was an ominous quality in the silence which I could not understand until a deep rumbling sound came from the very heart of the ocean, the earth shook and trembled underneath me, and with a deafening roar an immense wall of water rose into the air and dashed headlong towards us, towards the Sphinx and me, and overwhelmed us both.

*The Deluge!*

There was a pause, whether of one minute or of one thousand years I know not; and once again I sat at the feet of the great statue. I looked around and saw a sea no longer. Instead a vast expanse of half-dried marsh, with here and there large patches of white salty grains drying in the sun, could alone be seen. And the sun shone fiercely over the land until the patches increased in size and number. And still the sun threw its merciless fire upon everything, hunting the last drop of moisture from the marsh and turning all into soft dry land, which was burnt to the colour of pale yellow.

*The Desert!*

Still the Sphinx gazed out at the landscape; its thick, strong, unmutilated lips shaped as though they were about to break into a smile, itself apparently content with its solitary existence. How perfectly this lonely figure fitted in with its lonely surroundings! In this calm Colossus the very spirit of solitude seemed to have found a worthy incarnation.

And so it waited until one day a small fleet of drifting boats stopped at the riverside and disembarked a group of men who came slowly forward and then prostrated themselves with glad prayers before it.

From that day the spell of silence was broken and henceforward habitations were built on the lowland not far off, and kings came with their priests to pay court to one who was himself the courtless king of the desert.

And with their coming my vision went out, as the flame goes out of a wick when there is no more fuel.

# CHAPTER 11

## THE DESERT GUARDIAN

THE stars were still thick overhead, the crescent moon was still smiling gallantly upon us both, the Sphinx still rose transfigured and majestic in the silvery beams, when I turned my head away to the left, where, in my vision, I had watched the sea rise like a furious monster and devour the dry world.

A bat, mistaking my still body, perhaps, for part of the landscape, flapped its wings against my head and flew off, sending a slight shiver of repulsion down my spine. Apparently it had come up out of some opened subterranean mummy-tomb.

And I thought of the great ocean of sand which rolls across the three million square miles of the Sahara Desert every now and then, never breaking its flow until it reaches the long ridge of bare limestone hills which rise like rose-painted walls from the ground, hills which protect Egypt and guard the valley of the Nile for such a long distance. Nature, as of set purpose, seems to have thrust up the Libyan Hills to save Egypt from being overrun by the very desert which she has also made.

The danger is very real. About the period of early spring, each year, cyclonic winds of terrific force, the dreaded Khamseen, declare war against the northern portion of Africa and whistle furiously across the continent all the way from the Atlantic shores. As they move forward, like an invading army thirsting for loot and victory, the sand and dust move with them. The determined crowds of whirling sand grains spread themselves everywhere, covering the land with a golden shroud. Where no resistance is made to their encroachment, they bring desolation with the years, the sepulchral desolation of the grave, for they entomb huts, houses, monuments, temples and even whole cities. Thus the yellow sand holds imperious sway and rules the land with resistless sceptre. Such is the force of these

Khamseens that the sky may be obscured completely and the sun disappear from view. The swirling clouds of sand, often as impossible to see through as a real London fog, are driven rapidly forward and part of them is then deposited against and upon any objects which stand in their course; they gradually accumulate around and over those objects. I had seen villagers who live near the oases on the edge of the Libyan Desert forced to abandon their huts and to rebuild them on higher ground, such was the all-conquering drift of sand against the walls. I had seen a lofty old temple in Upper Egypt, which the excavators dug out lately, against which sand had piled up to the very roofs.

CARVINGS ON THOTHMES IV STELE, WHICH STANDS IN FRONT OF THE SPHINX

I looked back at the Sphinx, at the pathetic, half-sad expression around its seven-feet-wide mouth that was just faintly discernible in the starlight and which had replaced for ever the half-smiling look I had seen on the figure of my vision, the primeval Atlantean Sphinx. The desert winds, so dreadful in their force, had battered its face, which irreverent men likewise had disfigured.

Surely the flying sands had hurled themselves upon it from time to time, sometimes silently, sometimes howling with storm-fury, and had all but buried it? They had. I remembered the mysterious dream which the Pharaoh Thothmes IV has recorded in fascinating hieroglyphic characters upon the red granite stele which lies between its paws. I remembered, too, word for word, the pathetic plaint in that dream of the forlorn forgotten Sphinx, which was buried up to its neck in the pitiless sands.

*"The sand of the desert approaches me,"* cried its Spirit, *"and I am sunken deep in it. Hasten! Cause to be done that which shall clear the sand away, then I shall know that thou art my son and my helper."*

And after he awoke, Thothmes said to himself:

"The inhabitants of town and temple come to honour this god, but no one of them ever thinks of freeing his image from the sand."

The relief drawings at the top of the stone stele show the king offering incense to the Sphinx and then follows the full story of history's most amazing dream and of its amazing consequences. The young Thothmes was still a prince when he was hunting with friends in the desert fringe near Gizeh.

"He was amusing himself upon the south roads," run the hieroglyphics, "shooting at a target of copper, hunting lions and wild animals of the desert, and racing in his chariot, his horses swifter than the wind."

He dropped from his horse at midday, wearied and exhausted with his sport. After dining, he sought repose and sent his attendants away to rest. At the altar he offered a prayer to the gods and then went off to rest himself.

"The heaviness of sleep seized upon the prince in the hour when Ra is crowned. He found the majesty of this revered god speaking in his own voice, even as a father speaks to his son, saying:

*" 'Truly, I see thee, I behold thee, my son. Thothmes, I am thy father, Heru-Khut, who will give thee this kingdom. Thou shalt lift up its red crown and the land shall be thine throughout its whole extent. The diadem of the god shall shine upon thee, food from Egypt and costly presents from strange lands shall be given thee!' "*

The dream came to an end with the urgent request to dig the Sphinx out of its sandy tomb, if the young prince wished to have the promised crown bestowed upon him.

Thothmes dutifully obeyed the command received in his dream and set many men to the task of clearing the sand which filled the deep court and muffled the Breast of the Sphinx.

Heru-Khut, "the Rising Sun," Spirit or god of the Spinx, faithfully kept his promise in turn. Over the very heads of his elder brothers the prince received the Pharaonic crown as Thothmes IV and led armies out of Egypt which won victories wherever they went. His empire stretched from far-off

Mesopotamia in the east to the Second Nile Cataract of Nubia in the south; he overcame the Bedouins of Lybia in the west, while bearded Ethiopians brought him the promised costly presents. Under him Egypt became immensely rich, both toiling peasants and idling princes were prosperous; its civilization and culture flourished as never before. The predicted glories came magnificently true.

All this is not hearsay but history, not legend but living fact, for the Egyptians kept more careful records than any other nation of antiquity, while many of those records, being deeply inscribed on hard stone, will outlive those on paper and parchment.

¶

Nor was this the only time when a man has been moved to free the Sphinx.

Seven times have the ever-active sands buried the Sphinx; seven times has it been freed.

This, in historic times only, for the men of pre-history possessed a reverent regard for this image which caused them to protect its body with devoted care.

It was first excavated more than five thousand years ago by Khafra, a Fourth Dynasty Pharaoh who turned the Second Pyramid into a tomb to hold his granite sarcophagus. Less than two thousand years afterwards came the second effort to rescue the Sphinx from the sands, that of Thothmes IV, whose famous dream induced him to undertake the task. He even tried to protect it against future invasions by building a crude unburnt brick wall around it to act as a barrier.

To-day you may observe these bricks, some of which are still stamped with the King's prenomen. But once again the sand crept in and took possession of the stone giant, and this time it was an alien king, the philosophic Roman ruler Marcus Aurelius, who, finding the Sphinx buried up to the neck, extricated it once more. The slabbed masonry of the paws and underneath the chest, not being cut from rock as was the main body and head, had fallen into a ruinous state, and the king thoughtfully repaired that too, while parts where he restored the brick-girdled walls still stand out by their black colouring against a grey background.

Under the Arabs, naturally, the Sphinx was completely neglected again, until only the weary greyish-white face showed above the golden sands. Not till the beginning of last century did someone take pity upon it, when Captain Caviglia, an enthusiastic Italian archæologist and student of supernatural mysteries, attempted to excavate the upper part of its body, but such was the rapid invasion of sand that he had great difficulty in keeping the parts which he had already cleared from being reburied. In 1869 August Mariette, founder of the Egyptian Museum, in honour of the opening of the Suez Canal, made a partial effort, the fifth of its kind, to remove the ever-growing pile of sand, but he did not stay long at his task. Thirty-three years later Maspero, his successor at the Museum, raised a large fund in France by public subscription for the same purpose. Thus equipped, he was able yet again to bring the major proportion of the Sphinx to the light.

Maspero hoped to find at its base some opening that might lead into an interior chamber. He could not bring himself to believe that this unique statue did not possess some undiscovered architectural secrets. But not a single opening or entrance was found. He then began to question whether or not the Sphinx rested on a terrace, below which might lie the secret chamber that he sought. The magnitude of the task of excavating the base was, however, too great for his limited funds, and American millionaires having then scarcely begun to interest themselves in Egyptology, he was forced to leave the work to posterity.

The seventh and latest effort was made a few years ago, when the Egyptian Government decided on a final clearance of the sand and brought into view hitherto unseen parts of the base lying in the oblong basin. The diggers completely exhumed the lower part of the great stone block, which had so long been buried, and revealed in detail the vast platform of rock, paved with long slabs of stone, upon which it stands. The entire enclosure surrounding it and much of the forecourt was also cleared. The forty-feet-wide flight of steps which led down to this platform was brought to light. At last, the Sphinx could be seen in its true dignity. A steep, solid, concrete girdle wall was then built around parts of the enclosure, to defend the Sphinx and keep the sandy enemy at bay. Never again, let us hope, will the swift-growing pile of yellow grains collect by degrees against the flanks of the Sphinx, to render vain this praiseworthy work of excavation.

And yet, one must not be too harsh in condemning the enemy. If the sands bury the statues and temples of Egypt, they also perform the protective office of preserving them, embalming them and saving them from perishing. There is perhaps no better preservative for the stone monuments made by man than the warm, dry African sand.

¶

One by one, gently and perhaps reluctantly, the innumerable stars were vanishing, and I knew that my long vigil was soon to reach its end. I had set its term at the hour when one could no longer glimpse the mysterious march of constellations around the indigo sky, and when dawn would quiver over the country with a rosy light.

The air was chilly, too, and my throat dry and parched.

Once more I regarded steadily this grave stone guardian of ancient secrets, whose figure in the faint starlight was so emblematic of the Silent Watcher of our world. Had I turned a leaf in Egypt's pre-history which had rarely been turned before? Who dares to measure the age of the Sphinx? Once its Atlantean origin was accepted, who could affix a date to it?

And I saw no reason why such an origin, pictured so briefly in my vision under the stars, should not be accepted. Atlantis was no longer a fiction of Greek philosophers, Egyptian priests and American Indian tribes: individual scientists had collected a hundred proofs of its existence, and more. I saw, too, that when the Sphinx was first carved out of the rock, the surrounding lowlands could not have been covered with sand; for then the rocky escarpment itself, which stands at the foot of a hill whose summit is topped by the Pyramids, would also have been under the sand—a position full of obstacles which would render the work hardly possible. No, it was much more likely that the statue had been cut ere the sands had made their appearance, and when the Sahara was a gigantic sea, beyond which lay the great and tragic island of Atlantis.

The men who had inhabited prehistoric Egypt, who had carved the Sphinx and founded the world's oldest civilization, were men who had made their exodus from Atlantis to settle on this strip of land that bordered the Nile.[1] And they had left

[1] "All the facts lead to the conclusion that the Egyptians had already made very great progress in the arts of civilization before the age of Menes (first of the Pharaohs), and perhaps before they immigrated into the valley of the Nile," was the considered opinion of Sir J. G. Wilkinson, one of the best Egyptologists ever produced by English learning.

before their ill-fated continent sank to the bottom of the Atlantic Ocean, a catastrophe which had drained the Sahara and turned it into a desert. The shells which to-day litter the surface of the Sahara in places, as well as the fossil fish which are found among its sands, prove that it was once covered by the waters of a vast ocean.

It was a tremendous and astonishing thought that the Sphinx provided a solid, visible and enduring link between the people of to-day and the people of a lost world, the unknown Atlanteans.

This great symbol has lost its meaning for the modern world, for whom it is now but an object of local curiosity. What did it mean to the Atlanteans?

We must look for some hint of an answer in the few remnants of culture still surviving from peoples whose own histories claimed Atlantean origin. We must probe behind the degenerate rituals of races like the Incas and the Mayas, mounting to the purer worship of their distant ancestors, and we shall find that the loftiest object of their worship was Light, represented by the Sun. Hence they built pyramidal Temples of the Sun throughout ancient America. Such temples were either variants or slightly distorted copies of similar temples which had existed in Atlantis.

After Plato went to Egypt and settled for a while in the ancient School of Heliopolis, where he lived and studied during thirteen years, the priest-teachers, usually very guarded with foreigners, favoured the earnest young Greek enquirer with information drawn from their well-preserved secret records. Among other things they told him that a great flat-topped pyramid had stood in the centre of the island of Atlantis, and that on this top there had been built the chief temple of the continent—a sun temple.

The emigrants who sailed to Egypt took this religion with them and constructed similar temples; in the giant sloping pylons and in the pyramidal tombs of Egypt we may read to-day the characters of this Atlantean legacy. And ever the Sun found a first place among Egyptian gods.

One thing more these emigrants carried across the seas and that was the taste for gigantic statuary, the predilection for stone giants. Just as in the ruined, Atlantean-descended temples of Mexico, of Peru, and of Yucatan, massive as they are, built of stone blocks of immense size and with finely fitting joints, one can see the sister style of architecture to the Egyptian, so in the colossal figures which were to be found within the courts of, and along the approaches to those temples one recognizes the same family strain.

The stone figures of men, which were found by Captain Cook on Easter Island, that lone, desolate, mountain-top remnant of a sunken continent, measured only twenty-seven feet in height, less than one-third of the Sphinx's height; yet they, too, possess an ancestry linked with that of Egypt.

The purpose of the Sphinx had now become a little plainer. The Egyptian Atlanteans had built it as their grandest statue, their sublimest figure of remembrance, and they had dedicated it to their Light-god, the Sun. And somewhere, too, they had built its temple, equally therefore their grandest, their sublimest temple.

The Sphinx was the revered emblem in stone of a race which looked upon Light as the nearest thing to God in this dense material world. Light is the subtlest, most intangible of things which man can register by means of one of his five senses. It is the most ethereal kind of matter which he knows. It is the most ethereal element science can handle, and even the various kinds of invisible rays are but variants of light which vibrate beyond the power of our retinas to grasp. So in the Book of Genesis the first created element was Light, without which nothing else could be created. "The Spirit of God moved upon the face of the Deep," wrote Egyptian-trained Moses. "And God said, Let there be Light: and there was Light." Not only that, it is also a perfect symbol of that heavenly light which dawns within the deep places of man's soul when he yields heart and mind to God; it is a magnificent memorial to that divine illumination which awaits him secretly even amid the blackest despairs. Man, in turning instinctively to the face and presence of the sun, turns to the body of his Creator.

And from the sun, light is born: from the sun it comes streaming into our world. Without the sun we should remain perpetually in horrible darkness; crops would not grow: mankind would starve, die, and disappear from the face of this planet.

If this reverence for Light and for its agent, the sun, was the central tenet of Atlantean religion, so also was it the central tenet of early Egyptian religion. Ra, the sun-god, was first, the father and creator of all the other gods, the Maker of all things, the one, the self-born.

"Homage to thee, thou art the lord of heaven," sings the beautiful old *Hymn To Ra When He Riseth In The Eastern Sky*, "Thou stridest across the sky with heart expanded with joy. Thy rays are upon all faces. Hail my lord, thou that passest through eternity and whose being is everlasting."

If the Sphinx were connected with this religion of Light, it would surely have some relationship with the sun. It had!

For after I turned round to face the dawn-light which now appeared out of the darkness, clearly streaked against the flat horizon, I remembered the golden disk of my vision and saw this relationship as in a flash. To test the matter I bent down and scrutinized something on my left arm, a radium-lit wrist compass, safe guide and good friend.

And I found that the Sphinx had been set with its face exactly towards the east, its sightless eyes gazing exactly at the spot where the sun was beginning its diurnal reappearance upon the horizon!

The Sphinx was set eastwards to symbolize Life reborn, as the royal tombs of Egypt were set on the west bank of the Nile to symbolize Life passed, through analogy with the setting sun. And just as the risen sun ascends into mid-heaven, so man, after his resurrection, ascends into the spiritual world, and, as the sun traverses the royal arch of the heavens, and then proceeds on its unobserved course below the horizon, so man traverses both worlds.

¶

I turned back and resumed my watch. As the night slipped away, the face of the Sphinx became more and more distinct, while the massive girdling wall which surrounded it stood up clearer and clearer against the sands.

A pinkish light appeared in the sky, running in long lines as though marked with a crayon by an unseen hand. Upward rose the dawning sun, more and more disclosing to one's view the familiar Egyptian landscape and tinting the distant heights to a pale rose.

Seven miles away the muezzins of Cairo would be mounting the tall minarets of their mosques, to stand on circular platforms and call the Prophet's followers from their sleep, for it was now the hour of first prayer.

Here the Sphinx called too, albeit silently.

And as I gazed at its half-profile I wondered at the temerity of those men whose desecrating guns had knocked off half its nose. What thoughts must have run through the Sphinx's brain when these barbarians began to fire! First amazed, then affronted, finally it must have resumed its ancient philosophical resignation. The Egyptians blame this mutilation upon Napoleon's soldiers; the French archæologists attribute it to the Mameluke soldiers of the eighteenth century, declaring that the nose was used as a target for their artillery practices. But Napoleon would never have permitted such desecration of the oldest statue in the world. The little Corsican was too great a man, too much a lover of artistic things, too ardent an admirer of the outstanding works of antiquity, and too thoughtful not to have perceived and valued the significance of the stone dreamer of the desert. The Mamelukes would certainly have had less qualms, feeling as they did the Muhammedan detestation of idols. One Arab historian even mentions a fanatical sheikh who, in 1379, tried to break the Sphinx's nose in his zeal for Allah. The real truth is, however, that the damage was begun in a much earlier time than that of either Mameluke or Frenchman, and later centuries merely witnessed its completion. For during that long period which stretched from the fall of the Pharaohs till the nineteenth century, superstitious travellers did not hesitate to arm themselves with hammer and chisel and procure talismans and mementoes at the Sphinx's expense. Part of the mouth was thus chipped away by visitors who came at a time and under a rule which did not value the monuments and antiquities of the land as they are valued to-day, when visitors can no longer do what they please and when the authorities provide vigilant protection for Egypt's first monumental work of art.

Not all travellers betrayed such barbarous habits. A few, who came as long ago as the time of the Greek and Roman monarchs, could not resist the temptation of cutting their names on the side of the Sphinx or on the girdle-walls of the deep basin in which it stands, names which the curious may still observe and decipher in our own time. And on the second toe of the left paw, so faintly scratched as to be scarcely readable, certainly unseen by the crowds who come and go to-day, there is a charming original sonnet addressed to the Sphinx and signed by a celebrated name, none other than that of Arrian, the historian of Alexander the Great. The beautiful Greek verses deserve a printed record somewhere.

"The eternal gods have formed thy astonishing body," runs a rough prose translation of the lines, "in their solicitude for a region burnt by heat, where thou throwest thy benevolent shadow. They have placed thee like a rocky isle in the midst of a large plateau, whose sands thou dost arrest. This neighbour, which the gods have given to the Pyramids, is not, as at Thebes, the man-killing Sphinx of Œdipus; he is the sacred follower of the goddess Latona, the guardian of the benevolent Osiris, the august chief of the land of Egypt, the king of the dwellers in the sky like unto the sun, equal to Vulcan."

Perhaps the greatest loss which the Sphinx has suffered from the hands of its wretched mutilators is the loss of its famed smile, that gentle, inexplicable and inscrutable smile which puzzled generation after generation of the ancients. Even seven hundred years ago the destruction was not yet complete and Abdul Latif, the Baghdad physician, philosopher and traveller, could write in his accurate and observant notes, of the colossal head which he found on his visit an arrow's shot from the Pyramids, "This face is very beautiful and the mouth bears the impression of grace." Such praise, coming from a man whose work, *On the Human Body*, became a classic among the Arab peoples for centuries, is worth quoting. "An intellectual man asked me what I admired most of all I had seen in Egypt, which object had most excited my admiration," continues Abdul Latif, who began his Egyptian travels shortly before 1200 A.D., and for answer, he is compelled to point towards the Sphinx. Alas his praise might not be so easily won to-day! The nose has been shot away, the plaited square beard broken off, the mouth sadly chipped and even the sides of the headdress noticeably damaged. The once-benignant mouth now possesses but a half-wry expression, and has become a half-sad, half-mocking feature. But if the old Sphinx smiles no longer, it nevertheless continues to sit, despite its regrettable scars and injuries, in imperturbable disdain of the aeons.

§

Fitly, this strange creature, embodying the strength of a lion, the intellect of a man, and the spiritual serenity of a god, quietly teaches the inescapable truth of the necessity of self-control that man's being may surpass the animal in him and tame it. Who can glance at the great stone body, whose legs and claws of a creature of prey are linked to the head and face of a noble human being, without deducing that elementary lesson? Who can read the symbolism of the hooded snake which rises above the headdress, the uræus-emblem of Pharaonic sovereignty, without perceiving that the Sphinx's call is not alone to be a king over others but to be a king over oneself? It is a mute preacher in stone, delivering a silent sermon to all who have ears to hear.

That the Sphinx represents something or someone divine is suggested by the hieroglyph inscriptions on the walls of the Upper Egyptian temples, as at Edfu, where a god is pictured as changing himself into a lion with a human head in order to vanquish Set, the Egyptian Satan. That the Sphinx conceals some architectural secret and hides some mystery cut in stone is equally suggested by a curious fact. In every other part of Egypt small copies of the Sphinx were set up before their respective temples, as guardians and protectors of the threshold, or else lions were figured protectively at the gates of the temples. Even the *keys* of the temples bore the shape of a lion. But the Sphinx of Gizeh alone seems to stand without a temple at its rear. The so-called Temple of the Sphinx, that fortress-like structure of ruddy squared stone columns and plain massive walls, does not belong to it at all, as Professor Selim Hassan's latest excavations have finally and fully proved. It is now revealed as being really the temple of the Pyramid of Khafra, the Second Pyramid, with which it is connected by a paved sloping causeway, a causeway which had now been completely unearthed. Moreover, this curiously built sanctuary stands before and not behind the Sphinx.

The small open temple which Caviglia dug out from the space against the breast and between the paws but which has now nearly gone, was built but lately in comparison with the real date of the statue. It is made up of three fourteen-feet-high stelæ, which acted as roofless walls, two of which time and acquisitive hands have taken down and removed. Even the sacrificial altar which once fronted the entrance to this shrine and which now fronts the entrance to the paws, is of Roman work, although made from a piece of red granite taken from the far older Khafra temple close by.

Where, then, is the real temple of the Sphinx?

I raised my head a little and looked behind the statue. And I saw, from the angle where I was sitting, looming up in the early morning light, lifting its truncated apex to the sky, the world's largest building, the world's insoluble stone riddle, the world's first wonder to the Greeks as to us, that enigma of the ancients which continues to puzzle the moderns, the fit friend of the Sphinx.

The Great Pyramid!

Both, built in Atlantean times, stand as distinctive marks of the mysterious continent, and remain as mute legacies from a race of people who have departed as mysteriously as their own land.

Both remind the successors of the Atlanteans of the glories of that lost civilization.

¶

And then, both sun and Sphinx met again and renewed a glorious tryst kept daily for uncounted years. The sky went quickly through all those changes which follow dawn in Egypt; the horizon turned from pink to heliotrope, from heliotrope to violet, from violet to red, before it assumed that cloudless intense whitish-blue colour which is Egypt's perpetual canopy. I know now that the Sphinx, as the desert Watcher, was an emblem of the Sacred Four, the Silent Watchers of this World, the Four Gods who carry out the commands of Deity, the mysterious Guardians of Mankind and its destiny. The men who cut the Sphinx's figure knew of these lofty Beings but we, poor moderns, have forgotten them utterly.

A little tired of my long night vigil, I prepared to bid farewell to this titan's head raised above the sand. Its self-possession, its air of masterful composure, its radiation of spiritual repose, had somehow reacted upon me, and produced a subtle world-detached mood for which I could hardly find words. The Sphinx, so old that it had watched the childhood of the world, plunged in unbroken contemplation, had seen civilizations rise to glory and then slowly droop like withered flowers, had watched shouting invaders pass and repass, come and depart, come and stay. And yet it stood its ground, so utterly calm, so utterly removed from all human emotions. Something of that stony indifference to the mutations of fate seemed to have crept under my skin during the night's darkness. The Sphinx relieves one of all worry about the future, all burdens of the heart; and it turns the past into a cinema film, which one may watch in detachment, impersonally.

Under the limpid sapphire sky, I took my last look at the wide forehead, the deeply sunk eyes, the round plump cheeks, the massive projecting headdress made to imitate a real one of folded linen with horizontal bands running across it, one broad band between two narrower lines. I glanced anew at the rose-coloured streaks which still marked its cheeks, reminiscent of the Sphinx which the ancients saw, whose form was plastered over with smoothed limestone and whose surface was then coloured a dull red.

If the force of a lion and the intelligence of a man mingled their symbolisms in this crouching body, there was yet something neither bestial nor human in it, something beyond and above these, something divine! Though not a word had passed between us, nevertheless a spiritual healing had emanated from the Sphinx's presence. Though I had not dared to whisper into those great ears, so deaf to the world's bustle, I knew it had perfectly comprehended me. Yes, there was some supernatural element in this stone being, which had come down to the twentieth century like a creature from an unknown world. But those sealed heavy lips close in upon their Atlantean secrets. If the daylight had now fully revealed the Sphinx to me, it also increased the latter's mystery.

I stretched my cramped feet out upon the sands and then slowly stood up, speeding a valedictory word at the impassive face. And in its fixed eastward stare, ever watchful for the first rays of the sun, I read again the hopeful symbol of our certain resurrection, as certain and as inescapable as the sun's dawning.

*"Thou belongest to That Which Is Undying, and not merely to time alone,"* murmured the Sphinx, breaking its muteness at last. *"Thou art eternal, and not merely of the vanishing flesh. The soul in man cannot be killed, cannot die. It waits, shroud-wrapped, in thy heart, as I waited, sand-wrapped, in thy world. Know thyself, O mortal! For there is One within thee, as in all men, that comes and stands at the bar and bears witness that there IS a God!"*

# CHAPTER III

## THE PYRAMID

THE Pharaohs themselves are now but phantasms, thin vaporous spirits who dwell in Amenti, the Hidden Land, but the Pyramids are with us still; solid, bulky memorials which have become an enduring part of the rocky stone plateau upon which they were built. Ancient Egypt continues to hold the attention and to grip the interest of the modern world, chiefly because it has left us these stupendous testimonies to its existence, testimonies which are more tangible and more massive than any which have been left by other dead empires of the East.

Pliny the Roman wrote down somewhere that the three Pyramids had filled the earth with their renown, and now, two thousand years after he scribed that statement, we may say unhesitatingly that time has taken nothing away from that renown. I wrote, not long ago, to a few friends who live a semi-secluded existence in the remote interior of the South Indian peninsula, men who had hardly ever crossed the long ridge of hills that neighbour them, who scarcely ever troubled the world and who were scarcely ever troubled by the world, and I told them about some researches I was making at the Great Pyramid. It was not necessary for me to explain where and what the latter was; I knew that they knew, and the reply, when it came, proved that my assumption about these simple Indian folk was correct. The renown of the Pyramids had travelled farther even than in Pliny's time. Indeed, their fame is such that I wonder how many tourist business magnates have looked yearningly at those triangular sides with regret that such magnificent advertising should be wasted! Perhaps the day may not be far off when some enterprising manufacturer will offer a hundred thousand piastres yearly to the Egyptian Government for the sole right of erecting a tremendous hoarding across the north face of the Great Pyramid, and when we shall have the doubtful pleasure of reading thereon, a painted injunction in English, French and Arabic, to wash our faces with a soap whose renown is to-day hardly less than that of the Pyramids themselves!

These ancient time-defying monuments excite the interest of the learned and attract the curiosity of the layman, partly because they emerge out of the abyss of the centuries and partly because their immense size stupefies even a generation which has become familiar with massive structures. When we first glimpse the Pyramids, we seem to arrive at a strange, ancient epoch whose age is fitly expressed in the strangeness of these unfamiliar outlines; we are struck with amazement when we consider how the hands of primitive men could have raised such monstrous artificial mountains on a desert plateau to rival the creations of Nature herself.

When the Grecian conquerors first penetrated Egypt and sighted these incredible buildings, lifting their pointed peaks to the desert sky, they stared silently and caught their breath: and when the Grecian sages of Alexander's time drew up their list of the seven wonders of the world, they placed the Pyramids at its head. To-day, these alone are left standing out of the seven.

But age and size, impressive though they are, do not constitute the sole recommendation to such an honour. There are both well and little known facts about the first and greatest of the Pyramids which may cause us to wonder no less than the Greeks.

When the scientists and experts whom Napoleon took with him on his invasion of Egypt were commissioned to make a survey of the country, they fixed the Great Pyramid as the central meridian from which they would mark out the longitudes. After they had mapped out Lower Egypt, they were surprised at the apparent coincidence of this meridian exactly cutting the Delta region, formed by the mouth of the Nile and practically constituting the whole of Lower Egypt, into two equal portions. They were still more surprised when they found that two diagonal lines drawn from the Pyramid at right-angles to each other would completely enclose the entire Delta area. And they were profoundly astonished when reflection revealed to them that the Great Pyramid's position was not only suitable as a central meridian for Egypt, but also for the entire globe, *for the Great Pyramid stands exactly on the middle dividing line of the world map!*

This amazing fact results from its position; if a vertical
line is drawn through it, the land area lying to the east will
be found equal to the land area lying to the west of the line.
The meridian of the Great Pyramid is thus the natural zero of
longitude for the whole globe. Its position on the land surface
of our earth is therefore *unique*. And in perfect keeping with
that position, its four slanted sides front the four points of
the compass.

This extraordinary geographical position for a man-built
monument is either another meaningless coincidence or a
purposive achievement, and of a race as astute and intellectual
as the early inhabitants of Egypt one is forced to accept the
latter opinion. That the largest stone building in the world
should be set up on the world's central line, strikes the imagination with compelling force! That the most outstanding of all
structures erected upon the surface of this globe should have
been planted at such a point is, indeed, something to think
about!

The guides and handbooks will glibly tell you that the
Great Pyramid was built by a Fourth Dynasty Pharaoh, Khufu,
renamed Cheops by the Greeks, who wanted a first-class and
truly original tomb fit for a king, and that this is all there really
is to it. And for a handy, convenient and conventional theory,
this notion that it is nothing more than a grandiose grave is
doubtless the best you will find. It has the backing of all the
big men in Egyptology, archæology and ancient history; so
bend your head in respect before orthodox authorities and
accept their dicta.

There are unorthodox theories, too. The notions which
have been built around this ancient building—and they are
many—range from the completely improbable to the scientifically
plausible, because the Pyramids are large enough and important
enough to have become a happy hunting-ground for cranks.

The chief engineer of an Australian railway spent time and
trouble in collecting a lot of measurements and figures to prove
that the Pyramids were intended to be used in land surveying!
I picked up in Paris some heated correspondence between a
French professor and two noted Egyptologists, wherein the
former sought to show that the real object of the Pyramids was
to commemorate symbolically the fact that the River Nile had
been artificially created at some remote epoch! Some ingenious
historians see the Pyramids as gigantic granaries wherein Joseph,

the son of Jacob, had stored the corn destined to feed the people during lean years of famine. Had these historians ventured inside the Pyramids they might have discovered that the empty space available for storing could not have held more corn than might feed the people of an average street.

Fifty years ago Proctor, the astronomer, presented an interesting case on behalf of his theory that the Pyramids were built for purposes of astronomical observations, to provide suitable places for watching and noting the positions and movements of stars and planets. But such costly observatories had never before and never again will be erected!

Ingenious and delightful, too, are those arguments which perceive in the stone sarcophagus of the King's Chamber nothing less than a baptismal font, which was filled with water when in use. Another group, however, declare that this sarcophagus was filled with corn, and not water, because it was intended to serve as a standard of capacity measurement for all the nations of the world.

It is equally inconceivable that vast treasures of gold and jewels were secreted in its recesses, because the colossal expense of constructing it would have cost the very fortune it was intended to protect!

Other theorists were confident that the Pyramids had originally been gigantic lighthouses, erected for the benefit of ships navigating the Nile! While Monsieur de Persigny's advocacy of the notion that they were massive ramparts, put up to defend houses, tombs and temples against invading desert sands, can only make the modern Egyptians smile.

¶

But there are sedulous propagandists of other theories which wear a plausible face and which, indeed, have found a fairly wide acceptance in certain circles of England and America. These are interesting, even fascinating, and cleverly worked-out yet how far are they true?

Their propagandists read a peculiar significance into the internal measurements of the Great Pyramid; they see in its chambers, corridors and gallery a symbolical handwriting and a prophetic declaration pertaining to our own times, while they claim to have found the correct keys to the decipherment of its message. They find in the length and height and width of these passages, chambers and thresholds, mute presages of another dreadful Armageddon. They play with an incredible array of figures and link up the Anglo-Saxon race, the lost tribes of Israel, the books of the Bible and the early Egyptians, in a strange medley.

"When we measure the passages and Grand Gallery of the interior, we find they give in inches the exact number of years required to bring us into the period in which we are now living," they declare. "The length of the Grand Gallery is 1883 inches; add to this 31—the years denoted by the Pyramid as that of our Lord's atoning ministry—and you get 1914, the year when the Great War broke out." Such is a fair sample of their statements.

They are quite sure that the Pyramid was not built to benefit its builders, but instead, was unselfishly put up for the benefit of future ages, and that it had particular reference to the age of the so-called millennium. With confidence they await the coming of One indicated by the Pyramid's greatest revelation, the advent of the Messiah.

I wish I could follow my friends who believe these things. I wish I, too, could light up my heart with their great hopes. But reason, to which I must always hold, and common sense, which I must guard as a treasure, rise and bar the way.

The man whose untiring effort and persevering research did more to create these theories than that of anyone else, was Piazzi Smyth, one-time Astronomer of Scotland. Smyth's character was amazing: it trembled on the verge of inspired genius, but his hard Scottish dogmatism interfered with and distorted the message which his intuition was trying to communicate to his intellect.

Smyth went out and spent a whole winter at the Pyramid, measuring from point to point, taking angles and examining every detail of the structure. But he brought his theories ready-made with him, and those measures and figures had to fit these theories. The latter, like the Pyramid, were immovable; but the former, unlike the Pyramid, might be made to accommodate themselves to what they were expected to prove. Smyth worked quite honestly, of course, but was half-blinded by his partisanship. I know only that the late Sir Ernest Wallis Budge, formerly Keeper of the Egyptian Antiquities in the British Museum, could not accept his figures. I know also that Sir Flinders Petrie, doyen of English archæologists in Egypt, after a winter's careful surveying work at the Pyramids, found seventy-one inches difference between his figure and that of Piazzi Smyth of the most important measurement in the edifice. I know, finally, another man, a trained engineer, who lately re-examined all the external and internal dimensions of the Great Pyramid, as presented not only by Piazzi Smyth, but also by his chief modern successors, and found to be unreliable several of the computations given by the latter gentlemen. Indeed, Petrie tells an amusing story of his discovery of a

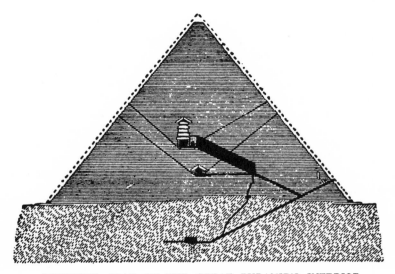

SECTIONAL PLAN OF THE GREAT PYRAMID'S INTERIOR

disappointed follower of Smyth's, whom he found trying to file down the granite boss in the ante-room to the King's Chamber to the size required for the theory!

But the weakness of their figures is not the only reason why one must be a little wary about going whither these enthusiastic people would lead us. Many years ago they used to give 2170 B.C. as the date of the Pyramid's construction, because in that year a certain Pole Star was in a straight line with the axis of the entrance passage, and they thought that this long dark passage had been set at an angle which would catch the light of this star. But, owing to that grand movement in the heavens called precession of equinoxes, the stars move from their original positions relative to our globe and do not reoccupy the same point in the sky until 25,827 years have passed. It might, therefore, be said with equal logic, that the Great Pyramid was built 25,827 years before 2170 B.C., when that Pole Star would again have looked down the axis of the entrance passage.

Actually, the entrance passage was set at an angle pointing towards the spot which would be occupied for some centuries by each star which came in turn to keep watch before the Pole. Thus the argument that it was set at Alpha, of the Dragon Constellation, means little, because it has faced other stars too.

The more distant figure was unacceptable because it implied that the human race was considerably older than the five to six thousand years of existence which our theorists thought the Bible gave to man, so they stuck to the nearer one. Every Egyptologist has rightly rejected the nearer date, well knowing from discovered historical inscriptions and records that the Pyramid could not possibly have been built so late.

The Bible is a collection of books more complicated and more profound than appears on the surface. The first five books—and especially the book of Genesis—cannot be correctly read without a key; that key, unfortunately, was thrown away many centuries ago.

Men misread the Biblical records and do violence to their reason in an effort to swallow what these records never attempt to teach. It was thus that we arrived at the delightful position of last century, when geologists, having discovered that the earth's deposits of fossilized animals plainly indicated how impossible was the six thousand years of age assigned to the world, other equally eminent theologians thereupon seriously maintained that God had purposely entombed those fossils in order to test the faithful!

Had our Pyramid theorists not misread their Bible too, they might have accepted the older date and perhaps come a good deal closer to the truth, for the solid stone body of the Pyramid is quite capable of having withstood the ravages of three hundred centuries of time: its strength and stability are such that it will remain standing when every other building on earth has crumbled.

It is, perhaps, in the predictive activities of this school that the reason for the wide ground it has gained may be seen. The sayings of the Hebrew prophets have been curiously mingled with the dimensions of the Great Pyramid in order to predict the outbreak of wars and the fall of governments, the reconstitution of the Christian Church and the return of Christ, the economic woes of the world and the divine mission of English-speaking peoples, the cataclysmic upheaval of land and sea, and so on.

One may remember, however, that Piazzi Smyth himself gave the date 1881 as the year of the millennium. One remembers, too, that May, 1928, was for long given by this school as the most fateful month in world history, but it passed uneventfully. The most fateful month was then transferred to September, 1936, which, we were told, had really been indicated by the Pyramid's dimensions. Nevertheless, neither Armageddon nor the Millennium was to be seen on that day. Thereupon the date was altered to August 10, 1953. Once again the prediction proved incorrect.

The claim that this massive structure was built at unprecedented expense and labour, not for the benefit of existing or proximate people, not even for the benefit of Egyptian posterity, but for the benefit of people who were to follow nearly five thousand years after and who were to dwell in alien continents, is naturally not easy for any rationalist to accept. Even granting that these theorists have correctly noted some of the mathematical proportions and interior features of the Great Pyramid, it seems that they have run off at a tangent and plunged into a plethora of predictions which have no visible link with those facts. The essence of their theory is that God persuaded the early Egyptians to write a stone message to our epoch, but He could quite as effectively have communicated that message to-day directly, simply and more successfully through some human prophet, rather than take the hazards of finding his cryptic stone message either unread, as it was through all past centuries, or misunderstood, as it may so easily have been in ours.

But if one is unable to accept these peculiar theories, one may respect the sincere motives of their propagandists, to whom we may even be grateful for the interest they have aroused in the spiritual significance of this unique structure.

The nature of the Pyramid's true purpose and the symbolical meaning of the Sphinx are two of the most fascinating and interesting riddles which Egypt has set her habitants and visitors alike, yet the two which are most difficult to solve.

¶

Was it then reared, this Egyptian skyscraper, merely to hold one Pharaoh's mummified flesh, as our handbooks tell us and as black-robed Arab dragomans tell their tourist clients? Was such vast bulk cut out of the limestone quarries of nearby Tourah and sawn out of the granite quarries of far-off Syene, merely to hide a single linen-wrapped corpse? Were over eighty million cubic feet of stone laboriously dragged and worked under a burning African sun to satisfy the caprice of a single king? Were two million, three hundred thousand blocks, each weighing about two and a half tons, carefully cemented together to cover what a few blocks could have covered just as well? And, finally, was Josephus, the Hebrew historian, right when he declared the Pyramids to be "vast and vain monuments"?

From what we know of the power of the Pharaohs and the after-death beliefs of the Egyptians, such a thing is quite possible, although it is not quite probable. No coffin, no body, no funerary appurtenances have ever been found inside the Great Pyramid, so far as careful historians know: although there is a tradition that one of the Caliphs used to keep a decorated wooden mummy-case standing outside a palace door and that this case had been brought out of the Pyramid. No lengthy hieroglyphic inscriptions, no chiselled bas-reliefs or painted representations of the life of the deceased appear upon any of the inner walls of the Pyramid, as they do upon the walls of every other early burial vault in Egypt. The interior structure is plain, devoid of the embellishment which the Pharaohs loved to lavish upon their tombs, free from the ornamentation which one might reasonably expect to find were this one of ancient Egypt's most important tombs.

Perhaps the point which is regarded as most conclusive evidence that here was the tomb of a pagan monarch, is the empty, coverless, red-granite box which lies on the floor of the King's Chamber. This, obviously, was the sarcophagus of the king, says your Egyptologist; who thereafter regards the matter as settled.

But why do not the sides of this sarcophagus carry the usual conventional texts and religious representations? Why do they not bear a single word or a single hieroglyphic inscription of any kind? All other sarcophagi usually carry some written or pictured memorial of their use; why not this one, if it was dedicated to one of Egypt's most celebrated kings?

Why were air channels, more than two hundred feet long, built to connect the burial vault which held this supposed sarcophagus with the outer air? Mummies do not need fresh air, while the workmen had no need to re-enter the chamber once they had roofed it in. I have seen no other chamber anywhere in Egypt, constructed to serve as a sepulchre of the royal dead, which possessed air channels.

Why was this presumed coffin placed in a room which is one hundred and fifty feet above the ground level, when all other Egyptian practice was to cut down into the rock below ground level for a burial vault? In fact, it was and is, a world-wide custom to dispose of the dead either under or on the ground. "Dust thou art and to dust thou shalt return," has ever been Nature's message to man.

Why should that lofty hall, the Grand Gallery, have been built to give access to the King's Chamber, and built over thirty feet high, when a continuation of the Ascending Passage, which is a mere four feet in height, would have served the purpose equally well and entailed much less labour through being far less complicated in construction than the Grand Gallery itself?

Why was a second room, the so-called Queen's Chamber, built near the first one? Pharaohs were never laid to rest near their queens, while a single mummy does not need two vaults. Had the Queen's Chamber contained the conventional wall paintings and inscriptions of Egyptian tombs, its existence as an ante-room might have been justified, but it is bare and as unornamented as the King's Chamber. And why, too, should the former have also been fitted with air shafts, sealed though their mouths were when discovered? Why should the builders have troubled to ventilate these two so-called tombs? It is a point worth repeating to oneself: the dead do not breathe.

No! One's intelligence, seeking the true cause of all this enormous expenditure of time, labour, material and money, refusing to accept either the prediction or tomb theories, must turn away in quest of some other explanation.

¶

I mused long and often over this mystery of the Pyramids' purpose and spent many an hour stumbling over the rocky debris which surrounds them or wandering through the dim passages and gloomy chambers which lie within them. I frequently sat on the white limestone blocks at the base of the Great Pyramid in the fierce heat of the afternoon sun or on the soft sand which lies to the east, and pondered the problem. I climbed course after course of masonry, searched carefully for clues, examined crevices and studied the general lay-out of the three buildings. I disturbed large lizards and huge cockroaches inside the dark, rarely visited tunnels of the Second and Third Pyramids. In short, I worked so hard at my researches that I became as familiar with these old structures, these stone mementoes of Egypt's earliest race, as I was with the rooms of my new flat in Cairo.

And the more I became acquainted with their details, the more I was compelled to admire them, while the better I understood their peculiar plans the better I realized their remarkable technical excellence.

The technical skill involved in quarrying, transporting and hoisting into position the immense stone blocks for these triangular legacies from remote antiquity, at a time when steam and electrical aids were not available, demanded and received my admiration. No travelling steam-crane could have moved along steel rails to hoist those mighty blocks of stone into place, for both steam and steel were alike unknown quantities in that epoch.

Certainly, if any Pharaoh had wished to leave a lasting tomb for posterity, he could not have chosen a more durable architectural form than the pyramid. The immense base, the sloping sides and the narrow top would protect his sepulchre against wind, sand and time, better than any other form, while the solid mass of the interior offered the greatest possible resistance to the violating hands of men.

Although the impressive skyscraping towers of New York have now outdistanced the Pyramid, the fact remains that throughout the known history of the world and until lately the Pyramid remained its highest man-made structure, dwarfing all others, a wonder for the ancients and a riddle for the moderns.

I quickly found, as all other investigators have before me, that the internal construction of the First Pyramid was far more complicated than that of the other two, as well as being infinitely more interesting, while its immense comparative size proclaimed its greater importance. It was not long, therefore, before I concentrated all further study upon this one, which I believed must contain the real secret of the Pyramids.

I came to know the Great Pyramid under every one of the marvellously changing lights of Egypt. At dawn the first rays would touch it a silver grey; the disappearing sun would leave it a pale violet; while under the mysterious light of a full moon every stone from base to apex would appear as if bathed in a bluish phosphorescence tinged with silver.

Yet the Great Pyramid which we see to-day is not the Pyramid that the ancients saw. Theirs was covered with a fine, white, smooth, polished limestone casing on each of its four sides that reflected the sun's rays with a fierce brilliance, and that physically justified its old Egyptian name of *The Light*. The beds and sides of these blocks were worked to a perfect surface and fitted together with such mosaic precision that the cemented joints were scarcely to be seen. The stone triangle, so unexpected, so arresting, set down on the yellow carpet of the desert, blazed out with light like a gigantic mirror, and therefore was visible at enormous distance under the strong Oriental sun. And even as late as the end of the twelfth century these white stones were still in place, bearing upon their surfaces hieroglyphs that drew from the pen of Abdul Latif the following quaint descriptions:

"The stones were inscribed with ancient characters, now unintelligible. I never met with a person in all Egypt who understood them. The inscriptions are so numerous that copies of those alone which may be seen upon the surface of the two Pyramids would occupy above six thousand pages."

To-day, its once-smooth sides are terraced into steps, while not a single inscription can be discovered, and of all the thousands of casing stones but a few bare base blocks remain in position. It is clear, from these vestiges, that the casing material was taken from the Mokattam Hills which lie to the south-east of Cairo. For two years after Abdul Latif's visit, Egypt shook and trembled as a great earthquake smashed the town of Cairo to pieces. And then the Arabs descended on the Great Pyramid for building material wherewith to set up anew their broken city, as the Turks and Greeks had once turned the noble Parthenon into a quarry and carted off most of its stones to build their houses. They avidly stripped off the polished, bevelled white lining blocks and carried them off to Cairo. How many old mansions, mosques and forts of the Egyptian capital hide within their thick walls to-day the hieroglyph inscriptions that once covered the four faces of the Great Pyramid? Part of the graceful mosque of Sultan Hassan, acknowledged to be the most beautiful of Cairo's three hundred mosques, was built with these casing-blocks.

There are enough stones in the structure to build the houses of a fair-sized town—such is the immense amount of material it contains, and they would have carried off the entire Pyramid, too, but they found that the cost and labour and time of unwedging even a single one of the enormous blocks which compose its body was so utterly disproportionate to its value and so difficult a task that they gave up the idea as hopeless. Nevertheless, they did not learn this lesson until they had removed the topmost courses of masonry and thus deprived the Pyramid of its apex.

Nor is the entrance which visitors use to-day the original entrance which was used by the ancient Egyptians themselves. The, latter remained a mystery, a secret kept and guarded by the Pyramid for several centuries before its rediscovery by a determined Arab king, who spent a fortune and set an army of labourers at work to wrest this secret of its sealed opening from its reluctant grasp. The innermost passages and chambers of the Great Pyramid had defied Greek and Roman ruler alike, as they had defied the uninitiated Egyptians, and with the passing of the Romans though the legend of its entrance persisted, the location of that entrance became unknown.

From the time that it was closed and sealed, centuries passed peacefully over its untouched interior, until, at last, it was broken into by men in quest of its fabled treasure, and the long sleep was disturbed. Not till the year 820 of our era was that location determined, when the Caliph Al Mamoun gathered his best engineers, architects, builders and workmen together on the little plateau of Gizeh and bade them open the Pyramid. "O king, it cannot possibly be done," said the chief men. "I will have it certainly done," he replied.

They had to work without chart or plan, but were guided by an old tradition that the entrance was on the northern side. They naturally chose a point in the middle of that side for their great attempt, goaded all the time by the watchful presence of the Caliph, who wanted to test the truth of old legends that vast treasures had been hidden inside the Pyramid by forgotten

Pharaohs. Incidentally, he was the son of Caliph Haroun Al Raschid, the famed character of the famous book *Arabian Nights*.

This Caliph Al Mamoun was no ordinary Caliph. He had ordered his scholars to translate the writings of the Greek sages into Arabic; he continually reminded his subjects of the virtues of study; and he himself took pleasure in joining the most learned men of his country in their discussions.

His imperial residence was in Baghdad and it was from this famous city that he came to Egypt. Not long after this attempt to open the Pyramid, he returned to Baghdad and there finished his life.

But the builders of the Great Pyramid, foreseeing that one day human cupidity would violate their structure, had placed the entrance several feet to one side of the centre and considerably higher than anyone might reasonably expect a doorway to be situated. As a result, Al Mamoun's men worked for several months to penetrate the interior of the Pyramid without finding any sign of passage or room; nothing but solid masonry presented itself to their view. And had they depended on hammer and chisel alone their undertaking would have endured as long as the reign of their king, and longer. But they were astute enough to build little bonfires against the stones and then, when the latter became red-hot, flung cold vinegar upon them until they cracked. To-day, one can still see the blackened charred surfaces of blocks which escaped the chisels that were so busy more than one thousand years ago. Two blacksmiths worked all day sharpening the chisels that blunted so quickly against the massive stones, while wooden engines were set up to assist the efforts of the weary men in forcing their way inside. Yet still the original entrance, the corridors and the inner rooms remained undiscovered.

The work of excavating in a narrow passage stifled the men with dust and heat, the difficulty of penetrating the hardest mass of solid masonry in the world with the primitive tools then available fatigued them almost beyond endurance, while the complete failure that was the only reward of their efforts disheartened them to the point of despair. They had tunnelled their way inwards for more than a hundred feet and at last they were on the point of putting down their tools in open mutiny and refusing to continue such useless labour, when the sound of a heavy stone falling out of place came to their ears

D

—it came from the interior just a little way beyond the farthest point to which they had penetrated.

Destiny had taken a hand in the game. Thereafter they worked with zest and zeal and soon broke through into the original entrance passage. The Great Pyramid had been reopened.

It was, then, easy enough to ascend this passage and find the hidden door: a door so cleverly concealed that it could never have been discovered from the outside. After so many centuries the secret door was no longer in working order; it had got irretrievably stuck. That door has disappeared to-day, lost in the general pillage which took place after the earthquake at Cairo. It was just such a door as the ancient Egyptians would have fixed at the opening to the most mysterious building they had erected. It was really a movable stone flap, self-replacing, and finished externally so as perfectly to resemble the surrounding casing stones; it fitted tightly into the opening and was itself a solid block of stone. When closed it could not be detected apart from the rest of the outer surface. When opened it wheeled round on its own length, revealing a cavity. It was finely balanced and worked on a pivot, the centre of gravity being placed under this pivot, while compensating weights were fitted to counteract its heavy weight. It could not be opened except with a strong push at one end followed by a powerful pull at the other; powerful enough to lift it outwards from the face and then up. This allowed the visitor to squirm his way, crawling on all fours, into the passage behind. The turning flap of stone then swung backwards on its pivots and completely concealed the entrance again.

Even that was not all, for a heavy wooden locked door then barred his onward way. And after this further obstruction, ten more doors had to be passed before he succeeded in reaching the King's Chamber. Most of these were wooden, while one was another movable secret stone flap. But all have since utterly disappeared.

§

Once inside the original entrance passage, Caliph Al Mamoun's men found that their labour was by no means over. They discovered that the passage came to a dead end before a huge block of granite. It did not seem likely that the opening and passage had been constructed merely to terminate in a cul-de-sac; therefore, they tried to cut their way through this formidable granite barrier; but they failed. The tools at their disposal could not penetrate this stone; the Pyramid builders must have searched the whole of Egypt for the hardest stone it could yield before they selected this particular variety.

Fortunately for the efforts of the invaders the material at the side of the dark granite block was white limestone, a much softer stone and therefore much easier through which to quarry. They turned their attention to this and hewed a tunnel through it parallel with the granite block. A few feet of cutting brought them to the end of the block and into another passage. It then became apparent that the entrance to the second passage had been purposely closed at some time by this gigantic granite plug, conical in shape and weighing many tons, which fitted tightly into its mouth.

This further passage ran upwards at an angle which was similar to that at which the first passage ran downwards, i.e. about twenty-six degrees. Al Mamoun's officers and men crept up this steep corridor, which was less than four feet high and a little over three feet wide. The light thrown by their torches revealed nothing but the bare walls until they reached a point where it went on horizontally. This point was really a junction where the passage was met by a lofty ascending corridor, seven times greater in height, and by a descending narrow shaft that lost itself in the very depths of the Pyramid.

Continuing along the horizontal passage, the stooping intruders, with heads bent towards the floor, found themselves eventually in a large room, which, to their disappointment, was completely empty. Its walls were quite plain, inscription-less, and only a large niche on the eastern side gave the slightest promise of any treasure to reward their labour. To enter it they had to mount a platform and then pass into a rough passage so low they were forced to crawl along like snakes. But the passage ended abruptly in the solid masonry core of the Pyramid and though in later days they considerable enlarged this terminus, the only treasure to be found consisted of blocks of limestone.

Retracing their steps to the junction, they began to explore the long and lofty corridor, which, in later times, has received the name of Grand Gallery. It had a peculiar sloping roof, built up with seven overlapping courses. Its floor inclined upwards at precisely the same angle as the passage which led to the Gallery. The men began to climb this smooth slippery

floor, moving between polished granite walls that led upward
for one hundred and fifty feet of unbroken ascent and whose
two sides were lined with long slotted stone banks.   At the
end of the Gallery a high step suddenly blocked their way.
They climbed it and walked across a level floor into a low
narrow passage which brought them to an antechamber.   A few
more paces, a stoop beneath a solid portcullis, and they entered
a large chamber which was located in the very heart of the
Pyramid, being equidistant from all sides.   This was the room
which they later named "The King's Chamber," as they also
called the first discovered room "The Queen's Chamber."
But such names were never used by the ancient Egyptians.

The King's Chamber was walled with squared dark granite
blocks of immense size. Its ceiling was formed of nine enormous
beams of the same material, now known to be the largest stones
in the whole Pyramid. One of them alone weighs seventy tons.
How the builders ever got it into position, two hundred feet
above ground level, without using our modern steam or
electrical hoists, is a problem about which our own architects
theorize but which they cannot solve.

The Caliph Al Mamoun and his men were again deeply
disappointed. For, apart from an open stone coffin, the
Chamber was entirely empty. The coffin contained nothing
but dust.

It seemed incredible that the ancient Egyptians had built
such a prodigious empty tomb as this Pyramid to no purpose,
they thought, so they feverishly tore up part of the stone
flooring, burrowed open one corner of the room, and hacked
vainly at the solid walls in their fierce quest of hidden treasure.
But they could not defeat the astuteness of those cunning
early builders and eventually retired baffled, chagrined and
disheartened.

Two more places were left for their exploration: the underground continuation of the original entrance passage and the
deep narrow shaft.   The first took them into a small tunnel,
along which they had to make a rapid descent and in which it
was easy for their feet to slip, for it had been cut downwards
into the solid rock for a distance of no less than three hundred
and fifty feet.   It ended in a roughly hewn chamber whose roof
was so low that it could be touched with the hands and whose
unfinished rocky floor was so rugged that they had to clamber
up and down to cross it. They named it "The Pit." It

contained nothing but debris and dust. At the farther side another small passage had been cut into the rock; they could enter it only by crawling on their stomachs, like snakes, with faces a few inches from the floor. Even this subterranean tunnel yielded nothing, for it abruptly terminated in a solid wall of rock.

Remained the shaft. It was almost entirely perpendicular and could be explored only by letting down one man at a time, suspended by ropes, into its inky depths. After sixty feet of descent a small chamber was encountered, a roughly hewn enlargement of the shaft. The latter was continued again from the floor of the chamber, leading apparently endlessly downwards. It looked like a deep well and this, in fact, the men decided that it was. They never completed its exploration.

Anyway, the vast treasures which, in their imagination, littered the Pyramid, did not exist.

Thus ended Caliph Al Mamoun's great adventure in reopening the Great Pyramid. The learned Arab historians of to-day will give you many variants of this last story, but these are the really authentic facts.

¶

Centuries rolled over the truncated head of the Pyramid after Haroun Al Raschid's son forced a hole into its northern side. Legend soon enwrapped it with superstitious dread and surrounded it with ghostly horrors, so that the Arabs shunned its interior as they shunned the leper. Only a few venturesome souls ever explored its heart and depth again. For the most part its dark passages and bare chambers lay undisturbed in majestic silence. Not till the second half of the eighteenth century, when stolid, matter-of-fact, unsuperstitious Europeans began to tread the surrounding sands, did the hammer and chisel of the excavator resound once more within the ancient building.

Enterprising Nathaniel Davison, His Britannic Majesty's Consul at Algiers in the seventeen-sixties, took a long vacation and went off to Egypt, where he gazed speculatively at the Great Pyramid. He knew that the ancient Egyptians usually buried a certain amount of jewels with their illustrious dead. He knew, too, that everyone said the Pyramids were just gigantic tombs.

And he had discovered, in the open doorway of the King's

Chamber, a curious echo which returned more than once every time he shouted loudly.   He suspected—and rightly—that somewhere behind the granite slabs of this gaunt room there existed another chamber.   It was just possible, indeed probable, that within that chamber there lay a linen-wrapped mummy with its accompanying jewels.

He gathered a few workmen together and set to work.   The floor of the King's Chamber had already been fruitlessly excavated by Al Mamoun centuries before; the echoes of Davison's own voice seemed to come from overhead; and so he turned his attention to the ceiling.   A careful examination of the layout of the Chamber and its adjoining passages showed that the easiest way to penetrate what lay above it was to force an opening through the top course of the eastern wall of the Grand Gallery and thus work through into the side of any chamber which existed there.   Procuring a tall ladder to examine the spot, he was surprised to discover that the opening already existed, so he crawled through.

A chamber, twenty feet long, was found.   Its position was exactly above that of the King's Chamber.   Its ceiling was so low that Davison had to crawl in on his knees to search for the treasure which lured him.   The room was completely empty.

Davison returned to Algiers, having gained nothing more than the problematical honour of having his name affixed to that of the newly discovered chamber by the archæologists who followed him.

He was succeeded at the Pyramid in the early years of the nineteenth century by a strange excavator, who was dreamer, mystic and archæologist in one.   This man was an Italian, Captain Caviglia, who put in so much time at the old building that he became, in his own words, *"tout-à-fait pyramidale."* Lord Lindsay encountered him during a visit to Egypt and wrote home to England:

"Caviglia told me that he had pushed his studies in magic, animal magnetism, etc., to an extent which nearly killed him— to the very verge, he said, of what is forbidden man to know; and it was only the purity of his intentions which saved him. . . . He has strange unearthly ideas.   He says it would be highly dangerous to communicate them."

Whilst engaged on his archæological work, Caviglia actually lived for a while in Davison's Chamber and turned that gloomy recess into a residential apartment!

Caviglia did not limit his work to the Great Pyramid alone. He made discoveries in the Second and Third Pyramids, explored burial vaults in the region between them and the Sphinx, and unearthed some interesting sarcophagi and smaller relics of ancient Egypt.

About the time that a beautiful young woman unexpectedly found herself crowned as Victoria, Queen of England, destiny sent to Egypt a gallant British officer, a perfect English gentleman, and a wealthy patron of the British Museum, triply combined in the courtly person of Colonel Howard Vyse. He employed hundreds of labourers upon the most extensive series of excavations that all three Pyramids and the surrounding region had witnessed for a thousand years, i.e. since the time of Caliph Al Mamoun. He secured the services of Caviglia for a time, but the temperaments of the highly strung Italian and the thoroughly conventional Englishman clashed: they soon parted.

Colonel Vyse gave £10,000 of his money freely for these Egyptian excavations, while he presented their tangible results to the British Museum. Boxes of interesting relics crossed the seas, but his most interesting discovery remained behind. He had found four rooms high up in the Great Pyramid and immediately above Davison's Chamber, though not without some difficulty and much danger; his workmen risked a thirty-foot fall much of the time, as they excavated a small passage upwards through the solid masonry. These rooms were as low, as confined in space, as the first one. And they, too, were empty, if dusty.

With their discovery and after a study of the gabled ceiling of sloping limestone beams over the topmost chamber, the purpose of the whole series of five low rooms became clear. They had been constructed to relieve the ceiling of the King's Chamber of the overwhelming pressure which thousands of tons of solid masonry overhead necessarily forced upon it; they acted as a cushioning device. Not only that, but they safeguarded the King's Chamber from the precipitation of this masonry upon its floor in the unlikely but possible event of an earthquake splitting the body of the Pyramid. They would then act as an admirable arrangement of buffers to take the shock of subsidence after the earthquake, thus preventing the King's Chamber from being crushed in by the enormous mass of stone overhead. The passage of thousands of years over the Pyramid has proved the excellence and ingenuity of this architectural plan.

One curious thing which Vyse found was the first and only series of hieroglyphs which have ever been discovered inside the Pyramid since the inscribed outer casing was stripped off. These were the quarry-masons' marks on the rough faces of the stones in the five construction chambers. Among these marks were the cartouches, or oval-framed picture-writing, of three royal names—Khufu, Khnem Khufu and Khnem. They were not inscribed, but drawn in red paint, as masons' marks generally were in ancient Egypt.

Egyptologists could only hazard guesses at the meaning of Khnem, and they had never heard of any Egyptian king bearing that name. They could give no proper explanation of the presence of this name. But they knew very well who Khufu was: that Fourth Dynasty Pharaoh to whom the later Greek historians unfortunately attached the name of Cheops. This discovery of Vyse's finally settled the date of the Pyramid's building for them; Khufu had erected it and none else.

But nowhere in the Pyramid has Khufu's mummy ever been found.

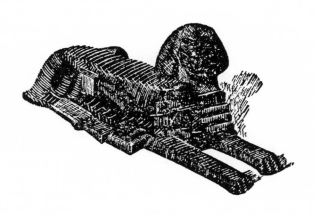

# CHAPTER IV

THE sleeping cats of Cairo opened their green eyes, yawned prodigiously, and then gracefully stretched their soft paws to the utmost possible limit. Dusk was arriving and with dusk began the activity which constituted their real existence—friendly chats, food-scavenging, mice-chasing, open battle and love-making. And with dusk, too, I was beginning one of the strangest activities of my life, albeit a silent one.

I had proposed to myself to spend an entire night inside the Great Pyramid, to sit, awake and alert, for twelve hours in the King's chamber, while the slow darkness moved across the African world. And here I was, at last, settling down within the strangest shelter yet built on our planet.

It had been no easy task to arrive at this point, either. I had discovered that, although the public could always approach it, the Great Pyramid was not public property. It belonged to the Government of Egypt. One could no more walk into it and spend an unconventional night inside any of its rooms than one could walk into any strange man's house and spend a night inside his best bedroom.

Each time one visits the interior of the Pyramid one has to buy a ticket for five piastres from the Department of Antiquities. I, therefore, walked into the Department of Antiquities and optimistically asked for permission to spend one night inside the Great Pyramid. Had I asked for permission to fly to the moon, the face of the official who listened to me could not have betrayed more utter stupefaction.

I entered into a brief and apologetic explanation of my request. Surprise gave way to amusement; he smiled. I felt that he regarded me as a fit candidate for a certain institution which few of us would care to enter as inmates. Finally:

"I have never had such a request before. I do not think it is within my power to grant it."

He sent me to another and higher official of the same Department. The comical scene which had taken place in his room was re-enacted once more. My optimism began to drain away out of my shoes.

"Impossible!" declared the second official kindly but firmly, thinking he had before him a tame lunatic. "The thing is unheard of. I regret—" his voice trailed off, the while he shrugged his shoulders.

He rose from his chair to bow me out of the room.

It was then that my journalistic and editorial training, lulled for several years but not dead, rose rebelliously into action. I began to argue with him, persisted in repeating my request in other ways, and refused to budge from the room. He got rid of me, finally, by saying that the matter did not come within the jurisdiction of the Antiquities Department.

Within whose jurisdiction did it come, then, I enquired. He was not quite sure but thought I had better apply to the police.

I realized that my request was eccentric at the least and sufficient to label me as insane at the most. Nevertheless I could not drop it. The determination to carry it out had become an obsession.

At Police Headquarters I discovered a Permit Section. For the third time I begged to be allowed to spend one night inside the Pyramid. The official did not know what to do with me so he sent me to his chief. The latter wanted a little time to consider the matter. When I returned next day he referred me to the Department of Antiquities!

I went home in momentary despair of ever achieving my object.

But "difficulties are often made to be overcome" is a saying whose wearying triteness does not diminish its undying truth. My next move was to secure an interview with the genial Commandant of the Cairo City Police, El Lewa Russell Pacha. I walked out of his office with a written authority, which requested the police chief of the area in which the Pyramid was situated to give me all the assistance necessary to achieve my purpose.

And so, early one evening, I reported at the Mena Police

Station to the local chief, Major Mackersey. I signed a book which was handed to me and which made the police responsible for my safety till the following day. A station constable was detailed to accompany me as far as the Pyramid, and to give instructions to the armed policeman who is placed outside the building to guard it at night.

"We are taking a risk in leaving you alone inside all night. You won't blow up the Pyramid, will you?" said Major Mackersey, humorously, as we shook hands in parting.

"I promise you not only that, but I shall not even run away with it!"

"I am afraid we shall have to lock you in," he added. "We always shut the entrance to the Pyramid at dusk with a locked iron grille. So you will be a prisoner for twelve hours."

"Excellent! To-day, no residence could be more desirable to me than such a prison."

¶

The approach to the Pyramids runs along a road shaded by *lebbek* trees. Houses appear on its sides at rare intervals. Finally the road winds gradually up the side of the plateau on which the Pyramids themselves are built, ending in a steep incline. As I drove up the avenue I reflected that of all the travellers who had taken the same direction for several centuries past, few if any had come on so curious a mission as mine.

I mounted the small hill across the western shore of the Nile to where the Great Pyramid and its good companion, the Sphinx, maintain silent watch over Northern Africa.

The giant monument loomed up ahead of me, as I walked across the mingled sand and stones. Once more I gazed at the triangular sloping flanks which enclose the oldest architecture that the world knows to-day, at the enormous blocks which stretch away from base to apex in diminishing perspective. The perfect simplicity of this building, its utter freedom from any trace of ornament, the absence of any curves amid all these straight lines—these things did not in any way detract from the massive grandeur of this creation.

I entered the silent Pyramid through the gaping hole which Caliph Al Mamoun had made in its side, and began my exploration of the titanic structure, not for the first time, it was true, but for the first time upon such a strange quest as had brought me again to Egypt. After making my way some distance, I reached the end of this horizontal hole and my path changed into the Pyramid's original entrance passage.

Then, torch in hand, with head bent down almost to my knees, I descended the long, low, steep, narrow and slippery continuation of the corridor. This awkward posture was exceedingly uncomfortable, while the declivity of the stone floor compulsorily hastened the speed of my descent.

I wanted to preface my sojourn in the King's Chamber with an examination of the underground region of the Pyramid, access to which in modern years has been barred by an iron portcullis which prevents the general public from entering this dismal region and being half suffocated. The old Latin tag, "Facilis descensus Averni," recurred unexpectedly to memory, but this time there was a grim sardonic humour in the words. I saw nothing in the yellowish beam of torchlight but the hewn rock through which this floor had been cut. When, at long last, I reached a small recess on the right, I seized the opportunity to slip into it and straighten out my body for a couple of minutes. I discovered that the recess was nothing else than the terminus of the nearly perpendicular shaft, the so-called Well, which descends from the junction of the ascending passage and the Grand Gallery. The old name still sticks to this shaft because for nearly two thousand years it was thought to have water at the bottom. Not till it was cleared out by Caviglia of the mass of debris which had accumulated in it was the bottom discovered to be perfectly dry.

It was narrower than the passage which I had just left, this unattractive, roughly excavated opening that yawned up into the solid rock. I discovered little niches cut into the sides, parallel with each other, which afforded foothold and handhold for the somewhat perilous climb.

It led upwards irregularly and tortuously for a considerable distance until it reached a large roughly cut chamber shaped like a bowl, the one now called the Grotto, which marked the level of the rocky plateau upon which the Pyramid had been built. The Grotto had been partly constructed in an enlarged natural fissure in the rock. Beyond this, the Well had evidently been cut through the masonry and not built up with blocks, as all the other overground passages were formed. This section of the Well widened out in diameter and was thus more difficult to climb than its narrower sub-Grotto section.

At last I emerged from the torn and ragged opening which formed the mouth of the shaft, and found myself in the north-western corner of the Grand Gallery.

Why and when had it been cut through the body of the Pyramid? The question automatically registered itself and as I meditated on it, the answer flashed up. Those ancient Egyptians who had closed down an epoch of the Pyramid's history by closing the entrance to the upper chambers and Grand Gallery with three monstrous granite plugs, had had to create a way of escape for themselves or they could never have got out of the Pyramid.

I knew from my own researches that the shaft and the Grotto had been cut at the same time as the building of the Pyramid, but that the Well did not descend any farther than the Grotto itself at the time. For thousands of years there was no direct link between the upper passages and the subterranean one.

When the Great Pyramid had fulfilled its mysterious purpose, those who were responsible sealed it. The sealing had been foreseen by the original builders, who had left the necessary material in place and had even made a contraction in the lower end of the ascending passage to hold the three granite plugs.

Working at their task, the last tenants cut the lower section of the Well through solid rock as a way of escape for themselves. When the work was finished and they had made their retreat, it was only necessary to block up the exit of the newly cut section securely, at the point where it joins the descending passage, and then ascend the 300-feet slope to the original entrance. Thus the Well, although originally created as a means of reaching the Grotto, finally became a means of leaving the blocked-up Pyramid.

I returned again by the easier route to the long slanting tunnel which connects the interior with the outer world, to resume my downward journey into the rocky plateau of Gizeh. Once, at a corner, an enlarged shadow was suddenly thrust across my path so that I drew back, startled, until I realized it was my own. In this weird place one expected everything; nothing was too strange to happen. Slipping and crawling the comparatively short remaining distance, I was relieved to find myself at the end of the descent and upon a level floor, but inside a still smaller tunnel. I crawled forward about ten more yards and then arrived at the open entrance to the strangest room I had ever seen—the so-called Pit. It was a little less than fifty feet from wall to wall on its longest side.

This gloomy vault, which lies beneath the exact centre of the Pyramid, gave to the eye an impression of a task hurriedly abandoned; it seemed to be a chamber whose excavation out of the solid rock was suddenly stopped. The ceiling had been well cut but the floor rolled up and down like a trench that had been bombarded. The old Egyptian masons usually worked downwards in cutting rock vaults and therefore finished the floors last; why this particular floor should never have been finished when more than a lifetime of labour at least was later devoted to building the superstructure that rose above the rock level, is an archæological nut which no one has yet been able to crack. But then, the whole Pyramid itself is really such a nut.

I flashed my torch into the turgid gloom of the vault and focused a beam of light upon the centre of the floor. I moved closer and peered over the edge of a deep yawning hole, mute testimony to the one-time presence of treasure-seekers, who had fruitlessly and laboriously excavated a pit within the Pit. I felt the unpleasant touch of the wings of a bat as it flew past my head and squawked around the airless room. Down in the hole I noticed the light disturb the sleep of three other bats, which hung upside down on the roughly cut sides. I moved away, awakening two more bats which hung suspended from the ceiling. Alarmed and bewildered as I thrust the light mercilessly upon them, they scurried to and fro, also squawking, and then disappeared into the gloom of the entrance passage.

I climbed over the hilly floor and reached the farther end of the chamber, where a tiny level tunnel presented itself in the wall. It was just wide enough to enable one to squirm inside but too low to permit anything else except crawling dead flat upon the stomach. The floor was thickly covered with the dust of several thousand years and the journey was anything but pleasant.    I endured it for the sake of examining the tunnel's terminus.    After penetrating nearly twenty yards into the rock I found it ended abruptly; apparently this tunnel, too, had never been finished.

Nearly suffocated, I groped my way back and returned to the airless Pit, took a final glance around the room, and began my return journey to the upper regions of the Pyramid.    When I reached the beginning of the low passage, which sloped upwards in a perfectly straight line for three hundred and fifty feet of solid rock before it continued as a built-up corridor, traversing the masonry, I stretched myself out on the floor and gazed up through the open exit into the darkened sky, as through a giant lens-less telescope.    There, an easily seen twinkling silver point in indigo-blue space, was the Pole Star.    I checked the direction by a wrist-compass, which indicated dead north. Those early builders had not only done a massive job but an accurate one.

I crawled back through the steep passage and reached, at length, the level corridor which conducts into the Queen's Chamber.    A score or more paces and I stood under its inclined arch roof, which meets in a ridge in the middle. I examined the two ventilating shafts which slant upwards from the northern and southern walls.    Here was clear proof that the room had never been a tomb, but was intended to be used.    Many have been puzzled by the circumstance of the discovery of these shafts, in 1872, when it was found that they stopped five inches short of the Chamber itself and apparently were not originally cut right through the walls.    In their discovered state, therefore, they could not admit air; so it is thought that they had some other and unknown use.    But the best explanation is that the time came when they had served their purpose and, like the rest of the upper passages of the Pyramid, were completely sealed at their orifices by new stone blocks.

Waynman Dixon, a civil engineer then employed on some works near the Pyramid, chanced to discover these air tubes while examining the walls of the Queen's Chamber out of curiosity.    He noticed that one wall, which sounded hollow at a particular spot, also seemed slightly cracked. He had the spot broken into and five inches from the surface found a small shaft; then, by the same process, he discovered its mate on the opposite wall of the Chamber. Both shafts extend right through the body of the Pyramid: this has lately been proved by means of probing-rods, which have been run up them for about two hundred feet.

I turned back to the level corridor and walked to the point where it meets the Grand Gallery. And then, for a hundred and fifty feet, I slowly progressed to the top of this steep, corbel-sided ascent. A slight weakness, engendered by a three days' fast, began to trouble me as I climbed that incline. Finally, I rested for a few seconds on the three-feet-high step which marked the end and which was so placed as to be exactly in line with the vertical axis of the Pyramid. A few paces forward through the Antechamber, a forced stoop under the granite block which hangs down from grooved side-walls, and which bars the exit of this horizontal corridor, and I had reached the most important room in the Pyramid, the famous King's Chamber.

¶

Here, too, the presence of a couple of air tubes, each about nine inches square, killed the tomb-chamber theory. Their openings into the room had never been sealed, as were those in the Queen's Chamber, but they had been completely filled with loose stones, which Colonel Vyse had to clear out when he wanted to determine the nature of these shafts. That this filling operation had been carried out at the same time as all the other attempts to conceal the internal arrangements of the overground portion of the Pyramid, was extremely probable.

I flashed the lamp over the bare walls and flat ceiling, noting anew the admirably accurate fitting of the immense polished granite blocks at their joints, and then began a slow circuit of the walls, carefully examining each individual stone. The rose-tinted rocks of far Syene had been split in twain to provide these blocks. Here and there treasure-seekers had scarred both floor and wall in their vain quests. On the eastern side of the floor, part of the stone flags had disappeared and beaten earth had taken its place, while on the north-western side a deep rectangular hole remained unfilled. A long rough stone block which had once formed part of the floor and covered this hole, stood against the wall on one side, left there by early Arab hands, perchance. Parallel with it, and but a few inches away, was the flat-sided, coffin-like sarcophagus: a lidless, lonely object, which was the only other thing to be found in this bare room. It was placed exactly north and south.

The dislodged flooring-block offered a possible seat, so I sat down on it, tailor-like, with folded feet, and settled there for the remainder of the night.

On my right I had placed my hat, jacket and shoes; on my left reposed the still-burning torch, a thermos flask with hot tea, a couple of bottles of iced water, a notebook and my Parker pen. A last look around the chamber, a final glimpse of the marble coffer beside me, and then I extinguished the light.

I kept beside me a powerful electric torch ready to be switched on.

The sudden plunge into total darkness brought with it the wondering question of what the night would bring forth. The only thing one could do in this strange position was to wait . . . and wait . . . and wait.

The minutes slowly dragged themselves along, the while I slowly "sensed" that the King's Chamber possessed a very strong atmosphere of its own, an atmosphere which I can only call "psychic." For I had deliberately made myself receptive in mind, passive in feeling and negative in attitude, so that I might become a perfect register of whatever super-physical event might transpire. I wanted no personal prejudice or preconception to interfere with the reception of anything that might come to me from some source inaccessible to the five physical senses of man. I gradually diminished the flow of thoughts until the mind entered a half-blank state.

And the stillness which descended on my brain rendered me acutely cognizant of the stillness which had descended on my life. The world, with its noise and bustle, was now as utterly remote as though it did not exist. No sound, no whisper, came to me out of the darkness. Silence is the real sovereign of the kingdom of the Pyramid, a silence that began in prehistoric antiquity and which no babble of visiting tourists can really break, for every night it returns anew with awe-inspiring completeness.

I became aware of the powerful atmosphere of the room. It is a perfectly normal and common experience for sensitive persons to become aware of the atmosphere of ancient houses, and my own experience began with something of this sort. The passage of time deepened it, enhanced the sense of immeasurable antiquity which environed me, and made me feel that the twentieth century was slipping away from under my feet.    Yet, following my self-imposed resolve, I did not resist the feeling, instead I let it grow stronger.

A strange feeling that I was not alone began to creep insidiously over me.    Under the cover of complete blackness, I felt that something animate and living was throbbing into existence.    It was a vague feeling but a real one, and it was this, coupled with the increasing sense of the returning Past, that constituted my consciousness of something "psychic."

Yet nothing clear-cut, definite, emerged from this vague and general sense of an eerie life that pulsated through the darkness. The hours slipped on and, contrary to my expectation, the advancing night brought increasing coldness with it.    The effects of the three-day fast which I had undertaken in order to increase my sensitivity, now showed themselves in growing chilliness.    Cold air was creeping into the King's Chamber through the narrow ventilation shafts, and then creeping past the thin barrier of my light garment.    My chilled flesh began to shiver under its thin shirt.    I got up and dressed myself in the jacket which I had put off only a few hours before on account of the intense heat.    Such is Eastern life at certain times of the year—tropical heat by day and a heavy fall of temperature by night.

To this day no one has discovered the mouths of these air channels on the outside of the Pyramid, although the approximate area of their positions is known.    Some Egyptologists have even doubted whether the channels were ever carried right through to the outside, but the complete chilling of the air during my experience finally settles the point.

I sat down for the second time upon my stone seat and surrendered myself anew to the oppressive death-like silence, and to the all-prevailing sombre darkness of the chamber. With pliant soul I waited and wondered.    For no reason at all I remembered irrelevantly that somewhere to the east the Suez Canal pursued its straight course through sand and marsh, and the stately Nile provided a backbone to this land.

The queer sepulchral stillness in the room, the empty stone coffin beside me, were not reassuring to one's nerves, while the break in my vigil seemed to have broken something else too, for very quickly I found that the sensing of invisible life around me rapidly rose into complete certainty. There *was* something throbbing and alive in my vicinity, although I could still see absolutely nothing. With this discovery the realization of my isolated and uncanny situation suddenly overwhelmed me. Here I was sitting alone in a queer room that was perched more than two hundred feet above the ground, high up above all the million people of Cairo, surrounded by total darkness, locked up and imprisoned in a strange building on the edge of a desert that stretched away for hundreds of miles, while outside this building—itself probably the oldest in the world—lay the grim tomb-cluttered necropolis of an ancient capital.

The great space of the King's Chamber became for me—who had investigated deeply into the psychic, into the mysteries of the occult, into the sorceries and wizardries of the Orient—peopled with unseen beings, with spirits who guarded this age-old building. One momentarily expected some ghostly voice to arise out of the all-embracing silence. I now thanked the early builders for those narrow vent-shafts which brought a steady but tiny supply of cool air into this hoary old room. That air travelled through nearly three hundred feet of the Pyramid before it arrived; no matter, it was still welcome. I am a man accustomed to solitude—indeed glad to enjoy it—but there was something uncanny and frightening in the solitude of this chamber.

The all-encompassing darkness began to press on my head like an iron weight. The shadow of uncalled-for fear flickered into me. I brushed it away immediately. To sit in the heart of this desert monument required no physical courage, but it did require some moral fortitude. No snakes were likely to emerge from holes or crevices, and no lawless wanderers were likely to climb its stepped sides and enter it at dead of night. Actually, the only signs of animal life I had seen came from a scared mouse which had met me early in the evening in the horizontal passage, and which had darted hither and thither between the creviceless granite walls in a frantic effort to escape out of reach of the dreaded beam of torchlight; from two incredibly aged yellowish-green lizards I had discovered clinging to the roof of the narrow cutting which extends inwards from the niche in the Queen's Chamber; and, lastly, from the bats in the subterranean vault. It was also true that a few crickets had chirped a good deal upon my entry into the Grand Gallery, but they had soon ceased. All that was over now, unbroken silence held the whole Pyramid as in a thrall. There was naught of a physical nature which could possibly injure one here, and yet—a vague uneasiness, a feeling that invisible eyes were watching me, recurred for the second time. The place possessed a dream-like mysteriousness, a ghostly unreality. . . .

¶

There are vibrations of force, sound and light which are beyond our normal range of detection. Laughing song and serious speech flash across the world to waiting wireless listeners, but they could never detect them were not their receiving sets properly tuned. I had now brought myself out of the state of mere receptive waiting into a forcefully concentrated condition of mind which focalized the whole of its attention upon an effort to pierce the black silence which surrounded it. If, in the result, my faculty of awareness was temporarily heightened to an abnormal extent by the intense inward concentration, who shall say that it is impossible I began to detect the presence of invisible forces?

I know only that as I "tuned-in" by a method of interiorized attention which I had learnt long before this second visit to Egypt, I became aware that hostile forces had invaded the chamber. There was something abroad which I sensed as evil, dangerous. A nameless dread flickered into my heart and returned again and again soon after it was driven away. I still following my method of intense, single-pointed, inward-turned concentration, feeling followed its usual trend and changed into vision. Shadows began to flit to and fro in the shadowless room; gradually these took more definite shape, and malevolent countenances appeared suddenly quite close to my own face. Sinister images rose plainly before my mind's eye. Then a dark apparition advanced, looked at me with fixed sinister regard and raised its hands in a gesture of menace, as though seeking to inspire me with awe. Age-old spirits seemed to have crept out of the neighbouring necropolis, a necropolis so old that mummies had crumbled away inside their stone sarcophagi; the shades that clung to them made their unwelcome ascent to the place of my vigil. All the legends of evil ghosts who haunt the areas around the Pyramids, came back to memory with the same unpleasant detail with which they had been related by Arabs in the village not far off. When I had told a young Arab friend there of my intention to spend a night in the old building, he had tried to dissuade me.

"Every inch of ground is haunted," had been his warning. "There is an army of ghosts and genii in that territory."

And now I could see that his warning was not a vain one. Spectral figures had begun to creep into and around the dark room wherein I sat, and the undefinable feeling of uneasiness which earlier had seized me was now receiving fit and full justification. Somewhere in the centre of that still thing which was my body, I knew that my heart beat like a hammer under the strain of it all. The dread of the supernatural, which lurks at the bottom of every human heart, touched me again. Fear, dread, horror persistently presented their evil visages to me in turn. Involuntarily my hands clenched themselves as tightly as a vice. But I was determined to go on, and although these phantom forms that moved across the room began by stirring in me a sense of alarm, they ended by provoking me to summon whatever reserves of courage and combativeness I could muster.

My eyes were closed and yet these grey, gliding, vaporous forms obtruded themselves across my vision. And always there came with them an implacable hostility, an ugly determination to deter me from my purpose.

A circle of antagonistic beings surrounded me. It would have been easy to end it all by switching on the light or by leaping up and dashing out of the chamber and running back a few hundred feet to the locked grille-entrance, where the armed guard would have provided gregarious comfort. It was an ordeal which imposed a subtle form of torture, that harried the soul and left the body untouched. Yet something inside me intimated just as implacably that I must see this thing through.

At last the climax came. Monstrous elemental creations, evil horrors of the underworld, forms of grotesque, insane, uncouth and fiendish aspect gathered around me and afflicted me with unimaginable repulsion. In a few minutes I lived through something which will leave a remembered record behind for all time. That incredible scene remains vividly photographed upon my memory.   Never again would I repeat such an experiment; never again would I take up a nocturnal abode within the Great Pyramid.

The end came with startling suddenness.   The malevolent ghostly invaders disappeared into the obscurity whence they had emerged, into the shadowy realms of the departed, taking with them their trail of noxious horrors.   My half-shattered nerves experienced overwhelming relief such as a soldier feels when a fierce bombardment ends abruptly.

I do not know how long a period elapsed before I became conscious of a new presence in the chamber, of someone friendly and benevolent who stood at the entrance and looked down upon me with kindly eyes.   With his arrival the atmosphere changed completely—and changed for the better.   Something clean and sane had come with him.   A new element began to play upon my overwrought sensitive being, soothing and calming it.   He approached my stony seat, and I saw that he was followed by another figure.   Both halted at my side and regarded me with grave looks, pregnant with prophetic meaning. I felt that some momentous hour of my life was at hand.

In my vision the apparition of these two beings presented an unforgettable picture.   Their white robes, their sandalled feet, their wise aspect, their tall figures—all these return at once to the mind's eye.   Withal they wore the unmistakable regalia of their office, High Priests of an ancient Egyptian cult.   There was light a-glimmer all around them, which in a most uncanny manner lit up the part of the room.   Indeed, they looked more than men, bearing the bright mien of demi-gods; for their faces were set in unique cloistral calm.

They stood motionless as statues, regarding me, their hands crossed upon their breasts, remaining absolutely silent.

Was I functioning in some fourth dimension, aware and awake in some far-off epoch of the past?   Had my sense of time regressed to the early days of Egypt?   No; that could not be, for I perceived quickly that these two could see me and even now were about to address me.

Their tall figures bent forward; the lips of one spirit seemed to move, his face close to mine, his eyes flashing spiritual fire, and his voice sounding in my ear.

"Why dost thou come to this place, seeking to evoke the secret powers?   Are not mortal ways enough for thee?" he asked.

I did not hear these words with any physical ear; certainly no sound-vibration disturbed the silence of the chamber. Yet I seemed to hear them much in the manner in which a deaf man, using an electric earphone, might hear the words sounding against his artificial ear-drum; but with this difference—that they were heard on the *inside* of the drum. Really, the voice which came to me might be termed a mental voice, because it was surely heard within my head, but that might give the wrong impression that it was a mere thought. Nothing could be farther from the truth. It *was* a voice.

And I answered: "They are not!"

And he said:

"The stir of many crowds in the cities comforts the trembling heart of man. Go back, mingle with thy fellows, and thou wilt soon forget the light fancy that brings thee here."

But I answered again: "No, that cannot be."

Still he strove once more.

"The way of Dream will draw thee far from the fold of reason. Some have gone upon it—and come back mad. Turn now, whilst there is yet time, and follow the path appointed for mortal feet."

But I shook my head and muttered: "I must follow this way. There is none other for me now."

Then the priestly figure stepped forward closer and bent down again to where I sat.

I saw his aged face outlined by the surrounding darkness. He whispered against my ear:

"He who gains touch with us loses kin with the world. Art thou able to walk alone?"

I replied: "I do not know."

Out of the darkness came his last words:

"So be it. Thou hast chosen. Abide by thy choice for there is now no recall. Farewell," and he was gone.

I was left alone with the other spirit, who so far had only played the part of a silent witness.

¶

He moved closer so that he stood now in front of the marble coffer. His face revealed itself as the face of a man, very very old. I dared place no guess of years upon him.

"My son, the mighty lords of the secret powers have taken thee into their hands. Thou art to be led into the Hall of Learning to-night," he explained dispassionately. "Stretch thyself out upon this stone! In olden days it would have been within that yonder, upon a bed of papyrus-reeds," and he pointed to the coffin-like sarcophagus.

It did not occur to me to do other than obey my mysterious visitant. I laid myself flat upon my back.

What happened immediately afterwards is still not very clear to me. It was as though he had unexpectedly given me a dose of some peculiar, slow-working, anæsthetic, for all my muscles became taut, after which a paralysing lethargy began to creep over my limbs. My entire body became heavy and numb. First, my feet became colder and colder. The feeling developed into a kind of iciness which moved by imperceptible degrees up my legs, reached the knees, whence it continued its mounting journey. It was as though I had sunk up to the waist in a pile of snow while on some mountain climb. All sensation in the lower limbs was numbed.

I appeared next to pass into a semi-somnolent condition and a mysterious intimation of approaching death crept into my mind. It did not trouble me, however, for I had long ago liberated myself from the ancient fear of death and arrived at a philosophic acceptance of its inevitability.

As this strange chilling sensation continued to grip me, to pass up my shivering spine, to overpower my entire body, I felt myself sinking inwards in consciousness to some central point within my brain, while my breathing became weaker and weaker.

When the chill reached my chest and the rest of my body was completely paralysed, something like a heart attack supervened, but it passed quickly and I knew that the supreme crisis was not far off.

Had I been able to move my stiff jaws, I might have laughed at the next thought which came to me. It was this:

"To-morrow, they will find my dead body inside the Great Pyramid—and that will be the end of me."

I was quite sure that all my sensations were due to the passage of my own spirit from physical life to the regions beyond death.

Although I knew perfectly well that I was passing through all the sensations of dying, all opposition had now vanished.

At last, my concentrated consciousness lay in the head alone, and there was a final mad whirl within my brain. I had the sensation of being caught up in a tropical whirlwind and seemed to pass upwards through a narrow hole; then there was a momentary dread of being launched in infinite space, I leapt into the unknown—and I was *Free!*

No other word will express the delightful sense of liberation which then became mine. I had changed into a mental being, a creature of thought and feeling yet without the clogging handicap of the heavy flesh body in which I had been shut up. I had gone ghost-like clean out of my earthly body, like a dead man rising out of his tomb, but had certainly gone into no sort of unconsciousness. My sense of existence in fact, was intensely more vivid than before. Above all, with this exodus to a higher dimension, I felt *free*, blissfully, languorously free, in this fourth dimension to which I had penetrated.

At first I found myself lying on my back, as horizontal as the body I had just vacated, floating above the stone floor-block. Then came a sensation of some invisible hand turning me upright on my heels, after pushing me forward a little, and placing me properly on my feet. Ultimately I had a curiously combined feeling of both standing and floating simultaneously.

I gazed down upon the deserted body of flesh and bone, which was lying prone and motionless on the stone block. The inexpressive face was upturned, the eyes were scarcely open, yet the pupils gleamed sufficiently to indicate that the lids were not really closed. The arms were folded across the breast—certainly not an attitude which I could remember having assumed. Had someone crossed those hands without my being aware of the movement? The legs and feet were stretched out side by side, touching each other. There lay the seemingly dead form of myself, the form from which I had withdrawn.

I noted a trail of faint silvery light projecting itself down from me, the new *me*, to the cataleptic creature who lay upon the block. This was surprising, but more surprising still was my discovery that this mysterious psychic umbilical cord was contributing towards the illumination of the corner of the King's Chamber where I hovered; showing up the wall-stones in a soft moonbeam-like light.

I was but a phantom, a bodiless creature sojourning in space. I knew, at last, why those wise Egyptians of old had given, in their hieroglyphs, the pictured symbol of the bird to man's soul-form. I had experienced a sense of increased height and breadth, a spreading out just as though I had a pair of wings. Had I not risen into the air and remained floating above my discarded body, even as a bird rises into the sky and remains circling around a point. Did I not have the sensation of being environed by a great void? Yes, the bird symbol was a true one.

Yes; I had risen into space, disentangled my soul from its mortal skein, separated myself into two twin parts, left the world which I had known so long. I experienced a sense of being etherealized, of intense lightness, in this duplicate body which I now inhabited. As I gazed down at the cold stone block upon which my body lay, a single idea obtained recognition in my mind, a single realization overwhelmed me. It expressed itself to me in a few brief, silent words:

"*This is the state of death. Now I know that I am a soul, that I can exist apart from the body. I shall always believe that, for I have proved it.*"

This notion clutched hold of me with an iron grip, the while I was poised lightly above my empty fleshly tenement. I had proved survival in what I thought the most satisfactory way— by actually dying and then surviving! I kept on looking at the recumbent relic which I had left behind. Somehow, it fascinated me. Was that discarded form the thing which, for so many years, I had considered as myself? I perceived then, with complete clarity, that it was nothing more than a mass of unintelligent, unconscious, fleshly matter. As I regarded those unseeing unresponsive eyes, the irony of the whole situation struck me forcibly. My earthly body had really imprisoned me, the real "me," but now I was free. I had been borne hither and thither upon this planet by an organism which I had long confused with my real central self.

The sense of gravity seemed to have gone, and I was literally floating on air, with that strange half-suspended, half-standing feeling.

Suddenly, by my side, appeared the old priest, grave and imperturbable. With upturned eyes, his face more ennobled still, with reverent mood, he prayed: "O Amen, O Amen, who art in Heaven, turn thy face upon the dead body of thy son, and make him well in the spirit-world. It is finished." And then he addressed me:

"Thou hast now learned the great lesson. *Man, whose soul was born out of the Undying, can never really die.* Set down this truth in words known to men. Behold!"

And out of space there came the half-remembered face of a woman whose funeral I had attended more than twenty years before; then the familiar countenance of a man who had been more than a friend and whom I had last seen laid to rest in his coffin twelve years previously; and, finally, the sweet smiling picture of a child I knew who had died in an accidental fall.

These three peered at me with tranquil faces, and their friendly voices sounded once again around me. I had the shortest of conversations with the so-called dead, who soon melted away and vanished.

"They too live, even as thou livest, even as this Pyramid, which has seen the death of half a world, lives on," said the High Priest.

"Know, my son, that in this ancient fane lies the lost record of the early races of man and of the Covenant which they made with their Creator through the first of His great prophets. Know, too, that chosen men were brought here of old to be shown this Covenant that they might return to their fellows and keep the great secret alive. Take back with thee the warning that when men forsake their Creator and look on their fellows with hate, as with the princes of Atlantis in whose time this Pyramid was built, they are destroyed by the weight of their own iniquity, even as the people of Atlantis were destroyed.

"It was not the Creator who sank Atlantis, but the selfishness, the cruelty, the spiritual blindness of the people who dwelt on those doomed islands. The Creator loves all; but the lives of men are governed by invisible laws which He has set over them. Take back this warning, then."

There surged up in me a great desire to see this mysterious Covenant and the spirit must have read my thought, for he quickly said:

"To all things there is an hour. Not yet, my son, not yet."

I was disappointed.

He looked at me for a few seconds.

"No man of thy people hath yet been permitted to behold such a thing, but because thou art a man versed in these things, and hast come among us bearing goodwill and understanding in thy heart, some satisfaction thou shalt have. Come with me!"

And then a strange thing happened. I seemed to fall into a

kind of semi-coma, my consciousness was momentarily blotted out, and the next thing I knew was that I had been transported to another place. I found myself in a long passage which was softly lit, although no lamp or window was visible: I fancied that the illuminant was none other than the halo-like emanation around my companion combined with the radiation from the luminous vibrant cord of ether which extended behind me, yet I realized that these would not sufficiently explain it. The walls were built up with a glowing pinkish terra-cotta coloured stone, slabbed with the thinnest of joints. The floor sloped downwards at precisely the same angle as the Pyramid entrance itself descends. The masonry was well finished. The passage was square and fairly low, but not uncomfortably so. I could not find the source of its mysterious illuminant, yet the interior was bright as though a lamp were playing on it.[1]

The High Priest bade me follow him a little way down the passage. "Look not backwards," he warned me, "nor turn thy head." We passed some distance down the incline and I saw a large temple-like chamber opening out of the farther end. I knew perfectly well that I was inside or below the Pyramid, but I had never seen such a passage or chamber before. Evidently they were secret and had defied discovery until this day. I could not help feeling tremendously excited about this startling find, and an equally tremendous curiosity seized me as to where and what the entrance was. Finally, I *had* to turn my head and take a swift look backwards at what I hoped was the secret door. I had entered the place by no visible entrance, but at the farther end I saw that what should have been an opening was closed with square blocks and apparently

[1] Dr. Abbate Pacha, Vice-President of the Institut Egyptien, spent a night in the desert near the Pyramids, together with Mr. William Groff, a member of the Institut. In the official report of their experiences, the latter said: "Towards eight o'clock, in the evening, I noticed a light which appeared to turn slowly around the Third Pyramid almost up to the apex; it was like a small flame. The light made three circuits round the Pyramid and then disappeared. For a good part of the night I attentively watched this Pyramid; towards eleven o'clock I again noticed the same light, but this time it was of a bluish colour; it mounted slowly almost in a straight line and arrived at a certain height above the Pyramid's summit and then disappeared." By pursuing enquiries among the Bedouins, Mr. Groff discovered that this mysterious light had been seen more or less frequently in the past, the traditions of its existence stretching back centuries. The Arabs put it down to guardian-spirits of the Pyramid, but Groff tried to find a natural explanation for it, though without success.

cemented. I found myself gazing at a blank wall; then, as swiftly whirled away by some irresistible force until the whole scene was blotted out and I had floated off into space again. I heard the words: "Not yet, not yet," repeated as in an echo and a few moments later saw my inert unconscious body lying on the stone.

"My son," came a murmur from the High Priest, "it matters not whether thou discoverest the door or not. Find but the secret passage within the mind that will lead thee to the hidden chamber within thine own soul, and thou shalt have found something worthy indeed. The mystery of the Great Pyramid is the mystery of thine own self. The secret chambers and ancient records are all contained in thine own nature. The lesson of the Pyramid is that man must turn inward, must venture to the unknown centre of his being to find his soul, even as he must venture to the unknown depths of this fane to find its profoundest secret. Farewell!"

My mind whirled into some vortex that caught me; I slipped helplessly, sucked downwards, ever downwards; heavy torpor overcame me, and I seemed to melt back into my physical body; I strained my will, pushing and trying to move its rigid muscles, but failed, and finally I swooned. . . .

I opened my eyes with a shock, in inky blackness. When the numbness passed, my hands groped for the torch and switched the light on. I was back in the King's Chamber, still tremendously excited, so excited in fact, that I jumped up and shouted, my voice echoing back in muffled tones. But, instead of feeling the floor beneath my feet, I found myself falling through space. Only by throwing both hands on the edge of the stone block and clinging to the sides did I save myself. I then realized what had happened. In rising I had unwittingly moved to the far end of the block and my feet were now dangling over the excavated hole in the north-west corner of the floor.

I picked myself up and got back to safety, secured the lamp and threw a beam of light upon my watch. The glass was cracked in two places, where I had struck my hand and wrist against the wall in jumping up, but the works still ticked merrily away; and then, as I noted the time I almost laughed outright despite the solemnity of my surroundings.

For it was precisely the melodramatic hour of midnight, both hands pointing to twelve, neither more nor less!

·      ·      ·      ·      ·      ·      ·

When the armed police guard unlocked the iron grille soon after dawn, a dusty, weary, tired-eyed figure stumbled out of the Great Pyramid's dark entrance.  He made his way down the large square blocks of stone into the early morning sunlight and gazed, with eyes that blinked, at the flat, familiar landscape. His first act was to take several deep breaths, one after the other. Then he instinctively turned his face upwards towards Ra, the sun, and silently thanked him for this blessed gift of light to mankind.

# CHAPTER V

## WITH A MAGICIAN OF CAIRO

THE life of Cairo is a life in two worlds. One moves into the ancient Arab world as soon as one begins to walk eastwards from its great central square, the Ataba el Khadra, and one returns to the modern European world as soon as one begins to walk westwards. It is a strange life, this, where Orient and Occident, medieval and modern, Eastern colour and squalor and Western greyness and cleanliness, meet and face each other under the irresistible pressure of our times.

And it was in Cairo that I discovered mediums and magicians, soothsayers and astrologers, sorcerers and fortune-tellers, fakirs and holy men in plenty. They were there in all of their fifty-seven varieties, despite the frowns and restrictions of a Government which had shown its displeasure by forbidding most of their activities by law and which does not hesitate to put this law into action quite frequently. I must confess that, despite my sympathy with some of the subjects concerned, the Government had every provocation in imposing these restrictions. Charlatans preyed upon the credulous, irresponsible babblers were listened to with awe, and self-deluded seers were accepted at their own valuation. The harm that was done by fortune-tellers whose prophecies were taken as guides of action will never be known to its full extent, but it was sufficiently known to force the Government's hand. There were, however, a few characters whose personalities interested me apart from their profession. There was a wizard who killed a hen before my eyes by his invocations and magic; there was a Sudanese negress witch-doctor who accurately named India as being a country of great good fortune to me and then made some totally inaccurate predictions; there was a young Egyptian of Syrian Christian ancestry who firmly believed he was a reincarnation of the prophet Elijah and who completely lived the world-scorning life of such a prophet; there was a French-woman in the European quarter who quite easily read print through heavily bandaged eyes when she was put into the hypnotic trance state; there was a queer old man who lived with his followers in a great house adjoining an immense mosque, and who was so lost to this world that he spent almost the whole of his time audibly conversing with spirits; there was a brave and bold lady who had defied King Ibn Saud's ban and had secretly taken cinema pictures of holy Mecca, but who was now engaged in studying sacred matters under angelic teachers; there was the famous fakir, Tahra Bey, who thought nothing of sticking a dagger through his own throat or stabbing his chest just above the heart, but who emerged unbloodied and unharmed from these unpleasant operations; and there were a few others who caught my interest and engaged my attention. If I cannot write about them all in the space at my command, at least I can give some of them this fleeting record of a paragraph.

There was another phase of Cairene life, too, which attracted me much and that was its religious side, because it had been the focal point for Muhammedan culture for over a thousand years. So little does the average Westerner know of the great religion of Islam, so distorted are his conceptions of it, that I have thought it worth while to devote an entire chapter to describing Islam as I found it.

## ⁊

The wizard who did the strange thing with the fowl will have to remain nameless in this record, because I have given a promise to a high Egyptian Government official not to bestow personal publicity upon him. The reasons for this request need not be entered into here, but I accept them as sufficient and so I shall let him remain incognito and also withdraw the excellent photographs which I had secured of the wizard, his house and his feat.

I discovered him, one sultry afternoon, after numerous enquiries and frequent prowling. I had walked through a main street still flagged with ancient stones; turned aside into that noisy, closely packed, narrow-alleyed, picturesque ancient quarter which lies between the El Azhar Mosque and the dismal cemetery of Bab el Wazir. A train of camels had come into the city. Little bells were tied to each animal so that the whole procession made a merry jingling noise. Through the dark lanes I threaded my way, afoot and alone, trying to find the wizard's house.

I traversed a labyrinth of teeming by-ways which were so narrow that the sky appeared as an irregular slit between the house roofs. Yet, the sunlight playing upon those irregular streets, created a picturesque study in strong light and shade.

I picked my route, at last, along the winding street which led to his door through thick-piled white dust, that blew in from the bleak Mokattam hills which overlooked the nearby city boundary.

His house was large and medieval, its front being built of oblong blocks of stone whose faces were gaily coloured. The upper part had several heavily shuttered windows. A pair of heavy, carved and moulded, double doors turned inwards on a small but high vestibule wherein I found a couple of chairs and a low coffee-table, but no sign of anyone present. I peeped through another door into an adjoining room; no one was there either. I, thereupon, walked through a small stone-flagged passage into an inner courtyard, which was cluttered up with piles of papers and large documents, all so utterly dust-laden as to suggest that this open courtyard was used as a repository for the magician's more ancient archives. I wandered disconsolately around the place for about five minutes, wondering when and where someone would put in an appearance; but, still being unable to find anyone, I returned to the street and brought back a neighbour, who ascended alone into the upper regions of the house. A couple of minutes later she descended, together with a young man of about seventeen.

The latter addressed me in a soft hesitant tone.

"What is it you want, please?"

When I mentioned the magician's name he drew back in surprise. It was evident that Europeans were not numbered among the clientele.

"My father!" he exclaimed. "What do you wish to see him about, please?"

I explained my business and proffered a pencilled note of introduction. When he saw the name at its foot his eyes lit up with welcome. "Come! Take a seat."

He led me into the room adjoining the vestibule, and pointed invitingly at a divan covered with plain white cloth.

He disappeared into the upper regions again, out of which presently he returned. I heard the sound of slow, shuffling footsteps and he was followed into the room by a heavily built man of about sixty, who touched his forehead in greeting as he appeared in the doorway.

His head and shoulders were wrapped in a white shawl, from which a lock of raven-black hair escaped; his face was large-featured, good-natured, heavily moustached, but slightly bearded. His eyes were probably large, but he kept looking on the floor and obviously consciously controlling the lids so that they appeared quite narrow. He pressed me to retain my seat and himself occupied a large easy-chair.

¶

I looked around the room, which was lofty and cool but contained a queer assortment of odds and ends. The walls were decorated with oblong panels in which beautifully lettered inscriptions from the *Quran* appeared in red on a yellow ground. Two stuffed brown otters reposed in a wall-recess; piles of documents littered the window-sills and, judging by the dust under which they were buried, they had not been touched for years; a printed Arabic almanack lay on a pillow beside me; while several empty ink-bottles were distributed all over the place.

In a few monosyllabic words the magician informed me how honoured he was by my visit and begged me to partake of some light refreshment before we proceeded to anything further. I thanked him, but, knowing the habits of Egyptian hosts, asked him not to trouble about coffee for me as I never drank it. He suggested Persian tea, a delightful beverage, and I readily accepted. And so, while an eager servant disappeared into the nearest bazaar, I tried to draw the old man into some communicative conversation. My efforts failed, for, beyond the merest monosyllables dictated by Egyptian etiquette, he would say nothing about himself. Instead, he turned the tables by putting me through a subtle cross-examination. I answered his questions frankly and freely, so that by the time the servant served up little dishes of typical Egyptian sweetmeats—large cakes of fried wheat-flour mixed with honey; bananas, biscuits and tiny glasses of Persian tea—he was just a shade less reserved. Indeed, when he discovered that I did not want to investigate

in order to ridicule his methods or expose his probable charlatanry, he became very pleasant. But, underneath his manner
I detected all the time a firm caution, as though he could not
risk yielding entry into his life to a probing stranger from an
alien land.

However, he suggested that he might cast my horoscope if
I would give him my name, my father's name, my birth-date and
place of birth. I tried to intimate that it was not for this that I
had come to him, and that anyway fortune-telling often produced so many contradictions with each fortune-teller that I
preferred to enjoy the bliss of ignorance rather than take the
trouble of attempting to reconcile what seemed hopelessly
irreconcilable. The old man would not be put off so easily and
declared that, whether I wanted one or not, he was now interested
enough in me to calculate the map of the heavens at my birth
and write out an interpretation that would satisfy his own
curiosity and, he hoped, mine. I yielded at last to his impor-
tunity, letting him have the data required.

He then asked me to place my hand on a sheet of paper and
traced an outline in pencil around the palm. Within this
outlined sketch he wrote a few Arabic words. Why he did this
I never found out.

I broached the subject of his magic, but he put me off with
a non-committal answer. I had heard that he was probably the
greatest magician in Cairo, whatever value could be put on such
a recommendation.

Skilfully he steered the conversation into another direction,
so that I had to spend the time telling him about life in Europe.

"Come back in five days' time," he said when he rose from
his chair.

I duly came back and, after the usual preliminary hospitalities
were over, he produced a few sheets of foolscap covered with
Arabic writing which, he informed me, contained my horoscope
in the form of verse. I was thus forced to accept something
for which I had never asked, and to offer payment which, after
some refusals, he took.

Then came an unexpected turn in his attitude. He offered
to show me something of his magic. "Give me your handkerchief," he said, and when I had obeyed him he returned it
almost immediately. "Good! Now tear it in half." I did so.
He then took one of the torn portions and wrote something on
it with a pen, which he inked from a bottle that stood on the

table. When his writing was completed he folded the piece of linen and, handing it back to me, asked me to put it on a copper ash-tray that was lying beside me on the divan.

I awaited the next operation with some interest. The old man took a piece of paper and drew a large triangle upon it; within the triangle he inscribed some mysterious signs, as well as a few Arabic letters. Handing me the paper he asked me to place it on the folded piece of linen. I obeyed. There was a lull of a minute or so, he muttered a few phrases of incomprehensible jargon, tightly closing his eyes the while, and then suddenly opened the heavy-lashed lids.

Almost immediately the torn handkerchief caught light and blazed up in the tray beside me. The flame shot high up in the air, to my amazement, and then turned into a dense cloud of smoke which completely filled the room. It became difficult to breathe, one's eyes smarted, and I rose hastily to retreat to the doorway. But the magician was there before me, called for his servant, and had the latter open all the windows and thus clear the air in the room.

Whether the feat was genuine magic or a piece of good conjuring involving the use of inflammable chemicals did not trouble me, as I could not see much point in the whole demonstration. But the old man was evidently quite proud of it.

"How did you set fire to the handkerchief?" I asked.

"With the help of my genii," was the explanation—which explained nothing. I let it go at that. It is the usual explanation one hears in Egypt of anything that is in the slightest degree supernatural.

"Come again in three days' time," he said, "but do not forget to bring a white fowl with you. Because I perceive something in you which pleases me, I shall render you a service quite freely. Bring me the white fowl and with it I shall do some magic to put a jinn-spirit at your service. Remember, the fowl should not be too young nor too old, nor should it be of any other colour."

Thinking of the African witch-doctors who cut the throats of white cocks and then fling the blood over their client's head, I declined his magnanimous offer. He pressed me repeatedly and confidently assured me that this magical operation which he had in view would attract the aid of a powerful genie who would work for my success. But I continued to refuse. At last, however, he "cornered" me; I told him that such ceremonies disgusted me and I preferred not to avail myself of their alleged benefits. He immediately promised that there would be no blood-letting whatsoever, and on this assurance I yielded.

¶

Once again I kicked up little dust-clouds as I walked through the narrow lane leading to the aged magician's rambling old house. This time I had come from the Poultry Bazaar which lies a short way behind the Ataba el Khadra Square, a plump little white fowl tucked under my right arm. I could feel the warm beating of its breast under the pressure of my hand and I wondered what malign fate the old man had designed for it.

When I arrived, the magician's face lost its usual gravity and broke into a smile. He expressed his pleasure at my obedience to his request. He asked me to set the fowl down in the centre of the floor-rug and then step three times over an incense brazier which stood in a corner. Having done this and passed through the cloud of fragrant smoke, I settled down on the divan and watched both man and bird. The former took a sheet of paper and drew a small square upon it, which was next subdivided into nine smaller squares. Within each of the latter he inscribed a kabbalistic sign or Arabic letter. Then he began to mutter some half-audible mystic incantation, with eyes fixedly regarding the fowl, while now and then his whispers were punctuated by a commanding gesture of the forefinger of his right hand, which was stretched out as though he were issuing an order. The poor creature became frightened and ran off into a corner of the room, where it took refuge underneath a chair. The magician thereupon asked me to seize it and bring it back to the centre of the floor. I did not care to touch it again and told him so. His son, who had now come in and joined us, captured the bird and put it down at the point whence it had fled.

Once more it twisted about and made as if to run back to the corner a second time, when the magician commanded it in a firm voice to return.

The fowl stopped at once.

I then noticed that it started to tremble all over its body, so that the feathers shook to and fro.

The magician asked me to step three times over the incense brazier, as I had done before. When I returned to the divan I noticed that the fowl no longer looked at the magician but had turned its beady eyes in my direction, a direction which it never thereafter changed.

And then I observed an extraordinary thing. The little creature's breathing became laboured and heavy; each breath came in a sharp gasp, while the beak was never once closed, as though the bird were constantly engaged in a struggle to get air.

The magician had placed his kabbalistic paper on the floor nearby, slowly he retreated until he had withdrawn from the room and stood in the open doorway, where he began to mutter his strange spells, intently watching the fowl all the time. His half-chanted incomprehensible words, uttered in a most commanding voice, gradually swelled in tone and were followed by the slow decline of the bird into a half-lifeless state.

At last, the animal weakened to such an extent that its legs gave way and it sank to the floor, though it was still able to maintain the upright posture of its body. Two minutes passed and then, even this became impossible. It turned over on its side and stretched itself out on the floor. And then its spirit revolted against its doom; it made a tremendous effort to struggle on to its legs again, only to fall back exhausted. Another couple of minutes passed and it made a convulsive gesture, moved its body in spasmodic jerks and fluttered its feathers feebly. Thereafter, its movements lessened until they finally stopped. The flesh became stiff, the head became rigid, and I realized that the warm little creature which I had brought from the bazaar only a half-hour ago was now a corpse. I stood up, speechless at the amazing sight. There was a sickly feeling in my heart.

The old man asked me to place my handkerchief over its body. He said impressively:

"The magic has been successful. Henceforth the genie who destroyed the life of this fowl as a sign that he was ready to serve you, will work for your benefit. Sometimes when I have practised this the fowl does not die, which is a sign that the genie refuses to help the person."

My uncanny host had persistently kept his eyes bent upon the floor, a fact which I had noted throughout the ceremony. His next remark offered a peculiar explanation of this fact.

"When I say my spells to evoke a genie, and when I command it after it has been evoked, I never look at it. That is one of the rules which must be obeyed. But the sacrifice is not yet finished. Listen! You must wrap up the fowl and take it home with you and keep it still enwrapped until to-morrow. Then when the hour of midnight arrives, you should stand on the Kasr-el-Nil bridge and throw its body into the Nile waters. As you throw it over the side do not forget to make a wish and one day the genie will cause your wish to come true."

My handkerchief was too small to cover the fowl completely, so, glancing around the room, I picked up a copy of *Al Ahram* (The Pyramid), the popular Cairo newspaper, and wrapped it around the half-covered bird. When I returned home I gave the latter to my young Arab servant, with instructions not to unwrap the parcel and not even to touch it again until the following night. But the warning injunction was unnecessary. I lightly mentioned that it was a sacrificial fowl which had been slain by a magician, and that it was on no account to be eaten. The servant drew back, affrighted; and thereafter avoided the neighbourhood of the bird as much as possible.

That evening, I was dining in a restaurant with a couple of friends, one American and the other Egyptian, and I told them the whole story of the fowl and its magical sacrifice. They were quite sure that it had been killed by some other means than magic, whilst I passed no judgment but kept an open mind. As I unfolded all the details to them, they roared with laughter and for the rest of the evening that fowl dominated our conversation. I must confess that I, too, had to smile at some of their witty sallies at the absent magician, who became the butt of their clever jokes. Suddenly every light in the restaurant went out, whilst we were still in the midst of our meal. Despite the best efforts of the proprietor, he could not restore the illumination; he finally had to send out for candles, and we finished our dinner in comparative gloom.

My Egyptian friend, a convinced sceptic who had been educated at the Sorbonne, temporarily lost his brilliance of wit and lightness of spirits.

"Your magician has done this!" he complained, and I detected a tinge of fear under his joking remark.

The thing might have been a merely accidental fusing of a wire, of course, but it took place under circumstances which reminded me of two other curious incidents not very unlike it in character. The first came within my own personal experience, the second I heard from the lips of Robert Hichens, the famous novelist, who knew the principal character concerned.

The first case occurred many years ago when I was investigating various cults which had raised their heads all over Europe and America. One of them was led by a man of dubious character, formerly a clergyman, expelled from the Church; yet a man of considerable knowledge and forceful personality. My investigations revealed the fact that he possessed strong hypnotic power and that he was abusing this power for unworthy ends, besides exploiting credulous people for money. Beyond warning those of his victims whom I knew, I kept this discovery to myself, acting on my usual belief that every scoundrel meets an eventual Nemesis. The climax came when, apparently by accident, I met in the street at ten o'clock in the evening someone whose husband I knew fairly well. The lady seemed so strange in manner that I stopped to converse with her and was astounded to hear that she was just then *en route* to the unfrocked clergyman with whom, she calmly told me, she was going to pass the night. I guided her to the nearest lamp-post, where I raised her face to the light and examined the whites and pupils of her eyes. What I saw therein was sufficient indication that she was completely hypnotized and I, therefore, thought it my duty to de-hypnotize her immediately and persuade her to return home.

The following day I visited a friend to consult him about the matter. He was an Indian and, in fact, none other than my friend of the second chapter of *A Search in Secret India*. I related to him all the details of what I had unearthed about this ex-clergyman's ravages among weak-natured people, adding that I felt such a dangerous man could no longer be allowed to pursue his spoliating path unchecked. The Indian agreed; indeed, he became exceedingly angry and proposed that he should lay a heavy curse upon the fellow. I knew that the Indian was learned in the ways of his native Yoga and the arts of Oriental fakirs, and that a curse issuing from his lips would be no light thing. Judging such action to be a little stronger than was necessary, I said he could do as he pleased but I had thought of a more lenient way, and that was to order the fellow to take himself off and never show his head again. The Indian said that I should do that, too, but he for his part was going to carry out the curse; which he did.

At the conclusion of this rite I immediately left to carry out my own plan and went in quest of its victim. I found the pseudo-prophet, together with a large body of his disciples, in a small hall where a scene of indescribable confusion was being enacted.

The hall was plunged in complete darkness.

People were stumbling over each other trying to get to the door, groanings and mutterings were coming from those who had tripped up on the floor, while above all the din and disorder came the strident voice of their master, a voice laden with fear and despair:

"The devil is here," he was shouting. "This is the devil's work."

I struck some matches and found him lying prone on the platform, apparently quite hysterical.

Candles were eventually brought and his disciples carried him off to a nearby hotel, where they tried to revive him with his favourite drink—whisky. Meanwhile I learnt from the others what had happened.

They had all been sitting peacefully upon their chairs listening to their leader's lecture when *all* the electric lamps had suddenly exploded with the force of bombs, shattering glass in every direction. The hall had instantly become dark and amidst the resulting gloom and chaos they had heard their leader fall heavily to the platform floor, uttering cries of fright.

I followed him to the hotel, went into the lounge and wrote a short note which I put into a sealed envelope. I handed the letter to the chief of his deluded followers and requested that it should be given to the leader as soon as he was well enough to read.

The envelope contained an ultimatum. The man must leave the town within twenty-four hours and never return again, or else I would put Police Headquarters on his track.

He left. Within twelve months I learned of his death in an obscure country village.

And now for the curious point of the whole story.

The hall had been plunged in darkness at the very moment when my Indian friend's rite of cursing reached its culminating point!

My second anecdote concerns the ill-fated Lord Carnarvon, who financed the excavations that led up to the opening of Tutankhamen's tomb. All the world is familiar with the story of that astonishing discovery, of how the unfortunate peer swiftly contracted blood-poisoning shortly after the opening. Some people also know that the ancients placed a curse on the violators of this tomb. The rapidity with which his illness developed was the cause of his being sent down to Cairo to receive the best medical attention that city could offer.

The patient was kept at the Continental Savoy, one of the largest hotels in Cairo. One evening, not long after his arrival, the electric light circuit failed and every lamp in the hotel was extinguished. For nearly an hour the place was plunged in darkness. When the lights were restored, Lord Carnarvon's nurse found him lying dead in his bed!

But I must return to my fowl.

At midnight, next day, someone might have been observed furtively reconnoitring the Kasr-el-Nil bridge, awaiting a favourable opportunity to dispose of a sacrificial fowl. It was not so easy as it seemed to carry out the task. For the bridge is in the heart of the European quarter of Cairo: a huge British soldiers' barracks faced it on one side, while the spacious, well-guarded, well-policed headquarters of the British High Commissioner fronts it on the other. To throw a mysterious-looking, paper-wrapped parcel into the sombre waters from such a height, and at such an hour, would lead any rational observer to but one conclusion, viz. that a murderer was trying to dispose of some portion of his victim's trunk or limbs! However, the moment came at last, the parcel was tossed over the bridge; as it hit the water with a slight gurgle, the midnight visitor heaved a sigh of relief and hurried safely away.

My Arab servant praised Allah for my safe return. He looked as happy as a kitten that had caught its first mouse.

§

I tried, on subsequent visits, to get my magician to explain his feats in more detail, so that one could discover whether they were mere conjuring tricks after all. But the old man would speak little on the subject and would relapse into long silences, as though he were wrapped up in some other world—perhaps the world of his genii. I realized that to get him to open those uncommunicative jaws would be a task indeed. His own son had once informed me, after some questioning, that his father never told his secrets to anyone and that he, the son, had long ago requested to be taught that he might follow the same profession; but the father had refused, saying that it was a profession both difficult and dangerous. His parents had told him, as typical of something that frequently happened, a story of a magician who had evoked a genie but could not banish it again, with the result that the latter turned on him and caused him severe injuries. The boy was put to the comparatively harmless study of law.

I understood why it was impossible to expect the old man to reveal his secrets, whether they were genuine or false, because it was their very mystery which gave him his power and reputation; I decided to press him no further. It was perfectly natural that he should be loath to let go information upon which his fame and fortune depended.

But if I could not break down his reticence, I thought, as I sat once again in his dusty room, perhaps I could persuade him to explain the general theories which lay behind those secrets; perhaps I could find out from the fountain-head of a reputed expert what all this talk of genii meant of which I had heard so much in Egypt. And, even whilst I talked to him I could hear, coming through the barred window, the steady, rhythmic tapping of a tom-tom drum. In a neighbour's house a minor witch-doctoring sheikh was trying to drive out of the body of a sick man, by means of drumming and incantations, the genie which was supposed to obsess him and to be responsible for the illness.

"Your people disbelieve in our ancient magic," he interposed upon my thoughts, "merely because it uses forces they do not understand, the forces of the genii."

I remained silent. I could comprehend his Oriental attitude without much difficulty, otherwise I should never have been interested in the East.

Genii were everywhere. If a man were ill, unlucky or unhappy, an evil genie was supposed to have invaded his body or life; if he were fortunate or powerful, a good genie was equally responsible.

"What are these genii?" I asked the old man at length.

I found him in a friendly mood.

"Know that these invisible creatures do truly exist, even though sight of them has almost entirely been lost to the people of our time," he explained. "Just as there exist animals in the world of matter, so there exist spirit-creatures in the other world who are not human, who have never been spirits of mortal men, but who were born directly into the spirit world. Such are the genii. Nevertheless, do not mistake them for the souls of animals, because they are of quite a different character. Some have almost the intelligence of a clever man, others are saintly in goodness, while many others exist who are truly 'of their father the devil.' In fact, the inhabitants of the spirit world may be divided into three chief classes: the genii, the humans and the angels. The angels are mostly good and have never lived on earth. The genii are good or evil and likewise have never lived on earth. The humans, of course, are those men and women who have lived on earth and passed out of their bodies after death.

"Know, too, that just as animals are often made to serve man on earth, just as the dog, the horse and the camel are brought to subserve his will, so there are certain kinds of genii which can be made to serve him, whether in the invisible or visible worlds. It is, of course, only certain orders of these genii which can be rendered submissive to the commands of a human master. The magic of ancient times was mostly—as is even that of the few real magicians who exist to-day—a knowledge of how to obtain the service of these genii. In short, it was a form of spiritualism."

"What methods are used to secure this control?"

"First, it is necessary to learn their names before you can command them. Then a charm must be written on paper, containing the name of the genie, a certain passage from the *Quran*, an arrangement of numbers inside a diagram—usually a double square but sometimes a triangle. Thirdly, the aid of burning incense and perfumes, varied in composition according to the kind of genie you are invoking, must be brought in. Fourthly, certain invocations, or 'words of power,' must be pronounced. Lastly, there is the power acquired by initiation through one's own teacher." He paused for a minute, and then continued.

"But to learn this mastership demands a hard and dangerous apprenticeship. Magic always was and ever must be an art for the few. I may tell you our beliefs, in so far as I am doing now, but to reveal the practical secrets of real value is something I have pledged myself to my own teacher never to do except to an accepted pupil of many years' pupilship. It would be a bad thing for mankind if our secrets were made known to all, for then evil men could use them to injure others for their own ends, whilst we ourselves would lose the position of power we have always enjoyed. Let me tell you, in fact, that so far I have refused to accept a single pupil. Eventually I shall be bound, by the laws that govern our fraternity, to initiate someone before I die, so that this knowledge may be kept alive among mankind. As, however, I know the exact date of my death, I shall carry out my obligations in good time."

The old man paused. I was pleased at having succeeded so marvellously in weaning him out of his reticence, but would he continue? I gave him another lead, this time in the form of a question about his own initiation.

"Let me tell you a little of my story," he answered. "I was born sixty years ago in the town of Suag, which is in the province of Girga. My own father was a famous professional magician and astrologer. Ever since I can remember, the art in which he dealt attracted me greatly; fascinated me, in fact. My father noted this tendency of mine and told me that he would initiate me eventually and bring me up to follow him in the same profession. He owned a number of ancient Arabic manuscripts and rare books on the magic arts which he let me read and study. As soon as he had initiated me at the age of eighteen, I left home and made my way to Cairo, where I joined the El Azhar University. Here, I devoted myself to literary and religious studies, but I kept my secrets entirely to myself. I had brought a few of my father's manuscripts with me and these I continued to study at home. One thing I learnt was the different kinds of human nature, until I became so expert that I could tell at a single glance what a man's character and desires were.

"I left the University at the age of twenty-eight and thereafter lived much alone, practising further until I felt strong enough to have complete command over my genii. It was then that I adopted this profession and let myself become known. And unless one can get this strength it is far better to leave the thing alone. My sons begged to be allowed to learn my knowledge, but I put them to other subjects, because I saw that they lacked the courage necessary to make a successful magician.

"I practised astrology also, and many Egyptians of high rank found me out in time and often came to have their fortunes told. Princes, ministers, Pashas and wealthy merchants have sought my advice. A Minister of the Court of Abyssinia has consulted me, while last year I had a visit from the daughter of the Abyssinian Emperor. Once the Sultan of Morocco sent a special envoy to me with certain letters.

"Another year four thieves broke into my house at night,

attempting to kill and rob me in the dark; but I drove them off with nothing more than a walking-stick. Next day, I sat down and used my magic to discover their names. When I had done this, I collected enough evidence to have them arrested and sent to prison for five years.

"Not long ago, I was called to a haunted house where chairs and carpets and kitchen-pots were thrown about during the night by unseen beings. I set up an incense brazier and whispered my invocation to the spirits. In fifteen minutes some genii appeared. They were the cause of the trouble and I bade them go away and leave the house in peace. After that the spirits disappeared and the haunting ceased."

¶

The old man clapped his hands, at which a servant appeared, bringing a dish of white jellied sweet, some cakes, and tiny glasses of Persian tea.

"Is it possible to make these genii visible to an ordinary person?" I enquired across the table.

"Yes, after long preparations and much effort it can be done. The preparations finish with burning incense and slowly chanted invocations and then a genie appears out of the smoke in the darkened room and speaks in a loud voice. I no longer touch that side of magic as I am getting too old to make such tremendous efforts."

I wondered once more at this strange character who claimed to contact such weird creatures. He was certainly most uncanny. And yet, he could be very human too. For when his little granddaughter, a prettily dressed child of six, ran into the room unexpectedly, he bent down and kissed her affectionately and even condescended to play with her for a few moments.

I resumed my quest.

"What about the dangers which you mentioned before?"

He looked at me gravely.

"It is true. Whoever gains ascendancy over the genii incurs risks. The genii are not mere puppets in his hands, they are beings with an intelligence and will of their own; therefore, it is always possible they may rebel against the man who has enslaved them. Although they are entirely obedient to their master and give willing service, if the magician loses his self-control and becomes weak in will, or if he misuses his powers for evil ends, or if he fails in the highest courage, then there is always the possibility that some of his genii will turn and rend him, bringing unforeseen troubles, accidents or even death itself. The greatest marvels can be shown by the help of such spirits, but where the magician has only imperfectly mastered these servants, they may be pitiless towards him should they rise in revolt."

"Do you think the ancient Egyptians knew of these genii, too?"

"Of course, such knowledge was the chief part of the power of their priests. Genii were used to act as guards over the most important tombs and treasures; they were invoked in temple ceremonies; and they were also used for the most evil purposes."

I told him of my experience in the Great Pyramid, when I had spent a night in the King's Chamber and, in vision, beheld two priestly spirits as well as a secret passage.

"Inside the Pyramid and connected with the Sphinx there is a peculiar order of genii," he commented. "They were captured by ancient Egyptian High Priests and imprisoned in those places to guard certain secrets. They throw a glamour over the mind of anyone likely to penetrate the secret places, and thus defend them from intrusion. Yes, I too believe that secret passages and chambers and hidden records are contained within the Great Pyramid. Once I went there with the object of investigating them, but, as the watchmen do not permit one to go down into the underground passage, I had to return disappointed. Still, the genii who guard the Pyramid and Sphinx secrets can be won over—only to do this it is essential to know their particular form, invocation, name and written sign. This knowledge, unfortunately, has been lost with the ancient Egyptians."

I raised a query concerning the alleged powers of the magician. The old man agreed that they were limited.

"Of course, we cannot claim to do everything. We can do certain things and no more. Allah alone knows and commands all. We can but try to use our art, but Allah's is the final word."

I wandered out into the dusty street, under the clear pearly light of Cairo's sky, carrying in my jacket pocket an enormous reddish-brown, polished agate shaped like an egg, which the magician had given me as a keepsake and which, he said, had once belonged to a Pharaoh. As my fingers stroked its sleek surface, I thought of the man whom I had just left and of the unseen servitors who, so he claimed, were ready to obey his will. It was obvious to me that here one was treading on dangerous ground, on the very boundaries of witchcraft, sorcery and the black art.

Were these genii but baseless ancient inventions? No—it was not difficult to accept the theory that the hidden realms of Nature were inhabited by other creatures beside man; one could arrive at this conclusion by merely analogical reasoning. It was also quite possible that such creatures contained within their ranks those who were darkly malignant equally as those who were peacefully beneficent. Whether they could do all that he claimed was another matter. Egypt's prolonged sun-bath might have affected his brain; I could not decide straightway.

In India a Yogi had mysteriously restored life to a dead bird before my eyes, although this return of animation was only temporary: here in Egypt I had watched an equally surprising reversal of this performance.

I did not attempt to write down all he had said to me, for some men are note-shy and I knew psychologically that he was one of them. I fixed his phrases in my memory and transferred them to paper the moment I was alone—and how strange they looked then! I had wanted to investigate the forms of native magic. This was the first, curious result.

# CHAPTER VI

## WONDER-WORKING BY HYPNOTISM

SOMETIMES one finds things where they are least expected and it was during my sojourn in the European quarter of Cairo that I found there another strange manifestation of those forces which we call supernatural, but which science may one day explain so glibly that we shall no longer regard them as such.

I discovered a remarkable young couple who lived in a street which led directly to the barracks of the British Garrison. Cairo is such a cosmopolitan hive that a single block of apartments will frequently house half a dozen different nationalities. The French are quite prominent in this quarter and this young couple had lived in Egypt for many years. The husband's name was Monsieur Eduard Ades and his wife was known as Madame Marguerite. He was gifted with some amount of hypnotic power, she being an exceptionally fine subject for his experiments. After some years of practice and training, they had arrived at a certain degree of competence in their power of demonstrating the extraordinary possibilities which lie untapped within the minds and bodies of mankind. I tested them in various ways and, though most of our experiments were quite unsensational and of interest to scientific researchers alone, nevertheless there were two or three feats of a character sufficient to startle any hide-bound materialist who has never explored such possibilities.

The first feat which I shall describe was done under test conditions and even when I invited the slightly sceptical wife of a prominent British official to witness it, she was compelled to confess that it seemed a perfectly genuine demonstration, and that no theory of trickery could explain it.

The four of us sat in the simply furnished study of Monsieur Ades. The latter was a handsome man in the early thirties. His head was covered with a thick mass of wavy hair, his forehead high and intellectual, the eyes were steady and penetrating, the nose was Greek in its straightness; while he spoke in the animated manner of his race. Unusually eloquent, he could keep up a torrent of conversation for hours, with the words tumbling over each other in their hurry to escape from his mouth. His entire personality conveyed an impression of force and strength.

Madame Marguerite, on the other hand, was all that one might expect a good hypnotic subject to be. She was gentle, sensitive, quiet, reserved and wistful. Her body was short and slightly plump, the eyes being noticeably large, soft and dreamy. She moved with slow, lethargic movements.

She sat on a straight-backed chair while Monsieur Ades stood next to her and began the demonstration. He pressed his right thumb between Madame Marguerite's eyebrows and kept it there for about two minutes, while steadily watching her face. He did no more than this, never attempting to make any passes over her with his hands nor using any other devices that usually form part of a hypnotist's technique.

"When I first commenced to hypnotize Madame Marguerite many years ago," he explained, speaking rapidly in French, "I used a complicated method and had to wait a considerable time before she passed into the first degree of the trance state. Now we have worked together so often that I can dispense with all other preparations and hypnotize her almost at once, although no other hypnotist could have the same success with her. Look! She is now hypnotized."

Madame Marguerite's body had become somewhat rigid, her eyes had closed and she appeared lost to her surroundings. I asked permission to examine her and, raising her eyelids, found the conventional signs of unsensitiveness—the eyeballs had turned upwards on their axes and were fixed in that unnatural position. This was scientific evidence that she had entered the first degree of hypnotic trance.

We began with simple unostentatious feats. Monsier Ades ordered her to look across the room. "What a terrible scene is there," he suggested to her. "Watch how that poor person is suffering grievously. How sad that such a thing should happen, how sad!"

Madame Marguerite gazed at the far corner of the room and began to look unhappy. Soon she was weeping. Within a minute or two tears were falling down her cheeks quite copiously.

Suddenly the hypnotist commanded her to see a gay procession in the other corner and to laugh at it.  A few seconds later her distress lessened, she soon smiled, and finally laughed outright in a hearty and natural manner.

So she became in turn a child of three, a soldier, and a man with a sprained knee; always responding perfectly to the spoken suggestions and seemingly living completely in the new characters taken on.

Then, at Monsieur Ades's suggestion, I securely closed her eyes by fastening pieces of gummed tape, which I had brought with me, across her eyebrows, eyelids and cheeks.  After such treatment it was absolutely impossible for her to open her eyes.  But to perfect the conditions of this experiment, I tied a thick red velvet bandage around her eyes and head: assurance was now doubly sure.

Ades asked me to whisper in his ear some instructions to be carried out by his subject.  Accordingly, I whispered: "Raise your right arm."  He returned to her side, held his own right hand a few inches away from hers, and then raised it in the air.  He bade her imitate this action.

Although Madame Marguerite's eyes were so carefully sealed that she could not possibly have witnessed what he did, she immediately raised her right arm even as he had done!

He came over to us and asked the lady visitor to suggest another movement.  She whispered: "Cross the fingers of both hands."  He returned to the unseeing subject with crossed fingers and she unhesitatingly imitated him!

¶

Now came the most interesting experiment.  Ades put his subject into the second degree of hypnotic trance by touching her forehead and giving her the spoken suggestion.  In this state the latent powers of the subconscious mind stir into striking activity.

He commanded her to sit down at his desk.  Immediately she obeyed.  She looked a strange figure with the heavy red bandage around her eyes.

He asked us to select at random any passage from any book we chose.  We selected a French scientific work, opened it by chance at page fifty-three, marked a certain paragraph, and set it down on the desk by the subject.

Madame Marguerite picked up a pencil while Monsieur Ades placed a sheet of paper on the desk. He said, in a firm voice:

"Now find the chosen passage in the book. You will read it without difficulty, then transcribe what you read, on to the paper beside you. Begin!"

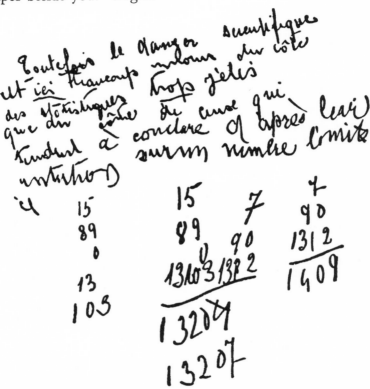

MADAME MARGUERITE'S ACTUAL WRITING WHILE BLINDFOLDED

The hypnotized woman poised her pencil in the air for a minute while she gazed through the bandage at the printed pages, then she began to write across the paper in a slow deliberate manner. Having written three or four words, she returned to the book and bent her face over the page, just as though her eyes were open and she could read every line. Yet we were satisfied that we had taken every precaution to prevent her doing this.

She continued this process of alternate reading and writing, a process which we watched with barely suppressed excitement. Ades assured us that she was accurately copying every word of the paragraph. He himself stood silent throughout. I asked him to command her to underline certain words: the second word of the second line and the third word of the third line. The command was given and we watched her slowly underscore two words.

The passage was finished at last and we eagerly walked over to the desk and inspected the written sheet, comparing it word for word with the printed original. The latter read:

"Toutefois le danger scientifique est ici beaucoup moins du côté des statisticiens trop zélés que du côté de ceus qui tendent à conclure d'après leur intuition sur un nombre limité. . . ."

A reference to the accompanying reproduction of the sheet in Madame Marguerite's handwriting reveals the fact that her copy was astonishingly accurate, and that she correctly underlined the two words indicated. She made a single error: instead of "statisticiens" she wrote "statistiques." A curious but understandable mistake.

Madame Marguerite did not complete the paragraph, because we thought sufficient had been written to demonstrate her strange faculty.

Another interesting experiment was to get her to write precisely the same paragraph but using her left hand. Normally she is not ambidextrous, but in the hypnotic state she carried through the task with ease.

After that, a series of figures were dictated to her by Monsieur Ades for addition, we supplying the figures to him previously. From the accompanying plate, which reproduces her actual writing, it will be seen that she misunderstood the last figures in the first sum, viz. 13,103, and had to make a fresh start. Though she was still heavily blindfolded, she was able to set down two sums with the digits in the proper columns, and to add them up correctly.

The next experiment indicated what immense possibilities lie latent and unfolded in us. The visitor whom I had brought took the subject's hand in hers and concentrated strongly upon the mental image of her husband. After a short time Madame Ades described the character, capacities, temperament, and even physical appearance of the absent man. Most extraordinary was her statement that he was a Government official.

"Correct!" was the surprised lady's comment on this reading of her own mind.

And yet, on another occasion, when I was with Madame Marguerite whilst she was in the same degree of hypnotic state, she ventured by her own desire to peer into futurity for me with extremely unsatisfactory results. I revolted inwardly at the falsity of some of her predictions, and within a few months she was definitely proved wrong. But when she attempted to read my character, aims, aspirations and ambitions, she proved quite correct. It is clear, therefore, that fortune-telling here, as elsewhere, is and must remain an extremely dubious procedure, although the general trend of events necessarily resulting from one's character may be read.

For the final experiment the subject was placed in the third stage of hypnotization, a deeper condition which made certain parts of the body insensible to pain, and which even enabled the hypnotizer to obtain control over organs that function involuntarily.

Ades rubbed a piece of cotton-wool upon the palm of her left hand, produced a needle for our inspection; then dug it into the fleshy part of the hand until the point came through on the other side and projected for half an inch. Apparently she felt no pain: on the contrary, when he suggested to her that a comedian was standing in front of us telling jokes, she began to shake her sides with laughter. A few minutes after he withdrew the needle from her hand. Not a single drop of blood was visible, either upon the skin or on the needle itself! A tiny black mark in the palm alone indicated where the needle had passed through.

§

I questioned Monsieur Ades upon the subject of hypnotism.

He was a well-educated man, a University graduate, and at one time a teacher of psychology in some college. Because of this he liked to be called Professor Eduard—a natural and harmless piece of vanity. It was by this title that I generally addressed him.

When I asked him for an explanation of his demonstrations, he turned his piercing regard upon me and exclaimed:

"Monsieur! I shall be perfectly frank with you. We really know nothing of the mysterious forces which cause the phenomena of hypnotism. Nevertheless, we understand the technique which can produce these phenomena and we know under what conditions success or failure will result.

"We have discovered that there resides in all persons a certain kind of force which we call magnetic influence, and that in some persons—as myself—this influence is so strongly developed that it can be used to affect others in the remarkable manner you have witnessed. On the other hand, it requires for its action people who are naturally receptive to it, who yield up their wills with the least resistance. When I discovered my own power I set out to strengthen it, until it reached the point you see to-day. And it was only by constant experiment with Madame Marguerite that we were able eventually to perform these feats. At first it took a long time to induce in her the hypnotized condition, only by continuous effort and experience I have succeeded in reducing the time to a few minutes.

"What happens when she is in that condition? She becomes a kind of somnambulist, a sleep-walker," he explained, "so that even if you were to fire off a pistol it would not awaken her from the semi-trance. The Doctors Preyer and Berger, who were able to make special studies of the cases of sleep-walkers, found that such persons could see quite well with their eyelids shut while in the somnambulic state. This mysterious condition proves that consciousness can be divided and that what psychologists call the subconscious mind does exist. And it appears, from our demonstrations, that this subconscious is very clairvoyant and untrammelled by the bonds of matter. It is then able to do with the body what the person in a conscious state believes impossible. This shows that our belief in limitations is a false one, and that we are all capable of much more than we think. Hypnotism frees the subject of such handicapping notions."

"What is your theory to explain Madame Marguerite's reading the book through sealed bandages?"

"I merely say that we dare not set limits to the powers of the subconscious, and that clairvoyance seems to be one of its natural faculties. In other words, the subconscious has its own powers of seeing, hearing and feeling, and is not dependent on the physical organs, such as the eyes and ears, for its operation.[1] The hypnotic condition draws the subject's attention away from these physical organs—from the whole body in fact—and thus concentrates it entirely on the subconscious mind, whose mysterious faculties thereupon come into play. But really, I cannot say much more than that. I can only provide the necessary conditions and then watch these faculties at work."

"You make no passes with the hands, I notice. Do you regard them as unnecessary?"

"I think they may well be necessary to some hypnotists, monsieur," he replied energetically, "but I can dispense with them. I rely entirely on the force of my will and on the spoken suggestions which I give to my subject. My experience makes me believe that the real secret of hypnotizing lies in these two methods, especially in suggestion, made calmly and authoritatively, and that magnetic passes are only necessary to those who do not feel expert enough to dispense with them."

¶

For a part of every year Cairo harbours a man who may safely be described as the most famous fakir of modern Egypt —none other than the illustrious Tahra Bey. Much controversy has raged around his feats; many critics have endeavoured to stab his reputation even as he stabs his own body with arrows and knives; yet the fact remains that a large number of distinguished people have found his achievements interesting at least, and convincing at most; that King Fuad of Egypt,

---

[1] The Yogis of India gave me a somewhat similar explanation of these phenomena. They claimed that every man had an invisible "soul-body" and that there were seven nervous centres in the latter, situated in an area approximating to the cerebro-spinal system and the upper brain, and that each of these unseen centres was the real controlling agency of our physical senses. Thus, they placed the first centre in the sacral region and this controlled smell; the second was in the spleen and governed taste; the third was at the navel and corresponded to sight, and so on. Their theory, was that the external sense-objects are really perceived by this "soul-body" which is the internal agent whose co-operation is essential to the successful functioning of all man's physical senses. The latter are merely instruments and without such co-operation become incapable of performing their offices. In other words, sight, hearing, etc., are primarily mental faculties and only secondarily physical. The Yogis claimed that by *conscious* control of attention, as in profound concentration, the feats performed by hypnotized subjects can be done at will, without a hypnotizer.

King Carol of Rumania and King Victor Emanuel of Italy, among others, honoured him with invitations, while Signor Benito Mussolini received him several times at the Chigi Palace; and that instead of shirking investigation he has usually courted it. I, who have seen several of his feats done by half a dozen unknown fakirs in different parts of India and Africa, find no difficulty in believing them possible; whereas, knowing the man, I know, also, that he actually does possess the powers which he claims. It is only when he stoops, as unfortunately he now does, to satisfy the popular craze for fortune-telling and charms, that he is indulging in an activity which I am unable to endorse. Perhaps he is not to blame, however. "The world has forced me to commercialize my powers, to become an artiste when I wanted to be a scientist," he sadly confessed to me once over the tea-table. Nevertheless, I admire him greatly, as being the first Oriental fakir with such extraordinary powers who has refused to clothe around them a dress of mystifying verbiage or religious irrelevancies. He himself wants to see the truth about the wonders of the fakirs separated from the nonsense with which it has been traditionally embroidered. He has a refreshingly sane and modern attitude towards his own achievements and the principles which underlie them, an attitude unique among that order of medieval-minded, unprogressive, irrational and mystery-loving human beings called fakirs. In short, he seeks to replace superstition by science.

Before one can adequately understand his feats one needs to understand the man, and the best way to do that is by a short sketch of his life. I shall set that down here, just as he told it me. But first meet him.

You may expect the lank emaciated figure of an ascetic. Instead, picture a short, distinguished-looking man with black hair and olive skin, grave, peaceful, bearded face, who sometimes wears the Arab burnous over his head, at others an ordinary European soft felt hat. He is slightly under medium height. He slips out of his Arab robes into a well-cut European tailored suit and finds himself equally at home in both. His piercing, beautiful eyes are exceptionally interesting because the white irises are strongly noticeable and lend depth and mystery to the jet-black pupils. His manner is always soft and gentle, while he is as courteous and as polished as all the better Egyptians invariably are. He murmurs his sentences so quietly and so humbly that no one might guess from his tone that he was a man with some of the most mysterious forces of Nature under his command and control. He carries himself with an unhurried ease and self-possession, a marked air of self-control, such as one always observes in really advanced fakirs. He smokes innumerable cigarettes during the course of a day.

"I was born in 1897, at Tanta, the busy little town in the Nile Delta which also contains the tomb of the famous thirteenth-century fakir Sheikh Ayid Ahmad el Badawi, visited by pilgrims from all parts of the East. My mother died while giving me birth, and my father belonged to the race of Copts, the Christians of Egypt. My father was himself well acquainted with the teachings of the fakirs, he had friends with similar tendencies; hence I grew up in an atmosphere favourable to my future work. At quite an early age I was initiated into the exercises and practices traditionally followed by fakirs, my own father being one of my teachers. Whilst I was yet a child, internal troubles in the country led to our change of residence, and so my father, myself and a teacher went to Turkey, where we settled down in Constantinople. Here I received a good modern education, studied medicine, and received a doctor's degree. This education was extremely valuable to me, psychologically, as it enabled me to submit my own psychic experiences to scientific analysis. I opened a clinic in Greece and conducted it for a short time, and it was there that I undertook the feat which I regard as the most marvellous of all that are within the capacities of fakirs—the resurrection. I permitted myself to be buried for no less than twenty-eight days, to be lowered into the very abyss of death, from which at the end of that time I emerged alive and unharmed. The Metropolitan and other Christian dignitaries were opposed to me and tried to prevent my feat, because they fancied they saw in it, and in the doctrines it illustrated, a menace to their religion. Nevertheless the government authorities defended me and answered that, being a doctor, I had the right to be buried if I wished. My scientific training and doctor's degree have been a help to smooth my path on other occasions, too.

"I visited Bulgaria and Serbia and Italy. In the latter country I permitted the best-known scientists to investigate my feats and allowed them to put me in a coffin made of lead. My body was completely covered with sand. The lid was nailed down and I was then sunk to the bottom of a swimming bath.

After about half an hour the police interfered and stopped the demonstration, but so far, of course, it was successful. Then I came to France, and there I was not only permitted to repeat the same experiment but actually to extend it. For twenty-four hours I remained in the coffin under water, my body in a state of catalepsy, while police and others guarded the demonstration all the time to prevent trickery. Here are two photographs which were taken on the spot. The first shows my rigid entranced body being laid in the coffin; the second shows the coffin being lifted out of the water where it had lain for twenty-four hours. I was glad to invite and undergo this test because so many critics have claimed to expose the performance of the Indian fakirs in being buried alive, a performance which you described in your own book on India. They say that the fakirs pre-arrange to have a secret air channel dug through the earth and that by this means they continue to breathe. No doubt this occurs in the case of pseudo-fakirs who are merely conjurers and illusionists, but it is totally unnecessary in the case of those who have learnt the genuine secrets of our art and can entrance the body at will. It is for this reason that I arranged a test under water, where the conditions are transparent and everything can be controlled by observers. Doctors were especially interested in this feat and they tried every means to test its genuineness, and quite rightly, but because it was based on natural laws I had nothing to fear.

"Although I am fond of the comforts of European life, I am also attached to my own country, and thus I make it a point to divide part of my time each year between Egypt and Europe. I like Europeans and some of them appreciate and welcome me. Once when the Queen of Spain telegraphed for me to go to her country, she even sent an official escort to conduct me. I do not feel vain about my achievements. The past now moves before my eyes like a wonderful film. A true fakir is above such things as vanity and greed; he lives an inner life detached from excessive worldly desires. You know the fakirs of the Orient, and I think you will agree that my case is almost unique because the others, where genuine, do not care to visit Europe and are too proud to submit themselves to critical investigations; in fact they think it is useless to show you their feats, as you Europeans are sure to attribute such to charlatanry or jugglery—in short, to anything but the right causes. And, much more important, they do not possess my knowledge of your languages—I know Italian and French—while I do not remember one of them who has taken a university course in medicine and the sciences and accepted modern education for what it is worth. As you have noticed, they generally despise such education and regard it as a hindrance. Of course, I do not agree with them."

¶

I collected a small group of doctors and other professional men whose interest I had engaged in these heterodox subjects, and we were privileged to watch a whole series of astonishing, if gruesome, demonstrations which Tahra Bey performed with an ease and swiftness that was astounding.

The fakir had dropped his European clothes; he wore a long robe of white linen. An Arab burnous was tied around his head with double blue and gold cords. A five-pointed, engraved gold star, the emblem of the order into which he had been initiated, hung suspended from a neck-chain, upon his breast. Around his waist there was a golden girdle. He stood with arms folded upon his chest. Around the floor of the room were distributed the various objects and materials to be used in his demonstrations—a table loaded with daggers, hat-pins, knives, needles, skewers and bits of glass; another table upon which rested a plank studded with the points of long, sharp nails; a block of heavy stone, a weighing machine and a large hammer; a white fowl and a grey rabbit, both tied by the feet and lying in a basket; two gleaming, polished scythe blades; a pair of trestles, a long coffin, a still longer and larger box, a heap of red sand and a pair of spades; a few hand-towels, some cotton-wool with other odds and ends. A brazier of burning incense filled the room with a soft perfume. Two young men in his employ stood by to act as assistants. Tahra Bey himself then came forward, but remained completely silent. He looked very distinguished under the soft illumination of the electric lamps.

Every article was carefully examined, to satisfy ourselves as to its genuineness and clear our minds of any suspicion of trickery, so far as these things were concerned.

The fakir touched the back of his neck and pressed the skin slightly higher than the nape firmly with his fingers; with the other hand he pressed the temples of his forehead. Then he seemed to suck air abruptly into his mouth, with the result that the Adam's apple of his throat was momentarily agitated. In a minute his eyes closed and he was entranced; at the same time he uttered a peculiar, sudden cry. His trance abruptly culminated in catalepsy so rigid that he would have fallen like a dead man to the floor, if his assistants had not caught him in their arms.

His body was now as stiff as a piece of wood.

For the first experiment he was stripped bare to the waist.

One of his assistants fixed the long scythe-blades to the tops of a pair of trestles with the sharpened sides uppermost. Upon these blades Tahra Bey was then placed so that one propped up his shoulders and the other his ankles. While he was in this condition a doctor took his pulse-beat and was surprised to find that it registered the abnormally high figure of 130.

The large block of stone was brought forward and weighed; it registered nearly ninety kilogrammes, or a little more than one hundredweight and a half in English weights. It was a rough cube of solid rock granite. The assistants placed it upon Tahra Bey's bare stomach; one of them took up the black-smith's hammer and vigorously delivered blow after blow upon the block. The fakir's body remained as taut and rigid as if it had been made of iron, never yielding once a fraction under the combination of terrific pressure and weight. Eventually the stone split into two pieces which fell resoundingly to the floor. Tahra Bey was lifted up, placed on his feet and supported by his two men. Apparently, he was quite unconscious of what had happened, and had not suffered any pain. Doctors examined him with interest and found that the scythe-blade edges had not left the slightest marks upon his skin! Nevertheless, the block of granite had left a strong red mark all over his abdomen.

He might have lain on a bed of flowers for all the effect this ordeal had upon him. It reminded me of the performances of lower orders of Yogis I had met with at Benares, who sit and sleep on sharp spikes, and from whom I had walked away, repelled rather than edified.

He was next placed upon the wooden plank studded with sharp nails of great length whose points jutted up in the air; an assistant jumped up and stood upon him, one foot on his chest and the other on his abdomen; yet when he was re-examined by the doctors, his bare back showed not the slightest mark of entry by the spikes! His pulse now registered 132.

He was lifted on to his feet.

We watched the fakir's eyelids tremble; slowly the eyes opened. For a couple of moments after he awoke his eyeballs rolled. He resembled someone just emerging from a dream which had taken him very far away. For the next half-hour those eyes remained uncannily fixed. Little by little he returned to life. He made a violent effort to inhale air, opening his mouth so wide that we noticed his tongue had been curled back into his throat. After the inhalation, he put his finger inside and thrust the tongue back to its normal position.

He had now wholly emerged from the cataleptic state into which he had so quickly thrown himself.

Having rested for a minute or two, he submitted to further tests which were to prove whether his flesh was really insensible to pain or not.

He asked the doctors to pierce his jaws with a pair of hat-pins, which one of them promptly did, running a hat-pin through each cheek, at such an angle that its end emerged through the mouth. Doctors are aware that there exist within the body certain places where the flesh between two muscles or two nerves may be pierced without injury. Therefore, good care was taken on this occasion to select really dangerous places in the fakir's face. Next they ran thick skewers through his jaws, Tahra Bey fully awake and perfectly realizing what was happening, yet he did not seem to feel in the least the painfulness of this procedure.

A more startling test was when he allowed another doctor to plunge a large dagger into his throat in front of the larynx, with the point reappearing after the dagger had passed through nearly one inch of flesh. Some of the doctors, who were, naturally and rightly, sceptical, took it upon themselves to watch the pupils of his eyes with the closest attention, in order to note whether or not they contracted or dilated. It was thus possible to establish the presence or absence of some drug in the body; they suspected that he might have secretly drugged himself before the performance, to render himself insensible to pain. They found his eyes were quite normal, however. When all these weapons had been withdrawn, not a single drop of blood could be seen on his skin. This was so astonishing to some of the doctors that they insisted on cutting his face with bits of glass and jabbing needles into his throat; still he emerged absolutely bloodless from the ordeal. They stuck arrows and hat-pins into his shoulders and breast with the same result.

To demonstrate another mysterious faculty which he possessed, Tahra Bey permitted a large sharp knife to be stuck into his chest and then withdrawn. The wound was bloodless. A doctor expressed a wish to see the blood flow to assure himself that the fakir had really been wounded. Immediately the latter caused the red fluid to stream out until it inundated his chest— a rather ghastly sight. When the doctor was satisfied, the Egyptian stopped all flow of blood by mere will power—an achievement which more than astonished some of those present. Ten minutes later the wound had practically healed.

One of the assistants produced a flaming torch and passed it along the entire length of the fakir's left leg as high as the middle of his thigh. We heard the skin and flesh crackle slightly in the heat, yet his face remained serene, unmoved, entirely undisturbed.

Another doctor, still unconvinced, believing that Tahra Bey had secretly taken some powerful drug, tested the man's heart-beats whilst the flame was being applied. They did not register the slightest change; had he suffered any pain and masked it, or even mastered it by a phenomenally strong will, the heart would, of course, have vastly accelerated its beats, his face would have turned pale, and other signs would have presented evidence of his secret suffering. Moreover, had he taken a drug like caffeine his breathing would no longer have remained normal, which was certainly the case with him now.

Other experiments included the sticking of long arrows through the flesh just above his heart, and right through his arms till they came out at the opposite side.

## ¶

He next showed a power over animals which Indian Yogis also sometimes display. I had brought a rabbit and a hen at Tahra Bey's request, and had placed them in a basket on one of his demonstrating tables. To these he now turned his attention.

He took hold of the rabbit and brought the hind paws round to its neck. The animal resisted two or three times, but the fakir pressed a nerve centre at the back of its neck, and made a couple of passes over it with his hands. At this the little creature lay stretched out on its back, exactly in the position in which he had put it, as still as though it had died. Its eyes remained quite open and we noticed that, despite the rigidity of the body, the eyeballs moved around from time to time, proving that it was very much awake, even if helpless. To test the matter, one of us approached the rabbit and touched its eye with a finger; immediately the eye closed and reopened, revealing that the animal was fully conscious of what was occurring, although unable to exert its will.

Tahra Bey gave it a gentle rap on the back of its neck and the creature uttered a cry, jumped up, regained its feet, and joyously ran around the table. It was quite unhurt and was none the worse for its distressing experience.

The same experiment was performed upon the hen, which responded as obediently as the other creature. Tahra Bey was able to put it and keep it in any position he desired, and for as long a time as he chose.

The fakir then informed us that his body was no longer insensible to pain, as this insensibility lasted for no longer than a period of about twenty to twenty-five minutes after his first entrancement. In other words, he had resumed complete normality. "If you were suddenly and unexpectedly to stab me with a knife now, I would undoubtedly cry out with pain," he confessed.

Finally, came the most noteworthy feat of the evening, none other than that of being buried alive. This extraordinary feat was done under test conditions which did not admit of the slightest doubt as to its genuineness.

Tahra Bey said that he would fix, beforehand, the exact hour and minute when he would emerge from the trance into which he would soon throw himself. He requested us, therefore, to keep him buried for no longer than exactly one and a half hours, as he would predetermine his awakening for five minutes after that time.

The coffin was brought into the centre of the scene, the floor of the apartment being first examined. It was laid with tiles and mosaic, as Egyptian floors frequently are, and it had nothing more than the ceiling of another room below it, for we happened to be in one of the blocks of modern flats which are springing up all over the European quarter of Cairo. The possibility of secret trapdoors was dismissed very quickly, but, to satisfy our last doubts, an ordinary rug was laid across the floor. The coffin was placed upon this rug.

Tahra Bey went through his usual procedure of entering the condition of auto-catalepsy. He pressed his fingers upon the arteries at the nape of his neck and upon nerve-centres in the temples. He curled his tongue towards the back of his throat and brusquely sucked in the air. Within a couple of minutes he became definitely cataleptic. His breathing stopped, the blood-stream ceased to flow and his entire body became numb. He fell back into the arms of his assistants, and while they supported him these facts were ascertained by the doctors who examined him: no heart beats, no breathing!

His ears, nostrils and mouth were then stuffed with cotton-wool by his assistants, his rigid, statue-like body being laid flat in the coffin. It would have been hard to say what was the difference between Tahra Bey in his coffin and any dead man in his coffin. Certainly, there was no sign of life in this ashen-faced "living corpse."

His assistants set to work with the spades, rapidly filling his coffin with the soft red sand. He was covered completely with it. The wooden lid was then brought and firmly nailed down.

Next, the long wooden trough was moved to the carpet and brought alongside the coffin. The latter was lifted up and transferred to the trough and placed inside. The assistants set to work again and piled up the sand over the coffin until the trough was filled right to the top.

We settled down for an hour and a half of waiting, while Tahra Bey lay immobile within his makeshift sandy tomb. We had examined everything used in the feat; we had carefully controlled every step of its performance. If he survived such a test we would be forced to pay tribute to his extraordinary powers.

At last the allotted period elapsed, and true to our promise, the sand was shovelled up and thrown aside; the coffin was disinterred, raised, and the lid opened. There lay the fakir, stretched out as stiff as a corpse, his skin the dull grey colour of one defunct. To all intents and purposes he was, certainly, a dead man.

He was taken out; the rigidity relapsed, and he was placed in a chair. After a few minutes the first signs of returning life appeared. His eyelids flickered; then the rhythm of quiet breathing manifested itself and, gradually, the whole body became reanimated.

Within a dozen minutes of his emergence from the coffin he was his usual self, and sat talking of his strange experience.

"My sleep was so profound that I know nothing of what you have done to me," he told us. "I recall only that I closed my eyes in this room and that, by the mysterious process of post-suggestion, I have awakened in this room again at the exact moment I set myself."

So ended our amazing evening with this amazing little man, who can work a miracle in a trice!

I came away with the feeling that the tottering figure of materialism would be brought to the execution block during this century. It had never done much to explain the mystery of mind.

There are pessimistic scientists who predict that the end of our earth will be a frozen planet rotating through emptiness. Maybe. But the end of man can never be so hopeless as his home, *because he is more than body.*

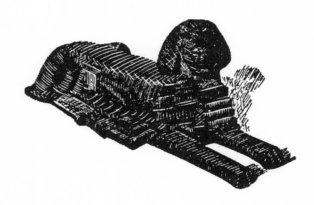

# CHAPTER VII

TAHRA BEY smoked one of his innumerable delicately scented Egyptian cigarettes, while he unfolded to me, one afternoon, the theories and principles which underlie his remarkable demonstrations. We sat in a luxurious flat in that growing quarter which is Cairo's inheritance from Europe. He had promised to tell me much, and so I anticipated his forthcoming revelations with a kind of mild thrill; I certainly received some illuminating answers to my questions.

It is always interesting, and sometimes profitable, to secure explanations of abnormal and extraordinary feats from those who have actually demonstrated them, and not from book-learned professors who can only theorize about them.

"We must begin by recognizing within ourselves the great possibilities which we all possess," he commenced; "and until we do this we must remain bound, hand and foot, to unnecessary limitations that prevent us exploiting our marvellous psychic and material powers. People, when confronted with the phenomena which I can produce, think it either some kind of conjuring or else something entirely supernatural. In both cases they are wrong. They do not seem to grasp the fact that these things are perfectly scientific, obeying the laws of nature herself. It is true that I am using psychic laws which are little understood, but, nevertheless, they *are* laws. Nothing that I do is arbitrary, supernatural, or against such laws. As for those who imagine I am a kind of stage illusionist, a conjurer, I must pity their narrow minds, their inability to envisage any higher possibility for mankind than the limited experience which has fallen to their lot."

My pen scribbled a stenographic note of the last sentence and I looked up, catching that wistful expression which sometimes stole into his mystic eyes when he alluded to his critics. One felt that he would rather make friends than enemies, would rather find understanding than incur misunderstanding.

"They think, for instance, that when I run hat-pins or skewers through my jaws if it is not a clever trick then it is a matter of being drugged, or if none of these things then it is a matter of forcing my will to resist the pain. Yet, if that were true, why is it that there are no scars on my body after I have been so badly wounded and cut? The fact is, that they cannot get away from their accustomed ways of thinking; they cannot grasp the possibility of the truth of my own explanations. Let them try to stick knives and skewers into their own throats and faces: they will soon see the difference. They may keep on saying to themselves that they do not feel it, and they may try their utmost not to, yet they will certainly do so."

He paused on this indignant note.

"But you want my explanations. The two secrets—although that is hardly the correct term, it will suffice—which enable me to perform all my feats are, first, pressure on certain nerve centres of the body; second, ability to enter into the cataleptic coma. Anyone who is suited and who will undergo the long training which I had to undergo in order to master and successfully practise the application of these two secrets, may perform the same feats. Without such application I could not claim to have the courage to resist the pain of these feats without a murmur, for I am not built like those Hindu fakirs you have seen who voluptuously seek to torture themselves and who endure voluntarily terrible sufferings dictated by their doctrines of asceticism. I have broken away from such barbarous doctrines and I definitely condemn the exaggerated exercises those ascetics set themselves. The only things I share with them are, on the doctrinal side, to live inwardly detached in spirit, and on the side of practices, the swallowing backwards of the tongue and the entry into catalepsy."

He spoke with a frankness which, knowing the ways of thought of Oriental fakirs, surprised me. However, I asked him:

"Will you please explain more fully your first secret?"

"Yes," came the soft voice in response. "Briefly, it is unnecessary for me to tell you that the nerves are the conductors of all pain, but it is necessary to point out that by finger pressure, to draw the blood away from the brain, on selected nerve centres, the latter are struck with anæsthesia. Mind you, I am not for a moment suggesting that anyone should practise this, because without the long and proper training requisite such unguided experiments would simply be foolhardy and dangerous.   When such pressure is combined with a concentration of thought on the state of losing consciousness, as well as with a complete relaxation of the muscles and nerves; when all this is followed by a complete swallowing backwards of the tongue and a brusque inhalation of air, rigid cataleptic coma is sure to supervene.  And then, for about twenty-five minutes afterwards, the flesh automatically will become totally insensible to pain, no matter how intense, how atrocious the latter ought to be."

"What are the nerves upon which you exercise pressure?"

"They are the main carotid arteries serving the head, the hypnotic centres of the temples, and the pneumogastric nerves. But, as I have said, these are not to be played with.   Anyone who tried to compress the carotids, for instance, and succeeded in drawing his blood away from the brain, would most probably find a buzzing produced inside his head through the blood leaving the nape of his neck; he would fall backwards helplessly, and inevitably he would faint.   I can do this quite safely because I have been trained since childhood by experts."

"And the tongue swallowing——?"

"Ah, that, of course, you have seen in India, among the Yogis.   Even so early as when I was a child of four months old, my father began to turn my tongue back with his finger. The result was a kind of convulsive fit.  When the latter became too violent it was a sign that the practice had been overdone and that it was necessary to stop it for a while.   To-day, I can swallow my tongue backwards with ease; though I still sometimes experience difficulty in returning it to its normal position and have to thrust it forward with my fingers.   Your Hindus occasionally indulge in tongue-lengthening exercises in order to be able to perform this difficult feat of curling the tongue back and sealing the windpipe; which also prevents the entrance of dangerous insects,[1] or even germs, whilst the body is lying helpless underground."

---

[1] I remember now that Brama, the Hindu Yogi in my book *A Search in Secret India*, who had studied along similar lines to Tahra Bey, once told me that any Yogi who undertook to be buried alive for a fixed period would refuse to be buried in a place teeming with the destructive little creatures known as white ants, which are capable of eating through wooden coffins and devouring the entranced body.

¶

"Assuming you have entered the coma, what happens?"

"Before I enter this state, I always fix beforehand the moment of my awakening. When that moment arrives, I awake. Many people employ this form of auto-suggestion in a simple manner, as when they tell themselves at night to awaken from sleep at a certain hour, in time to proceed to their work next day. This is a proof that the subconscious mind never goes to sleep; it is only the conscious mind which has such a lapse, which also explains why sleep-walkers often perform quite intelligent actions without remembering afterwards what they did.

"To return. The commencement of the cataleptic trance brings about a cessation of the two important vital functions of breathing and blood-circulation. We know well that most people will declare that death must inevitably supervene should this happen, but I need not stop to argue the point with you because you have already given public testimony to having witnessed the contrary in India. The fakirs alone can stop breath and blood movements and yet live on. Let it suffice to say that all circulation of the blood completely stops whilst I am in a cataleptic coma. In fact, the whole rhythm of my life is suspended. It is essential that I emphasize the fact that this is not the catalepsy sometimes attained in hypnotic experiments upon other persons, because in such cases the circulation of blood is frequently intensified. Why so? Because the methods used are totally different and quite unrelated. You will see this difference most clearly in the method which employs hypnotic suggestion alone, whereas I use purely physiological means, that is the nerve pressures and the tongue-swallowing. Another difference is that my insensibility against pain lasts not more than twenty-five minutes after I awaken from the second degree of trance. No such fixed period marks the cases of hypnotized subjects. Hypnotic states induced by suggestion frequently render the subject's body insensible to pain, it is true, but to be insensible to the pain after the state has passed, as I am, is another thing altogether. But the most important difference, after all, is that I put myself into the trance state entirely at my own will, whereas what hypnotist can hypnotize himself?"

"It is remarkable that your body is so unscarred, after the

numerous stabs you must have received during the course of your career.   How do you explain that, Doctor?"

"To achieve that, I do two things.   The first is to accelerate, temporarily, the blood circulation.   You know that the doctors found it rose up to 130 during the experiment the other evening. That accelerates my heart but does not over-drive it, and its rapidity does not fatigue me.   Such swiftness of blood-flow naturally helps to heal the wounds with amazing celerity. Remember I do this by mere will.   The second is to raise the temperature of the blood to fever-heat.   This destroys all germs which may have been introduced into the wounds and actually disinfects the latter.   My wounds never suppurate, and always heal completely within a few minutes or, in more serious cases, within a few hours at most."

I next raised the subject of his greater feat, that of being buried alive.

He threw away the remnant of a cigarette and immediately proceeded to light another.

"I need not tell you that thousands of years ago in ancient Egypt, as in ancient India, the same feat was performed quite commonly," he replied.   "In those days the universal materialism which prevails to-day had scarcely begun; everyone believed in the soul and, therefore, experiences such as mine were thoroughly understood.   Everyone believed then, as we fakirs do to-day, that it is the soul which mysteriously guides the life of the body and the consciousness of the mind.   We believe that the soul can live apart from the body, that if the chemical atoms which compose the body return to earth in the form of carbon, potassium, hydrogen, oxygen and so on, then the soul, which is their vital force, returns to its source, the Unknown Force, which is eternal.   I need hardly tell you, further, that the danger of modern materialism is that it gives false habits of thinking which deprive men of that incalculable force, the power of the soul.   So much for theory.

"In brief, I may say that by the profoundest cataleptic entrancement physical life is suspended, but the unseen spark of the soul continues, nevertheless, to function.   To demonstrate this demands a long and severe training, which is usually begun at a very early age.   I mentioned that my own father began to train me when I was only four months old.   Now I can allow myself to be buried for a few days, if I desire, and emerge quite unharmed."

"Sceptics always raise one objection," I murmured. "They always enquire how it is possible to live underground without breathing?"

"Take a simple case.  The pearl-fishers off the coast of East Africa can stay under water without breathing for eight or nine minutes.  That represents the highest record for normal human beings, as far as I know.  Now turn to the animal kingdom.  The frog is a rapid breather, yet it will remain under water without air for as long as four hours.  How can it do that?  Examine it and you will find its body rigid.  In fact it is cataleptic.  You will notice, too, that the eyes are closed, though not by the eyelids; by a special protective skin which wards off the danger of prolonged contact with the water.  Take the water-turtle.  It lives quite freely in the air and yet it, too, can spend several hours under water.  If, however, you deprive a turtle of air and force it to remain under water against its will, it suffocates and dies.  The reason is that it has not had time to prepare itself for its underwater experience.  Crocodiles which have somewhat similar powers of living in both elements, hibernate without breathing during certain months of diminished vitality.  Science can scarcely explain how these creatures can live without oxygen.  Some kinds of bats, of course, provide well-known cases of winter hibernation when they remain suspended without breathing.

"Let me tell you, at once, that the key to the incomprehensible performances of these animals is that they enter a state of special catalepsy.  And, if the animals can do this, why not human beings, who, after all, possess animal bodies?  If human beings will apply this key they, too, can obtain the same results.  This we fakirs have proved.  Were I not in cataleptic trance during the experiment of being buried alive, I would be suffocated within ten minutes.  There do exist circumstances in which we can live without breathing."

§

I watched him blow the grey smoke from his fragrant cigarette, and then I asked:

"If, as you say, during the period of burial the soul is detached from the body, does it enter the Beyond?  And what can you tell us of your experiences in that sphere?"

"Unfortunately, I can tell you almost nothing.    I do not wish to pose as a man knowing the secrets of the Beyond.    Although we have awakened the marvellous powers of the subconscious mind to such an extent, there are still mysterious depths which we have been unable to penetrate.    The trouble is that when we fakirs escape from the body we pass into a condition similar to that of sleep-walkers, that is we are unconscious of our existence and yet we exist, and when we return to bodily life we are unable to remember anything of our apparently supernatural adventure.    It may be that we have explored the regions of the world of spirits, but as we do not remember our experiences we can say nothing of that world.    Our slumber is so deep that it is just like the animal hibernation of those animals I have mentioned to you."

This was indeed to be regretted.    That a man who had "died" not a few times, as had Tahra Bey, should be unable to bring back any brighter report was decidedly disappointing. If complete blankness, sheer unconsciousness, lay beyond the grave—it was paradoxically a living blankness.    I expressed my disappointment at such negative result.

He shrugged his shoulders.

"We must respect facts as we find them," he replied.    "However, I believe that I returned, as in real death, to reunite my soul with the Universal Soul, the Unknown Force.    In that sense, I believe we are immortal."

I wondered how the Universal Force—or God, if you like— could be an infinite state of complete unconsciousness, for I could not conceive how a conscious being—Man—could derive his mind from an unconscious Being—God.    But I did not raise the point because it would land me in a theological argument, and I was dealing, here, with scientific facts.    Nevertheless, I respected Dr. Tahra Bey's frank explanations as I was sure he described his experiences exactly as they had occurred.

He proceeded to tell me the story of a curious case of burial. A well-known fakir had been buried alive, in the year 1899, at Tanta; Dr. Tahra Bey's native town.    He had predetermined to awake not before the 17th May, 1925.    When the allotted date arrived, he was disinterred and found to be still alive.    The flesh was in perfect condition and all his organs sound, except that he had lost the power of speech.    Six months later the man died.

I asked Dr. Tahra Bey why the man had died so soon.

He said:

"It was on account of the wearing-out of his body underground. Such prolonged burials shorten a fakir's life. On the other hand, if a man is buried for not more than very short periods, say one to three days, a marvellously invigorating and healing effect is the result. Centuries ago the Egyptian Dervishes discovered this. In those days they were entrusted with the punishment of certain criminals who were, instead of being sentenced to death, made to undergo long periods of burial after the Dervishes had properly prepared their bodies. The periods varied in length according to the nature of the crime. It was discovered that although this ordeal shortened their lives, on the other hand, they were marvellously cured of their diseases, no matter what kind, whilst they lay buried in the hot sand. My explanation is that such burials provide all the benefits of prolonged rest and of fasting. The fasting cure, so popular nowadays, allows Nature to set to work and heal the body of its maladies. A burial for a couple of days is equivalent to a fast for the same period, with the added benefit of complete repose for every bodily function, a benefit which our overworked organs can alone appreciate. This profound lethargy of a short burial sets potent healing forces at work, thus proving the power of soul over matter and the striking intelligence which rests in our subconscious minds."

"But are there no dangers in being buried alive?"

He spread out his hands with an air of acceptance.

"Of course they exist, but, by proper precautions, they can be forestalled. The process used must be carried out with the utmost care, for here we are playing with life and death. There was a young fakir named Said who met his death in this way. He was a most promising young man of eighteen who had unreservedly dedicated himself to the life of a fakir and had been trained in the process of auto-catalepsy you have seen me practise. He decided one day to undertake the courageous feat of being buried underground for no less than six years. Well, that was done, his body being placed in a special tomb. To exercise some control over the feat and to help him, some devout Muhammedans opened his tomb once every year during the holy festival of Ramadan, examined the condition of his body and then said prayers over it. During the first two years his body was found in a perfect state of preservation, but at the third opening they discovered, to their dismay, that worms had penetrated the coffin in which he was encased and destroyed a part of his body."

"How do you explain that, Doctor?"

He turned away from me to look out of the window. I followed his gaze and saw that it rested on the Nile, that wondrous river which has fed and supported millions of people through thousands of years, which has taken Egypt into its kindly arms as into a father's. Then he turned back.

"I have two theories. The first is that the preparations before entombment were not properly carried out. A fakir who is to undergo such a long interment should have his body completely covered with soft wax, as though a wax cast were being taken of the entire body. Then he should be deposited in a closed and sealed coffin out of which all dust has been drawn as though by a vacuum cleaner. Poor Said did not have these precautions taken. My theory is that the hole in his coffin had been made by a snake, of a very small but powerful species which exists in Egypt; that this snake had crawled inside, and over his body, eventually making its way into one of his nostrils and thence penetrating to the brain. This injury to Said's body would have allowed oxygen to enter his body. I attribute part of the efficacy of the cataleptic state to the fact that it deprives the body of oxygen. I am confident that so long as oxygen is kept out of the entranced body, no microbe, and even no worm, will touch it. The result of this entry was that he lost, to some extent, his defence of catalepsy against worms. These crept into the coffin and began to live upon the flesh, first making their way to the inside organs."

Dr. Tahra Bey had painted a ghastly picture of the dangers which await the fakir who does not successfully conclude his voluntary interment. One began to understand why the ancient Egyptians, wishing to preserve their royal and aristocratic and priestly dead, not only embalmed and mummified their bodies, but also enclosed them in thick stone sarcophagi, of almost indestructible granite which it was impossible to penetrate.

"After this you will understand why one must characterize as nonsense the criticisms that, when I perform my own feat of being buried, I have secret pipes conveying air to me. When I was some years younger, I let myself be buried for one hour in an open-air garden, and people danced over my grave. Nevertheless, my object is not to astonish people as do stage conjurers, but to demonstrate what great powers lie, little known and less understood, within us.

"It has sometimes happened that I have failed when about to give a demonstration, and I have always been frank enough to admit the fact. But, because of my long training and experience, such failure happens rarely."

¶

"Is it possible, Doctor, to perform an internal operation upon you while you are in the cataleptic coma without using anæsthetic?" I enquired.

"My belief is that it is perfectly possible, but I have never tested the point. A doctor once suggested that my wounds with the daggers and hat-pins might only be superficial; he asked whether I could support an operation without pain. I answered that I thought so and was willing to submit to one, provided it was not a dangerous operation. As the doctor replied that the law of the country forbade an operation not necessitated by illness or disease, and as I was neither ill nor diseased, we were unable to proceed further with the matter."

We had covered the ground of his special experiences; now I wanted to touch on his general attitude towards these things. His independent views were so outstanding among fakirs of the Orient that I sought to elucidate them still further. He smiled when I mentioned the subject and did not let me finish my last sentence. Making a slight gesture of the hand, he rejoined:

"I would like to see them placed on a scientific basis, stripped of all the false suggestions and auto-suggestions, mostly religious or superstitious, with which they have generally been inextricably mixed. I have witnessed the harm done to the cause of truth thereby. I have broken away entirely from the traditions of the fakirs. Our science is one thing, religion is another; they ought to be kept separate. It is not that I do not believe in religion—far from it; I regard it with respect and as something necessary to the life of man, since it bestows moral power. But, as you have noted in India, the tendency of man to ascribe to God or to spirits or to angels what arises solely out of his own soul powers, his subconscious, is so strong that I feel a complete break-away is necessary if our teachings are to be purified from superstition and scientifically explained. Many fakirs are the victims of their own self-suggestions, while others are the victims of the suggestions given them by their traditions. They may produce genuine feats, but false theoretical explanations. Look at the dancing Dervishes who whirl themselves into a hypnotic state and then cut themselves with daggers and knives without feeling pain. They preface this feat with elaborate ceremonial rituals and the saying of many prayers— in my opinion all needless and simply a form of creating auto-suggestion to arrive at a state which I can enter quickly and without prayers, solely by understanding the natural laws involved. My conviction is that fakirs have frequently used their marvellous feats to impress the minds of people, before imposing upon them their religious beliefs. They have adopted a mystery-making attitude to increase the force of such impressions they make. All that is futile in these days, when science and education have made so much progress. These mystery-mongers would do better to study science and explain their feats scientifically."

Dr. Tahra Bey was right. The age of abracadabras is past. Mystery and mystification belong to a dimmer time than ours. In these enlightened days, truth must be straightly expressed, not by the crooked and devious methods of fable and fiction, symbol and simile, broken hints and awe-inspiring whispers.

"But what of those fakirs who claim to enter into religious ecstasies?"

"I do not deny that they may have had these experiences, but the latter belong to the sphere of religion, which is outside my experimental researches. It is enough for me to work within the field I have undertaken. It is enough that I can demonstrate how the subconscious, the soul, survives and returns after the body passes through a state equivalent to death. In that alone I find instruction enough. Who can doubt the reality of the soul after such an experience? It is enough that I can demonstrate the wonderful powers of this soul, which will support my body when a large stone is smashed to bits upon it without harming me in any way. When a friend of mine, a trained athlete, thought he could imitate this feat and tried to do so he had his spine smashed. He had developed his body but forgot to develop the powers of his subconscious mind. The hope held out to mankind by the nurture of these powers is so sublime that I sometimes think they could bring about a new golden age. Science can no longer regard the wonders of the subconscious as the product of diseased imagination; it must study them seriously and earnestly, thus paying tribute to the Unknown Force which, uncreated itself, has nevertheless created the universe."

Thus the eternal Sphinx of man's own mind challenges our enquiry and courts our investigations. We need not fear. Man, who rises from protoplasm to paradise, is an ancient riddle that is destined to be solved by modern enquiry. The twentieth century will amply verify this prediction.

# CHAPTER VIII

I FELL upon my knees behind one of the noble pillars of the mosque and let the wings of my heart flap their way silently upwards in reverent devotion to that Higher Power which the men around me called Allah, the Power to which I had never been able to assign any name but which I, too, had agreed to call Allah during my sojourn in Egypt. I knew that we all in this respect meant the same thing, the same Supreme Being Who holds us all in the hollow of His unseen hands, and I could very well accept Him by one name as by none.

I do not know how long a time passed before someone began to read from a ponderous ancient folio of the *Quran*, Allah's sacred writ for this land, in barely-heard chanted tones. And, as the pleasant Arabic murmurs fell from his lips, I looked up and glanced around at those others who had obeyed the Prophet's command to gather at the onset of dusk and remember for a few minutes the Divine Source to which we owe our very life and being. There was an old man beside me dressed in a long robe of blue-striped white silk. His skin was the colour of pale walnut and provided excellent background for a row of splendid white teeth. He touched the soft red carpet with his forehead the while he whispered his prayers; and constantly lifted himself up, again to repeat the prostration. Anon he placed his hands flat upon his thighs, continued his whispering, and, before long, bent his brow to the floor once more.

There was another old man who entered and invoked the mercy of Allah even as I gazed around and who was also soon swaying to and fro at his devotions. He looked extremely poor and his tattered robe, which had once been white but was now dull grey, was in danger of becoming a heap of rags. His scarred and wrinkled face seemed a little tired with the battle which life and Allah had imposed upon him; but here,

in this venerable building dedicated to tranquil world-forgetting
devotion, his mind intent on the afternoon prayer, some of the
lines disappeared from his skin and a mellow peace crept slowly
across his face.   One could read his feelings so easily.   Did
they not say:

"O Allah, the Victorious, the Pardoner, verily Thou has
ordained Thy servant's life to run hardly, yet surely Thou
knowest what is best for him.   It is good once more to prostrate
oneself before Thee and to praise Thee.   Hath not Thy Prophet,
upon whom be peace, declared: 'Fear not, neither be ye grieved,
but rejoice in the hope of Paradise which hath been promised
unto you.'   Exalted, therefore, be Allah, the Almighty King,
the Truth!"

Here was a man who had the courage to confide his life,
blindly, if you like, to the all-powerful care of Allah; and,
evidently, he never regretted it.   He accepted whatever came;
the good along with the bad, with the venerable phrase:
"Inshallah!" (if God wills!).

I turned my face away and caught sight of a pious Moslem,
who looked like a merchant just arrived from his bazaar booth.
He stood in the prescribed attitude with his face towards the
east and his feet slightly apart, his open hands raised on each
side of his face and touching his ears, and then, sonorously,
uttered the salutation: "God is most great!"   He dropped his
hands to his waist and murmured for a while the opening chapter
of the *Quran*.   Then he slipped his hands to his knees, inclining
his body a little and spreading his fingers, and said: "May
God hear him who praiseth Him!"   And, thus, he continued,
bowing in accompaniment to his prayer, dropping to the floor
from time to time in the thirteen-hundred-year-old postures
prescribed for the orthodox Muslim.   At the end, he turned his
head and looked down at his right shoulder and said, as though
addressing the rest of the congregation: "Peace be upon you,
and the mercy of God."   Turning his head to the left, he
repeated the same blessing.   He remained squatting for a while
before he got up and quietly left the mosque.   His soul had
poured out its love to Allah and now he could return in peace
to his wares.

There were several others, too, all men, engaged in prayers
that seemed all-absorbing, and who betrayed no awareness of
their external surroundings.   Eyes and thoughts must be stayed
on Allah, the Prophet Muhammed had said, and they carried

out this injunction with a literalness that was highly com-
mendable. They had come here, not to examine their fellow-
worshippers, nor to be examined; their only business was
with Allah, and to Him they gave themselves up with a fervour
that was unforgettable to a sympathetic alien observer.

Long-robed Cairenes sat, bowed or prostrated themselves
near tarbush-topped, European-attired business men; the
fortuneless poor paid their homage to Allah while mingling
with the fortunate rich; and the scholar, his head packed with
the lore of a thousand tomes, did not disdain to take his place
behind the illiterate street-gamin. Their profound reverence
and complete concentration could not but impress a looker-on.
Such was the democracy which Muhammed had established
within these old, red, white and gold walls and under the
pointed Saracenic arches of this beautiful mosque.

For the mosques of Cairo imprisoned a heart-appealing
beauty that caught me in turn helpless each time I lingered in
them. Who could look from base to capital of the hundred odd
exquisite white marble columns that arcaded this building and
then turn his eyes towards the noble arches of the domed,
ornamented, brown and gold roof without yielding his
unreserved admiration? Who could set eyes on the geometrical
arabesques which adorned the stones of the main arch without
feeling real pleasure?

I got up and moved reluctantly away. My slippered feet
took the slowest of steps, the while I gazed anew upon the
colourful scene. There were the carpeted parapet-surrounded
dais whence a white-bearded man had chanted verses from the
*Quran* to us; the holy praying niche, flanked by two slender
columns, and the delicately carved wooden pulpit, whose
ivory-inlaid walnut door bore an ancient inscription—all
bearing the imprint of that artistry with which the Arabs have
enriched the world. Around the walls stretched friezes of
gleaming gold-lettered Arabic sentences taken from the *Quran*,
the shapely characters providing a decoration in themselves.
The lower part of the walls was lined with many-coloured
marbles. Everything was grandly spacious, as though the
builders had not stinted land for the house where men might
foregather to worship Allah.

I crossed the tile and mosaic pavement and reached the vast
court—nearly two hundred feet broad—where a marble quadrangle lay roofless to the winds of heaven. Four wide colonnades

I

closed it in, themselves enclosed within lofty crenellated walls, that shut out the world beyond so effectively that this might well have been one of the Quranic courts of Paradise, instead of a court in noisy Cairo.    Soft mats ran from pier to pier and squatting or reclining upon them were little groups of grave-faced men; pious, turbaned scholars, perhaps, or poor citizens with plenty of time and little to do.    Some prayed, some read; some slept, and others simply lounged.    Twittering sparrows darted hither and thither among the rounded columns in excitement when the scholars dropped their studies and brought out their food.

A covered, ornamented, marble fountain stood in the centre of the court, its white cupola-shaped roof supported by round columns, inlaid with coloured enamels, while palms raised their tall heads to form a shelter around it.    The immense quadrangle presented an attractive picture of simplicity, beauty and tranquillity.    Peace, as well as Allah, was its reigning sovereign. One heard, of course, the chirruping and trilling of little birds which had long made their nests under the arched roofs and among the carved capitals of the pillars—but their incessant soothing music provided an excellent background for the silence itself.    Near the fountain there was a small trough of fresh water, where the feathered songsters perched and preened themselves and satisfied their thirst.    They splashed their tiny bodies upon the surface, and performed their ablutions like the true believers that they were, and flew off to resume their hereditary occupation of chorus-making.

The bright morning sun thrust huge shadows here and there across the open court; the idlers looked at me, a momentary question in their eyes, to be swiftly dismissed as not worth the trouble of mental effort, and then they went on with the business of graceful idling.    The scene I saw to-day was exactly the same scene which some invading helmeted, armoured and triumphant Crusader must have witnessed so many hundred years ago when he dismounted from his prancing horse and entered the old mosque.    Cairo is rapidly changing, but its numerous mosques still stand, like so many fortified towers against which the soldiers of modernity dash themselves in vain.    And perhaps it is as well that these places should exist to-day, thus reminding our hurried and harried generation of what tranquillity could be found in an epoch when men were a little less clever than they are now.    Under those shady palms or within those covered arcades, they might remember the shelter of God or indulge in the luxury of dreams; at any rate, they could, if they wished, find here a pleasant place whence to view the city's activities in perspective and whence to take an inventory of life at its true valuation. I savoured subtly the ancient peace of this place.

At the entrance to this vast cloister I took off my slippers, for it was rightly ordained that none may walk with booted feet upon the sacred soil of a mosque and there deposit the unwelcome dirt of streets. I handed the slippers to a mosque attendant who emerged from a darkened room, descended a flight of stone steps whose flat surfaces had been worn into curves by the tread of hundreds of thousands of pious feet, and emerged once more in the narrow crowded lane.

¶

I walked a few paces away and stopped, turning to view the face and setting of this old building consecrated to the worship of Allah. It seemed a pity that part of the long frontal wall was hidden behind a row of old houses, but ample compensation remained in the sight of the towering minarets and the great heavy dome, the gleaming bulbous cupolas and the high latticed windows; and, lastly, the enormous and elaborate entrance gates.

Those minarets had no less than eight sides each, as well as three balconies, and they soared upwards out of their square bases on the mosque as thoughts and aspirations soared upwards within the mosque itself. They were like two tall, rosy fingers pointing to the sky. The cupolas had flattened tops and queerly resembled gigantic white turbans in comparison with the immense coloured central dome. They gleamed, as I watched them, in the blazing sun until my eyes smarted in the glare. The battlemented wall-tops stretched themselves out to form a perfect square. The high buff and red walls shut out our world of business and barter.

My eyes looked down again. Here in the street, sellers of sweetmeats, of Turkish delight and flat cakes, lined both sides of the entrance, displaying their offerings upon tiny, temporary tables, or even upon cloth laid on the bare sidewalk itself. The stall-keepers sat patiently awaiting their occasional customers with an expression of placid contentment. A few beggars squatted close to the steps, and two or three worshippers stopped on their way to or from the mosque to exchange scraps of conversation. A lemonade-seller, wearing the gaudy striped crimson robe of his trade, and carrying a huge tilted brass urn and a row of tumblers, looked quizzically at me, and then moved away. A quaint old man with an enormous beard sat on a little grey donkey which trotted past with its patriarchal burden. The usual street multitude stirred hither and thither. The air was tremulous in the afternoon heat, while the sun hung in a bowl of glorious blue.

Within the sacred precinct of the mosque was century-old peace; without it was this seething, jostling, trafficking crowd noisily bent on its business. Thus the two faces of life, with Allah sheltering both beneath his ample wings.

¶

I was walking early one evening across the Square of Ismailia when I noticed a carriage driver leave his empty carriage on the stand and climb the low green-painted iron railing which fenced off a small locked-up, municipal-owned garden. He prostrated himself upon the ground under the setting sun in the direction of Mecca, and proceeded to pray for six or seven minutes quite oblivious of the world around. He was lost in his devotions, looking neither to right nor left; obviously overwhelmed by his religious feeling. This beautiful action touched me deeply, both on account of its artistic effect and as evidence of spiritual loyalty. A policeman, stationed for traffic duty in the Square, watched him unconcernedly and let his trespass go without the slightest interference.

Another night, about the hour of ten, I wandered over to a lonely stretch of road along the Nile bank for a quiet stroll. Under the electric light of a solitary lamp-post, I discovered a young lad with a birch broom, a street sweeper employed by the town authorities. His back was propped against the iron post; and he was evidently taking a brief respite from his toil beneath a night sky which was like a cupola of lapis-lazuli. He sang aloud in joyful tones as he read the tattered pages of a small book, at which he peered with short-sighted eyes by the lamplight. He sang with such real fervour, and was so rapt in his words, that he was oblivious of my approach. His eyes glowed with the fire of joyous aspiration to Allah. I took the liberty of glancing at his book: it was a cheap, paper-covered copy of the _Quran_. The boy's clothes were dirty and torn, for his work was poorly paid; yet his face was a picture of happiness. I did not need to give him the greeting: "Upon you be peace!" He had found peace already.

A third evening I varied my habitual menu by dining in a restaurant off the Sharia Muhammed Ali which Europeans never patronized. It was in the heart of the old quarter and therefore kept its old customs well. I came to know and respect its red-tarbushed proprietor, who possessed a fine character and an innate politeness which sprang, not from his pocket, but his heart. The white-robed waiter had barely laid my dishes upon the table when he suddenly withdrew to a corner and took hold of something which leant against the wall. He treated it with such tenderness that one might have thought it to be his most treasured possession. It turned out to be nothing more than a faded straw mat, which he unrolled and spread upon the floor, laying its end in an easterly direction towards Mecca; which accomplished, he let himself sink down upon the hard, comfortless surface. For the next ten minutes he went through all the prostrations of the devout, reciting his prayers the while in low but clearly audible tones. His thoughts were now wrapped in Allah. There were seven or eight other patrons in the restaurant at the time, and only one more waiter. It was the hour when a substantial increase in patrons might momentarily be expected. Yet the old proprietor looked on approvingly, even nodded his head, so that the tassels of his tarbush swung to and fro in unison with his approval. He never left his little partitioned vantage-platform where he sat and surveyed the homely scene as any Sultan might have sat and surveyed the interior of his palace. He himself never waited at table nor directly accepted money. He was just an Oriental potentate who gave orders, but let others carry them out. As for the patrons, they accepted the present situation as good Muslims should, and were perfectly content to await the waiter's convenience. When at last the latter had emphatically, repeatedly and fervently assured himself—and incidentally his audience—that "There is no God but The One" and that "To God is the Victory" he returned to consciousness of his surroundings, remembered that after all he was only a waiter, rolled up his mat and replaced it in the corner. He looked round, mildly happy; caught my eye, smiled, and came up to

get my next order.    And when I left the restaurant he bade me
farewell with a simple "May God preserve you."

One can only understand the religion of Islam when it is
thus made manifest, put into action and practice.    I remember
travelling on the railway line that links Cairo to the port of
Suez and arriving at a wayside station.    As I thrust my head out
of the window to check my whereabouts I noticed a humbly
clad workman, one of a gang of labourers working on the line,
detach himself from the group with a chant from the *Quran* on
his lips and touch the ground with his forehead. He settled
down at prayer on the sandy soil only a few inches away from
the steel rails. His work was important for it gave him bread;
but not so important that he could afford to forget his duty to
Allah. I studied his face and found it the face of a man who lived
by the light of conscience; who had attained some sort of inner
peace, common labourer though he was.

I walked, at noon, into one of those cafés which abound in
Cairo, for a pot of tea and a couple of Egyptian cakes.    Whilst
I stirred the cubical sugar to assist its dissolution in the pleasant
brown infusion, the café owner dropped to the floor and began
his midday prayer. The latter was almost a silent one, whispered
to himself alone; or rather, to Allah.    I could not but admire
the fervour he showed, and I could not but respect the wisdom
of the Prophet Muhammed for so deftly teaching his followers
to mingle the life of religious devotion with the life of the
busy world.    I could not but contrast the practical value of
Islam with the less apparent value of those far Eastern faiths
which I knew so well, which seek too often to separate
the wordly life from the spiritual life into watertight
compartments.

These are but four cases out of many; four cases which
showed me what Islam meant to the poor and humble, to the
illiterate and uneducated, and to the so-called ignorant classes.
What did it mean to the middle and upper classes?    As far as
I could discern it meant a faith less strongly held, because the
onset of Western scientific education had weakened the bases
of religion here as in every other Oriental land which it had
touched.    I make no criticism, but merely note the fact as an
inevitable phenomenon, because I firmly believe that both
faith and science are necessary to life.    The broader minds
among the Muhammedans are now arriving at the same
conclusion.    They see that sooner or later Islam must succumb

to the twentieth century and the modern spirit, but they know
that it need not drink the poison of complete spirit-denying
materialism in order to do so.   Yet, making all this allowance,
the fact remains that the higher classes of Egypt hold to their
religion more strongly than the higher classes of Europe and
America.  The will to believe dwells in the very blood corpuscles
of the Eastern man, and he cannot get rid of it, try as he may.

But I will relate what I saw in the office of a friend, as typical
of what I saw in both offices and mansions alike.   I had occasion
to call on him not long before noon and partook of the inevitable
glass of Persian tea whilst he dispatched his business, he being
a busy man and an Inspector-General under the Government.

The office of His Excellency Khaled Hassanein Bey was
perfectly up to date and, save for a large framed Arabic text
from the *Quran*, much like any office in Europe might be.   His
Excellency sat at a glass-topped table, was constantly using
the telephone, and kept his papers in automatic roll-shuttered
filing cabinets.

Just before noon another visitor called, one of his own
inspectors in fact, and a few minutes later His Excellency
asked:

"You have no objection if I say my prayers now?" and of
course I reassured him on the point.

Rugs were unrolled, both men slipped off their shoes, and
prostrated themselves in the usual manner. For fully a dozen
minutes they were occupied with their prayers, while clerks
went on working, messengers entered, left papers, and departed
in an atmosphere of complete unconcern.   The two prayed as
men who were utterly alone, utterly in ignorance of my presence.
When their devotions were ended they rose and resumed their
seats at the glass-topped table, and continued to discuss their
business.

The thing impressed me intensely, as something which I had
never seen in any Western office. Nowhere in Europe or
America could one see the like.   There, at midday, men would
begin rushing out for lunch; here, in Egypt, these two men
prayed first and then thought of lunch.

If we in the West really believed, I thought, then this
incident was both an example to be followed and a rebuke to
be heeded.  But could we carry our faith thus far?  I doubted.

It was this point which struck me so much in Egypt.   God,
Allah, to the Muslim was a very real Being, and no mere

philosophical abstraction.   Merchants, servants and workmen; nobles, pashas and officials, thought nothing of stopping in the midst of their activities and kneeling prostrate before Allah in office, shop, street or home; quite apart from the mosque. Men who never dreamt of arising in the morning or retiring at night without bending themselves in brief reverence before Allah, might have nothing more to teach us, but at least they had this one thing to teach the Western world, so busy and so preoccupied with other matters.   I am not here raising the point of Islamic doctrines, which I shall explain in their proper place, but the point of what our faith in a Higher Power is worth; call that Power whatever we wish.

Imagine a man in London or New York getting down on his knees in an open street or space, thus publicly worshipping God; because he felt the call to do so, to remember the existence of Him who permits our own existence to continue!   The man would either be laughed at, ridiculed and perhaps pitied by our over-clever moderns, or else he would be arrested as a nuisance for obstructing the traffic of passengers or vehicles!

¶

The Sign of the Crescent hangs over the Near and Middle and Far East; while lately some of its rays have spread rapidly over the most distant parts of Africa.   Yet, the strength of the religion of Islam is not to be measured by the number of its adherents, but by the ardent devotion which each of those adherents gives to it.   We, in the West, usually like to insert the qualifying adjective "fanatical" before the word Muhammedan, and, if we are not altogether right, we are also not altogether wrong.   Here are people who hold to the tenets of their religion with a fervour that we have lost.

Why?

Let us begin at the beginning.   A man once knelt in a rocky cave on the rugged slopes of Mount Hira, in Arabia, and prayed to the Almighty that the pure, undefiled faith of the first patriarchs might one again be made known to his people, who were sunk in the grossest idol-worship, in a superstitious materialism which they mistook for religion.

That man was Muhammed.

He was of middle height, with long flowing hair, a pale face, which had just a touch of colour in the cheeks; both brow and mouth were wide, and the nose somewhat prominent. His dress was simpler than his position in life called for. He had been a merchant and had made a name in many towns for perfect integrity, fair dealing and absolute reliability. He had taken merchandise in the camel caravans as far off as Syria. Year after year his long line of plodding camels had made their way with measured steps across undulating, tawny sand-dunes and over rocky gorges, carrying great loads of goods which the black-turbaned caravan leader would sell in distant markets. At night, while his men lay sleeping, Muhammed would wander off by himself and sit for a while on the soft desert floor to reflect upon the mysteries of life and the nature of God. And the mystic stars threw their silver rays upon his solitary upturned face, bathing it in their own mystery, and marked him for their own child of destiny.

After his marriage to the widow Khadjia, he developed more and more a habit of profound meditation upon the gravest topics of human existence. It was thus that he became so grievously aware of the shortcomings of the crude religion of his time, and of its inability to satisfy the deeper instincts of his fellow-men. At last he turned to his favourite retreat—a lonely cave on Mount Hira, near the city of Mecca—and there spent an entire night lifting his heart until dawn in piteous prayer to the Infinite, not asking selfishly for personal illumination alone, but also on behalf of his people. Prayer passed after a time into entranced vision, and vision into transformation, and transformation into conscious communion with God. Veil after veil was rent asunder. Strange paradox—that he should find luminous Truth inside that gloomy cave!

And a Voice came unto him and said:

"Thou art the Man. Thou art the Prophet of Allah!"

Henceforth, the merchant, Muhammed, accepted the mantle which had been proffered him, deserted his bales of merchandise, and became the new Sayer of the Word, that Word whose echo would rumble over three continents within one century.

The Sibylline oracles of Rome had announced the future coming of Christ, and were thereafter silent. Christ came eventually, spoke His words to such as cared to hear Him, and then departed at an age when most men have hardly found their place in material life, let alone in spiritual life. Less than six hundred years after this event there came this other Prophet of the Unknown God.

¶

He was fortunate enough to find his first disciple in his own wife, for a wife can do much to mar or make a man's life.   The next man to whom he related his experience in the cave was Waraquah; an old bent and blind sage who warned him:

"Of a surety they will drive thee into exile, for never hath mortal man brought what thou bringest without falling a victim to bitterest persecution. Ah! If God deigned to lengthen my days until then, I would devote all my strength to helping thee triumph over thy enemies."

But the inspired prophet must always put up with the cross of loneliness and misunderstanding; there are compensations for him which are too invisible and too intangible to be comprehended by the masses.

Every new religion must prepare to be stoned at its birth by the stolid and stupid.

His friends and relatives formed the earliest group of converts.   They met and prayed in a quiet house outside the city.

In Mecca itself the people were following their rite of primitive magic, attempting to propitiate the unseen powers of the psychic threshold, worshipping a multitude of fetishes; here they were worshipping the One God.

For three years the gradually increasing group met and prayed in the utmost secrecy; for the appointed hour of public revelation, the date set by Destiny, had not yet come.   And then the Voice spoke again to the Prophet, saying:

"Make known the Command which hath been given thee." Whereupon he did not hesitate to call a great meeting of his people together and to warn them that if they did not fling away their ancestral caricature of religion and return to true worship, the wrath of Allah would fall upon them.   They listened unconverted, and left in disgust.

But the fire was now ablaze within him and he went from place to place, preaching the message which had been entrusted to him.   He dressed in coarse cloth and ate simply.   He gave away almost everything he had to the poor.   He even went among the three hundred and sixty-six idols of the holy shrine of the Kaaba itself to remonstrate with the idolaters there present, as Jesus bravely went into the Temple to remonstrate with the money-changers. An angry mob attacked him, and one of his followers was slain in trying to protect him.

The prophet's cross can only be carried by one who believes all he has prophesied, down to the last letter of the last word.

The authorities, finding they could not muzzle this outspoken man, tried to bribe him with wealth and position. Muhammed's reply was to warn them more strongly still of the coming wrath of Allah.

Thenceforth he was openly persecuted and he advised a number of his followers to seek refuge in Abyssinia, which they did. The vengeance of the Meccan authorities pursued them even there, and the Black Emperor was asked to deliver up the fugitives. Instead of complying, he called for their spokesman, one Jafar, and asked: "What is this religion by reason of which you have separated from your people?"

And Jafar told how they had been formerly leading a semi-savage life, worshipping idols, eating carrion, and oppressing the weak. Then came Muhammed as the Prophet of Allah, bidding them be truly spiritual, devoted towards the One alone, truthful, charitable and moral. He ended by reciting some passages from the *Quran*, which caused the Emperor to remark: "Verily this, and that which Moses brought, arise from one lamp. Go! for, by God, I will not suffer them to get at you. Go to thy dwellings and live and worship in thine own way, and none shall interfere with you."

Meanwhile, the persecution of Muslims in Arabia grew worse. When some of his persecutors asked Muhammed for a miracle to prove his apostleship, he lifted his gaze to the sky and replied:

"God has not sent me to work wonders. He has sent me to you. I am only the bringer of Allah's message to mankind."

It was during this bitter time that Muhammed reported an extraordinary experience which had come to him in the night. He had been taken out of the body in spirit by the angel Gabriel, and had met the spirits of the great Prophets of old—Adam, Abraham, Moses, Jesus and others—in the invisible world of the angels. He had, also, been shown how the destiny of the world is written down.

Not long after, this experience was followed by the rapid spread of Muhammed's doctrines, with an inevitable increase in persecution as its result. And just before a number of men had decided to slay the Prophet, the latter was inspired to leave

Mecca secretly and make his way across the desert to the city of Medina, where he had a great welcome and laid the foundation of the first mosque ever built. The day of his entry became the first day of the first year of the new Muslim calendar, although it was in the year 622 of the Christian calendar.

That was the turning point in Islam's fortunes.

The Meccans declared war upon the inhabitants of Medina. A small force led by Muhammed left the latter town and encountered the enemy, completely defeating them. The victors marched on and fought a further battle, which ended indecisively. Still more battles occurred resulting in a strengthening of Muhammed's position. He sent envoys with letters to the King of Greece, the Emperor of Abyssinia, the King of Persia, and the King of Egypt, informing them of the Prophet's mission and message, and inviting them to embrace the religion of Islam.

Seven years after his flight from Mecca, Muhammed set out with his army to return to the city. Because he did not wish to shed blood unnecessarily, he made his followers pile their weapons eight miles away from the city and enter as peaceful men. They were permitted to make their visit and to leave again unmolested. But, not long after, the Meccans assisted some tribesmen to massacre Muslims who sought sanctuary in their temple, and Muhammed was compelled to lead his army eastwards to Mecca once again. He took the city, broke up the stone images, peacefully converted the inhabitants, and set up his government there.

Islam now spread all over Arabia, bringing the wild tribes to sit at his feet and learn a higher faith. Muhammed gave his last address to his followers from the back of his camel, on the hill of Arafa.

"I leave the book, the *Quran*, for you," he told them, in his customary, slow, deliberate manner; "hold fast to it, or you shall go astray. For this is probably my last pilgrimage. Do not adopt your pre-Islamic habits and begin to rush at each other's throats after I go; for one day you will have to face Allah, who shall require you to answer for your sins." He reminded them that the Prophet was one like unto them, a man, though a messenger of Allah, and warned them not to worship mere graves.

On an afternoon soon after, he returned to the great Unknown whence he had come; his last words being:

"There is now none so great a friend as He."

This happened in the six hundred and thirty-second year of our era and in the sixty-first year of Muhammed's life. He had disproved the infallibility of the saying that a prophet is without honour in his own country.

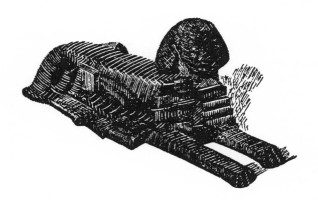

# CHAPTER IX

I WAS curious to know the authoritative answers to a number of questions upon Islam about which I had formed my own notions, based upon the rough guide of experience, but upon which I did not know the exact rulings of the Prophet and his book. So I took my way to His Eminence the Sheikh el Islam, the man who presides over the headquarters of the religion in Egypt under the rounded minarets and battlemented walls of El Azhar Mosque-University. His personal name is Sheikh Moustapha el Maraghi, and the institution of which he is Grand Rector is venerable with a thousand years of authority as the Muhammedan centre whose word on questions of faith and creed is final. He is a man of pontifical powers. It is true that Arabia holds the Holy Stone, the Kaaba of Mecca, the Sacred Place to which every devout Muslim hopes to make pilgrimage one day; nevertheless, it is Egypt which holds the Living Stone, the brain and nerve-centre of Islam. The Grand Rector is not only the chief dignitary of Islam in Egypt, but, because of the international character of El Azhar, an authority for other countries as well. At El Azhar the pride of Muslims, the deeper aspects of the religion have been taught since its early days to those who wish to perfect themselves in its doctrines, and who wish to understand in complete detail the message of their revelator, Muhammed.

"The *Quran*, rightly read, encourages scientific researches into the knowledge of God and of the universe," said Sheikh el Maraghi to me during the interview recorded below. "There is no science which can be foreign to the Creator and His creation, and nothing in any which can be contrary to the precepts of Islam. And the question faces us of purifying our religion of superstitious and fantastic interpretations. These studies assist us to do so. It is to the interests of Islam in this century when science has made such progress, to place at the disposal of its students the same sources of learning."

"Things are somewhat better than a century ago, when Edward Lane reported that 'the Muslims are very averse from giving information on subjects connected with their religion to persons whom they suspect of differing from them in sentiments,' but some of the old reserve still remains."

It was not easy for a man who was not a Muhammedan—in the orthodox sense, anyway—to obtain the interview that I desired; but, after some preliminaries, the good offices of mutual friends brought it about at last.

The way took me through the oldest swarming quarter of Cairo, along a wide street that split the bazaar area into two and deposited me at the very doors of the oldest centre of Muslim learning in the world, at the entrance to El Azhar itself. I passed under intertwined arabesques and spacious arches into a large, sunny courtyard, just as hundreds of thousands of students had passed before me during the long history of the place, students who emerged later to teach the words of the Prophet Muhammed across the Eastern world; to provide authentic interpretations of the holy *Quran*, and to keep the flame of Muslim culture ever burning.

When I was ushered into an audience hall and thus into the presence of His Eminence and after we had exchanged the usual greetings, I found time to study this grave-faced man of medium height who enjoys a unique prestige in the world of Muhammedans.

Sheikh el Maraghi, formerly Grand Cadi of the Sudan, has considerable influence not only in religious circles but also among a section of prominent public men.

Under a white turban, I saw a pair of steady, piercing eyes; a straight, regular nose, a small grey moustache, a firm mouth, and a stubble of grey growth on the chin.

The great institution over which His Eminence presided gave its instruction free to thousands of students, future upholders of Muhammed's doctrine, receiving its own funds from endowments and Government grants. The poorer students were fed and lodged free, or else received allowances of money. No longer could the old buildings house them all, so several branches had been built in other districts, and with these extensions had come a change in the teaching itself. Modern scientific studies had been introduced, well-equipped laboratories and amphitheatres for physics and chemistry provided, and up-to-date methods of teaching were now in practice. Yet, these reforms had been carefully introduced—so carefully that the ancient atmosphere was still retained, and both old and new educational methods dwelt side by side.

Once inside the walls, which enclose an array of colonnades and cloisters, of galleries and minarets, I saw black-bearded figures who sat and pored over their Arabic books. The echoes of the students' voices as they chanted their lessons, slightly swaying to and fro in rhythm with their sing-song, reached my ears. They squatted upon mats in small groups under the shade of cloistered roofs, while in their centre sat the teacher.

That is the traditional method of teaching, fittingly retained in the ancient buildings. But, in the great modern extensions elsewhere, I had already found that His Eminence had caused his religious university to take on a new lease of life by adapting it to present-day conditions. In this he had the enthusiastic support of the younger generation of Muslims, but he had to battle for a time against crusted theologians who did not realize that El Azhar must fit itself anew to work in a changing world. The battle was long drawn out but his victory complete.

Just as sunlight is forcing its way into the slummy narrow alleys of old Cairo, bit by bit, just as sanitation is winning its old battle with ancient quarters, and fresh air is diminishing the strength of century-old odours, so modern thought is forcibly making its impression on the old Oriental. The rising generation is spurring ahead on the journey towards that union of old-new ideas which is inevitable.

These students come from every corner of the Muslim world, from Persia to Zanzibar, drawn like steel filings to the magnet of El Azhar's authoritative culture. They are dressed in red tarbush and white turban and every colour of robe. I expected to see some Chinese students among the host and I found them, but I was surprised to discover young Japanese too.

Sheikh el Maraghi was dressed in a long black and white striped silk shirt, over which he wore a longer robe, with ample sleeves, made of black silk. A white girdle was wound around his waist. He wore a pair of soft yellow morocco shoes which turned up at the toes. The whole effect of his dress was one of simple effectiveness.

The grave quietude of his countenance pleased me.

I began by enquiring as to the central message of Islam.

His Eminence meditated his answer with much deliberation. "The first principle is that there is only One God. That was Muhammed's chief message. That is the message which God had given the Prophets (Moses and Christ) before Muhammed was given it also. Muhammed repeated this message to the Jews and Christians as a call to their priests to be united, whereas he found them at loggerheads.

"The belief in the oneness of a creating God who has no partner; a God who alone is to be glorified and worshipped, and who needs no mediation between Him and the people whom He created. Prophets and apostles are only intermediaries who communicate His laws and orders, and who call upon people to obey and worship Him. He is the only One whose succour is sought for the relief of shortcomings, and none other is to be appealed to for forgiveness or solicited in time of need. The Lord (be He exalted!) saith:

" 'Neither invoke, besides Allah, that which can neither profit thee nor hurt thee; for, if thou do, thou wilt then certainly become one of the unjust,' and:

" 'If Allah should afflict thee with misfortune, then there is none to lift it but He; and if He willeth thee any good, there is none to stop his favour; He will bestow His grace on whomsoever He pleaseth among His servants, and He is the Forgiving, the Merciful.' "

"What does Your Eminence understand by the idea of the soul?"

"The *Quran* does not define the word, so the Heads of Islam have entertained different opinions about it at different times. Such opinions may be studied intellectually; but they must not be added to the *Quran*, the Inspired Book. Yet we believe, of course, in the Day of Judgment for every soul, when the righteous shall reap their reward and ill-doers shall receive their punishment, establishing thereby the foundation of a moral sense. Thus saith Allah:

" 'And whomsoever doth an atom's weight of good shall be recompensed for it; and whomsoever doth an atom's weight of evil shall be punished for it.' "

"In what way did Muhammed differ from the Prophets sent by God?"

"The Prophet Muhammed did not differ from other Prophets since they were all chosen by the Lord to deliver His message to mankind, and as they all received revelation from Him. Muslims are enjoined to believe in the prophethood of all of them, without distinction. Thus saith the Lord:

> " 'Say ye believers: "We believe in Allah and that which hath been sent down unto us, and that which hath been sent down unto Abraham and Ismael and Isaac and Jacob and his offspring and that which was given to Moses and Jesus, and that which was given to the Prophets from their Lord. We make no distinction between any of them and to Allah we are resigned." ' "

Again the answer had come only after His Eminence had thought it over well.

"Do you think that no man can help another to find God? I mention this because the absence of priests in your religion is so striking."

"Yes, there are no priests between man and God in Islam, but, nevertheless, we have learned Muslims who can teach others the way of God as it is laid down in the *Quran*, and in the sayings and doings of the Prophet Muhammed.

"These are some of the principles ordained by Islam, without which no one could be worthy of being called a Muslim, and which do not differ from the principles of all religions that Allah has sent down to us through His Apostles. Islam, which is not the only religion that enjoins the belief in the unity of God, and which ordains obedience to God's injunctions, was not sent exclusively to Muhammed (Peace be upon him) but it is God's religion which He has sent down through all Prophets and Apostles. Saith Allah:

> " ' Verily the true Religion with Allah is Islam and none other is acceptable unto Him; and those who were given the Scriptures differed not concerning it until they knew the truth, through enmity and mutual jealousy.'

"Thus we group our people into those who have studied deeply our religious lore, and those who have not done so. We respect and listen to the first class; but we do not regard them as inspired men—only as intellectual men. No Muslim can say this or that is forbidden to you, because God alone possesses the authority to do so. There are no intermediaries with God, in our faith. That is a foundation stone of Islam. But we recognize and respect those who devote their lives to sacred study, and we go to them for their opinions and advice.

Hence a negro who is well learned in Muslim matters has the right to obtain a respectful hearing for his opinions. In our history there is such a case where a Caliph on the throne took advice from a black slave who was well versed in the Prophet's teachings and sayings. Of course, such a man was not kept a slave after that."

"May I ask, Your Eminence, whether mosques are essential to your religion?"

"No, people use them as places in which to pray, and they go there to hear a sermon on Fridays, but, as there are no priests or ceremonies, the mosques are not essential to the practice of Islam. Muslims may pray anywhere, not necessarily in a mosque—any piece of clean ground will do. Our object in building mosques is to bring unity by social fellowship in worship. Nevertheless, although not essential, worship in a mosque is naturally preferable."

"What is the nature of your prayers?"

Came the quiet restrained voice:

"When a Muslim prays it is understood that he repeats a section of the *Quran* which he has learnt by memory. Usually it contains certain sentences which are traditionally known to contain the things a man should think of when he prays. I must say and repeat that the object of our prayers is not only to do our duty towards God, but also to be spiritually educated during the time we say them. The Muslim who repeats these words, day after day, is thus constantly reminded of them. There could not be better words to use in prayer than those set him by the *Quran* for this purpose. 'We pray to Thee and only Thee. We ask for no help except from Thee.' Such are two sentences often used. Besides, set sentences help ignorant men.

"Our prayers are quite short, they consist of the opening paragraph of the *Quran* and seven other texts; but those who wish to do so can add any other texts they select. But no prayers of a man's own making may be added to these texts.

"The Muslim must pray five times a day. Should force of circumstances stop him from saying his prayers at the right time, then he must make up for it later. It is forbidden to miss a single hour of prayer."

¶

"What of a man who is seriously ill?"

"If he is quite unable to stand or squat in the prescribed postures for prayer, then he must say them whilst lying down. And if he is unable to speak, then he must raise both hands to his temples as a sign of reverence to God. Do not forget that our postures make men show humility before God, by causing them to prostrate themselves. It is good for men thus to acknowledge the greatness of God."

"Five times a day seems much to ask of men?"

"No; these prayers are essential to remind men frequently of God, and also to educate them spiritually, as I said before. Thus, when they address God as the Merciful, they learn that mercy is acceptable in His eyes and it is a suggestion for them to become merciful in their own lives. Similarly with the other qualities which we ascribe to God."

An official entered. He took the Grand Rector's proffered hand, bent down and kissed it fervently, then touched it with his forehead. After he had seated himself, I asked:

"What is the object of the pilgrimage to Mecca?"

"Just as mosques increase local fellowship in Islam, so the Mecca prilgrimage increases international fellowship in Islam. All men are brothers in Islam, and both mosque and pilgrimage enable them to come together as such. Equality is a principle of Islam. Islam is essentially democratic and destroys class hatred. Islam has solved the problem of pauperism by prescribing ordained alms, by taking a certain percentage of the money of the rich to be distributed to the needy. If all did this, good-will, peace and compassion would reign supreme among mankind; a sound equilibrium between classes would be established. Every man who believes in Allah meets in the mosque or on pilgrimage every other believer as an equal. Thus a king may walk beside a beggar, or pray beside him. Islam calls upon people to lay aside racial and other distinctions, while it makes religious unity and humane principles the tie that binds people together. No credit is given by Islam to anyone except for righteousness and good deeds. For so saith Allah (be He exalted):

" 'O men, We have created you all of Adam and Eve, and we have made you into peoples and tribes that you might know one another. Verily the most worthy of honour among you in the sight of Allah, is the most righteous; Allah is all-knowing and cognisant of your innermost thoughts.' "

"There is a common idea in the West that Muhammedans are fanatics and intolerant. Is this correct? Also that Islàm was propagated entirely by the sword. What comment do you care to make on this?"

Sheikh el Maraghi smiled.

"Islam has become a firm and unshakable belief; Muslims have become reputed strict upholders of their faith. The biased critics of Islam have, therefore, accused it falsely of fanaticism. In point of fact, what its enemies term fanaticism is nothing but firm belief—no matter what they may call it.

"As to the allegation that Islam was propagated entirely by the sword, one has only to refer to historical facts, analysing the real causes of the wars in which Islam engaged in its early days. One thus realizes that these wars had nothing to do with the spread of Islam. They were mostly in defence of self and kin, for the protection of the Faithful and to defend them against persecution and tyranny inflicted upon them by the unbelievers who drove them out of their homes. For these reasons God permitted His Prophet to take up arms against the offenders. Saith the Lord:

" 'Allah doth not forbid you to be charitable and to deal justly with those who have not waged war against you on account of your religion and have not driven you out of your homes; verily Allah loveth the equitable. Only doth Allah forbid you to make friends of those who, on account of your religion, have waged war against you, and have driven you out of your homes and have aided those who drove you forth.'

And:

" 'Permission is granted unto those who have taken up arms against the unbelievers, for they have suffered persecution; and verily Allah is well able to succour them. Those who have been driven out of their homes wrongfully, only because they say: Our Lord is Allah.'

"These are, briefly, some of the causes that forced the Prophet and his Companions to take up arms. At first he suggested that his Companions should leave him alone to call upon the Arabs to adopt Islam. But he was met with abuses and they refused to accept the new faith, molested him and contrived to distort his message. He had no alternative other than defending himself and his followers against the attacks of his enemies in order to uphold the cause of Allah.

"The war and conquests that took place later were meant, no doubt, to protect Islam. The conquerors gave the vanquished three alternatives: (*a*) to adopt Islam and be their equal, (*b*) to pay tribute which would mitigate the poverty of the Arabs, and in return receive protection of life and property, (*c*) or else to continue to fight them.

"No doubt, however, these wars were brought about partly by political, partly by social, and partly by economic reasons. The allegation, however, that Islam was propagated entirely by the sword is false; later on, Islam spread without any recourse to war. Did not the Mongols and the Tartars, who swept over Asia and destroyed the magnificent Islamic civilization, and who were the Muslims' bitter enemies, embrace Islam and become zealous supporters of it? If we refer to history and impartially examine its records, we are bound to find in it sufficient proof to refute the above allegation."

"What is Your Eminence's personal opinion of the Western people and institutions from an Oriental standpoint, so far as you have seen or heard of them?" was my next query.

"My personal opinion of Western people is that they have reached a high standard of culture, both scientific and social, but I remark that Western civilization lacks spiritual motives. We cannot consider civilization as perfect unless both the material and spiritual nature of men are taken into account, since they are complementary to each other and are mutually counterbalanced.

"As to European institutions, we admire and try to adopt many of them, urged by the very text of our Holy Book:

" 'Announce glad tidings unto my servants who hearken unto exhortation and follow that is best thereof. These are they whom Allah guideth unto His Religion and these are men of understanding.'

"Our Prophet supports this, too; he said:

" 'Wisdom is the lost treasure of the true believer, he taketh it wherever he findeth it.'

"All we object to in Western institutions is the excess in the individual freedom, as it leads to serious improprieties which tend to undermine the very existence of these institutions.

"While we admit that this principle of individual freedom

is a natural right of man, we cannot say that it is properly applied. In Islam this principle is properly applied, and one is allowed to do anything that is neither harmful to oneself nor to one's fellow-creatures.

¶

"In the early days of Islam it was the practice of the authorities to set apart portions of mosques for the teaching of religious and laic knowledge. Large mosques assumed the appearance of universities, especially when students' hostels and teachers' rooms were annexed to them. Money was bequeathed for the maintenance of these institutions. El Azhar was one of those mosques. When, in the seventh century of the Flight of the Prophet, Baghdad lay in ruins at the feet of the invading Tartars and the Caliph was abolished, King Alsahir Bibars took under his protection one of the sons of the Abbaside princes and made him Caliph. King Bibars reopened El Azhar after teaching in it had been suspended for a time, showering his grants on it. Consequently, El Azhar gained renown, and attracted many students who repaired to it from far and near in quest of learning. In due course, it became the largest and most important of Islamic universities in the world. It gradually developed until it became a public institution for Muslims in their entirety. No doubt this is a great distinction, which was not attained by any other mosque.

"The reforms I am introducing into El Azhar are to afford the students the opportunity of extending their mental and cultural horizon in all branches of knowledge.

"In its search for the truth, Islam commends logical reasoning. It condemns blind imitation and upbraids those who practise it. Saith the Lord:

" 'And when it is said to them: "Follow ye that which God hath sent down," they say: "Nay, we follow the usages which we found with our fathers." What, though their fathers knew nothing and were devoid of guidance.' "

"Can Islam fit the needs of the modern age, increasingly educated in science and tending to be entirely practical?"

"How could Islam, which is based on requirements of human nature and reason; which requires its followers to seek and augment their knowledge and to discharge their duties properly—

how could such a faith be unfit, or inconsistent with, the needs of our modern age of science and culture? Indeed, Islam urges people to pursue knowledge. Saith the Lord, in this connection:

" 'Say: Consider whatever is in the Heavens and the Earth.'

"The true believers are described in the *Quran* as those who 'meditate upon the creation of the Heavens and the Earth.'

"Early Muslims gave proof that it was possible to reconcile religion with practical life and science without going astray. They made use of Greek and Roman works on philosophy and science; they translated them, criticized them, and improved on them. They practised all branches of worldly occupations, including agriculture, commerce and industry.

"One of the reasons for its early and rapid spread was that Islam is a practical and not a theoretical religion. It put forth laws and orders that should be obeyed, and principles that could be applied to life.

"It took into account the relevant requirements of human nature, and established principles in which the needs of both body and soul were equally considered. It did not trespass upon one of them to the benefit of the other. When Islam made lawful the enjoyment of the good things of life, it prescribed limits to check man's appetites, and forbade him to do what might harm and corrupt him. Nor has it neglected the spiritual side of man; Islam gave this side its full due too."

"Why are women veiled, and will this custom cease? It is a common Western idea that women in Muhammedan countries have been kept down, half enslaved, treated as totally inferior beings. What have you to say to this?"

"As to the veiling of women," came the rejoinder, "Islam has specified a certain form of it, namely that women should not display their attractions to strangers and array themselves ostentatiously in public. In this way women retain their decorum and men are guarded against falling under their spell. No doubt, Islam, by ordaining this, was successful in laying down a sound principle to save both man and woman the evil of temptation and sin.

"Islam, however, did not carry the veiling of women too far; it permitted them to uncover their faces and their hands, unless temptation be feared.

"The Western view that Muslim women are kept down, half enslaved and treated as totally inferior beings, is neither true nor in accordance with our religious teachings, for Islam has given women full rights. It has allowed them, within reasonable limits, everything that would make them happy. It has permitted them a conservative form of liberty and made them mistresses in their own domain. It has not forbidden them education of any degree whatsoever. On the contrary, it has recommended that they should perfect themselves as much as possible. It has allowed them to have property of their own, and has given them the right to dispose of it. Women can have the power-of-attorney, can be guardians, can be trustees, can be judges except in criminal cases. Some Muslim women had a considerable amount of learning, some have been known for their righteousness, while others have attained distinction in literature. The rumour that Muslim women are half enslaved has originated from the fact that some ignorant people have, under the influence of their environment, acquired this wicked practice of ill-treating their women. Needless to say, Islam could not be held responsible for such abuses."

¶

The ignorance of the average European about this great religion is something for which he should not be blamed, but his misconceptions of it are less to his credit. Many of my friends in England know only that a Muhammedan is a man whose faith allows him to have four wives; beyond that they know nothing! I have no doubt that, at the back of their minds, is the thought that if Islam (to give the religion the name that is given it by its own people and not the artificial name of Muhammedanism which we have bestowed on it) has spread widely in the East, then the attraction of those four wives has a good deal to do with the matter. To a reflective man, who perceives in them four added responsibilities, four more financial burdens, the attraction of these possible wives is less obvious. Personally, I have met only two Muhammedans who had four wives, and they were Maharajahs, who possessed a good deal more than forty apiece. I know a few commoners who have two wives, but I have never met one with a harem of four. About 97 per cent of all the Muhammedans I have ever encountered possessed no more than one wife. It is thus, with some regret, that I must dispel an illusion which we

Westerners have rather fondly cherished. With this illusion gone, there is not much left of our knowledge of Islam.

The charge of polygamous practices, so often brought against Islam, so often employed to confuse its issues, is nothing of which Muslims need be afraid. Polygamy, in itself, is not necessarily heinous or immoral; from a psychological and scientific standpoint it may even sometimes be desirable. Anyhow, the percentage of polygamous marriages in the East is really extremely small, no higher than in the West where such unions certainly exist, but under conditions of shame, secrecy and illegality. In any case, public opinion is, nowadays, generally against polygamous unions in Egypt, and if 5 per cent is my guess for Egypt, 2 per cent is probably true for Persia, and 5 per cent again for the Indian Muslims.

I remembered that polygamy was widely practised among the ancient peoples and that Muhammed found it as an established institution in Arabia. He did not introduce or propagate it as a new doctrine, but simply accepted the situation and tried to regularize it in an ethical way. I remembered, too, that he found a somewhat barbarous marital condition among the Arabs of those early days, which compared unfavourably with the condition he established later. A man's wives, for instance, might be inherited by his son. He found temporary unions established by custom and forbade them. He found divorce was as easy as drawing water from a well. Though he did not attempt to make it much more difficult, nevertheless he warned his followers that "divorce was the most detestable to God of all permitted things." And he placed it under a code that should be fairer to both parties. It is an open question whether or not this is to be preferred to the legalized hypocrisy of our own divorce code.

The charge that he allowed men to pander to their passions is ludicrous. He imposed fasts upon every one of his followers to assist them to detach themselves from the passions. He banned alcoholic drinks in order to assist their efforts at self-control.

But I wanted to know what Muhammed had really laid down about this question of several marriages, so I asked His Eminence:

"What is the teaching concerning polygamy? What is the actual practice?"

His answer was:

"Islam allows polygamy if the husband could treat his wives impartially and equally. The Holy *Quran* forbids polygamy if impartiality on the part of the husband is impossible of attainment. Saith Allah, may He be exalted:

" 'And ye will not have it all in your power to treat your wives alike, even though you fain would do so.'

"At any rate, Islam did not favour polygamy; never unconditionally allowed it. It only intended to prevent the lustful, who could not content themselves with one wife, from falling into the sin of adultery. These were allowed polygamy only if they could fulfil the condition of impartiality.

"The present practice among the greatest majority of Muslims is to have a single wife, except for a few who by force of physical or material circumstances have to marry more than one, in order either to guard themselves against adultery or to support poor women who have no one to provide for them."

Before I left I was shown the priceless library, kept in rooms with exquisitely carved cedarwood ceilings. Ancient *Qurans* written on parchment, books with illuminated pages and gilded initials, manuscripts of great antiquity passed by the thousand before my gaze. Fifteen thousand of these manuscripts were kept here alone.

And with that my audience was closed. I had listened intently, for Sheikh el Maraghi's high prestige gave unique authority to every statement he made.

I had begun to understand more clearly why Muhammed's faith spread; why Islam quickly came to receive the reverence of wild desert Bedouins, no less than that of cultured city Persians, and of the host of tribes and peoples who dwelt in the Near and Middle East.

Muhammed, like Moses, but unlike Buddha, aimed chiefly at establishing a visible, tangible heaven on earth, with organizing a society of people who would go on with normal daily living but apply to it such rules as he, a messenger of God, had brought them. Buddha, and even Jesus, were preoccupied with giving voice to ascetic themes, to intuitions which concerned themselves with the secret recesses of the human spirit; Muhammed, like Jesus, passionately lived in God, but, whereas Jesus gave his passion to the finding of the inner kingdom, Muhammed gave his to founding an outer kingdom. We are not competent to set ourselves up in judgment, but simply to note these facts. Muhammed, Moses, Jesus and Buddha were truly all-inspired Ambassadors of God, but Muhammed's marked difference from most Oriental prophets was that he opposed the tendency to withdraw from the social and public duties of life which usually accompanies extreme religious devotion; he made it clear that monks and monasteries were undesirable in Islam; and he extended no approval to monkish doctrines involving the death of human affections.

It is a matter of regret that so little is known of the Islamic faith by the average Westerner; even that little is usually partly erroneous, if not wholly incorrect.

Muhammed taught men not to be ashamed to kneel and worship this Invisible King, to go down on their knees in the open street.

It is time we got rid of some of these misconceptions of this great man, Muhammed, and of his great religion, Islam, which becloud our minds. It is time that we understood why the magic of his name is such that millions, comprising nearly one-seventh of the human race, from the western shores of Africa to the eastern shores of China, call down daily blessings upon him. It is time we recognized the reality of the fervour of these men, the Muslims, and why the quickly uttered "Allah" of European pronunciation is a pitiful caricature of the fervent, long-drawn, heartfelt, two-syllabled "Al—lah" of the Oriental; who devoutly prolongs the second syllable.

Night had opened her eyes, twinkling with thousands of starry jewels as her adornment, when I stood again in the street outside El Azhar, gazing absent-mindedly at nothing in particular. The crescent moon shone through a mist surrounded by indigo-blue sky. Then, the strong tenor voice of the mosques' Muezzin rang out upon the air, resonantly proclaiming, from his high turret, the oneness of God.

Now throughout this city of carved gateways, fretted geometrical arches and tiled courtyards, watched over by Allah and His Angels, men were falling on their knees, with faces turned towards Mecca and repeating those simple words: "GOD IS MOST GREAT!"

# CHAPTER X

## IN THE PEACE OF OLD ABYDOS

MUCH more than seven thousand years before Muhammed awoke the wandering tribes of Arabia to the worship of a purely spiritual God, there flourished in this land of transparent skies a religion whose adherents carved those giant stone idols which he detested. And yet, the best minds of this religion worshipped the same Unknown God as he did; their faith was not, therefore, a mere credo of idol-worship. The learned Egyptologists of our time can say little more about that religion because it belongs to the epoch of prehistory, an epoch so scanty of material that they cannot lift its veil and can only guess cautiously at its people and events.

There are places in modern Egypt where the temple of the ancients and the mosque of the Muslims stand side by side—as at Luxor—regarding that, we find a striking contrast in this land.

My ears, as I write, seem to catch the thud of pawing hoofs, and my mind's eye can perceive the lithe-horsed cavalry of Arab invaders planting the green banner of the Prophet throughout Egypt. Time waits with ominous patience . . . and the green yields to red, white and blue—then back again to green. But, behind all—the faint jingling of ancient temple sistrums!

Egypt cannot shake off the emblems of her aboriginal faith. The Past, like a phœnix, arises before our gaze under the marvellous work of the archæologists. These visible stone tokens remind her of a Past to which she sometimes clings but which more often she ignores.

Yet the borderline between Past and Present is uncertain. The atmosphere of those vanished peoples and of their hoary worship hangs heavily over the land, as every sensitive person will testify. If their temples are now sadly diminished, and often stand broken or roofless at that, with large-winged bats

whirring around their pillars in the inky night; if they, themselves, have left only a few buried bodies to tell of their existence,
bodies drained of their blood, with entrails removed, and
turned into bandage-swathed mummies by skilled embalmers;
nevertheless, many of their spirits still haunt the old places
which they knew so well.   The power of the so-called dead
persists in Egypt above all other lands I know.

I discovered anew the presence of this intangible legacy when
I sat on crossed legs inside one of the seven wall-niches within
a pillared hall of Seti's Temple at Abydos, while strange figures
stared down at me from or displayed themselves upon the
pictured walls.   After two hours' riding along the raised causeway that cut across sugar-cane plantations and bean-bearing
fields, I had left the pleasant, fresh and vivifying early morning
air—for I had set out before the rise of dawn—and crossed the
flagged threshold of the old sanctuary built by the first of the
Seti Pharaohs.   The powerful sense of the Past crept quickly
over me, thrusting its visions of a vanished epoch before my
mind's eye as I sat there.

Involuntarily I saw the old processions pass along the paved
stone floor and take their measured, rhythmic way to the altar
chambers.   Inevitably, I felt the strong impress of those ancient
priest-magicians, who made this place one of their focal points
for the calling down of the benedictions of Osiris—the god
whom they symboled as wearing a triple-crested high headdress.   And some of their invocations possessed echoes which
had reverberated through the heavens for century after century;
for the great calm of a high presence began to enfold and
enchant me, and under its benign wings I saw my earthly
desire-filled existence slip away as sand slips through one's
fingers.

Fittingly had Strabo, the classic geographer, written of his
own dust-covered epoch: "At Abydos Osiris is worshipped,
but in the temple no singer, no player on the pipe, nor on the
cithara, is permitted to perform at the commencement of the
ceremonies celebrated in honour of the god, as is usual in rites
celebrated in honour of the gods."   Peace pervaded the white
walls of this hall, a dreaming peace that the outer world did not
know and could not understand.   Martha, for all her hustle and
bustle, received Christ's rebuke; Mary, the quiet and con-
templative, received His praise.   Not in noise and excitement
do we find our finest hours; only when serenity descends

quietly upon the soul do we enter into intimate union with Happiness, with Wisdom and with divine Power.

I squatted comfortably in my little wall-niche, as perhaps some brown priest of the temple had squatted in it a hundred generations ago, and let its gentle influence rest upon me like a spell. Oh! it was good to be alone for a while and forget the many noises which progress had brought in inexorable attendance upon its many benefits; it was good, too, to forget the gross selfishness, inevitable misunderstandings, unworthy hatreds and bitter jealousies which would raise their heads, cobra-like, to spit and strike when one returned to the world of un-illumined men.

Why should one return, I wondered?

We regard loneliness as a curse, but, achieving wisdom, we learn to look upon it as a blessing. We must climb the Mount Everests of our dreams and become accustomed to living among the pinnacles of loneliness. For if among the crowds we search for soul, we find only soullessness; if we look for truth, we discover mostly insincerity.

Society is of the soul, not of the body. We may spend an evening in a large drawing-room, filled with forty people, and yet move as lonely as though we were in the Sahara. Bodies may come near to one another, but while hearts and minds remain distant we are still, each of us, alone. Someone thinks it his duty to invite us to his house, thanks to the rules of a formal etiquette; we arrive but our host is not there to receive us. He has merely left his body behind to meet us, knowing well that the gulf between our minds is too broad to induce him to stay. An introduction to such a man will do everything else except introduce us. Whom God hath put asunder, let no man join together!

I have taken a ticket for the Celestial Empire, that grand country to which our petty and trivial news does not percolate. Am I then a hater of my fellows? How can he be said to be a misanthrope, who plays with little children and shares his pence with the poor?

Why not remain apart and accept the proffered blessings of a solitary retired existence, free from unnecessary anxieties, in calm places such as this sanctuary at Abydos?

We fling our scorn at the man who deserts society to seek a higher life, though perhaps he retires only that he may return to impart some good news to his race. For memory brought back the solemn pledge which had been extracted from me by those whom I respected—nay, revered—and I knew that the return was inescapable.  The knowledge did not sadden me, however, for I knew also that when the world tired me, I could plunge into the deep well of my spiritual being and later withdraw refreshed, serene, satisfied and happy.  In that great consecrated silence within I could hear the clear voice of God, even as in the great silence of this temple hall I could hear the more feeble voices of the vanished gods.  When we turn outwards to the world we wander amid shadows and perplexities, but when we turn inwards we may move amid sublime certitudes and eternal beatitudes.  "Be still," the Psalmist had counselled, "and know that I am God."

We have lost the old art of being alone and do not know what to do with ourselves in solitude.  We do not know how to make ourselves happy out of our inner resources, and so we must pay entertainers or other persons to make us temporarily happy.  We are not only unable to be alone, but less able to sit still.  Yet, if we could keep the body in one posture for a time and use our mind in the right manner, we might win a deep wisdom worth having, and draw a deep peace into our hearts.

Thus I rested for nearly a couple of hours until the incessant tick-tock of time sounded again in my ears and I opened my eyes once more.

I looked around at the thick reeded pillars which dotted the hall and supported the heavy roof, curiously resembling giant papyrus-plants holding up solid domes.  Their shafts were lit up here and there by rays of sunlight that penetrated holes in the roof and revealed their pictured and coloured bas-reliefs. Here was the Pharaoh standing ceremonially in the presence of one of his time-honoured gods or being led before the great Osiris himself; there was row upon row of lined hieroglyphs —so mysterious to the uninitiated eye.  Seti himself had seen those selfsame inscriptive pillars with their projecting bases.

I stretched out my stiff feet for a minute and then got up to move around the place.  Through lofty chambers and past vaulted sanctuaries, I crossed to the closer study of wall paintings whose blue, green, red and yellow colourings looked not less fresh against their white, marble-like calcareous limestone background than when they left the artist's hand three thousand five hundred years ago.

The delicate, skin-touched beauty of women must sooner or

THE BIRD-MAN—
SYMBOL OF THE
FREED HUMAN
SOUL

Painted by N. V. Hayward

THE GREAT PYRAMID AND THE "CITY OF THE DEAD"

*Egypt Travel Bureau*

THE SPHINX

THE SUDANESE NEGRESS WITCH-DOCTOR

THE YOUNG SYRIAN "ELYAH"

PROFESSOR EDUARD ADES:
THE HYPNOTIST

MADAME MARGUERITE:
HIS "SUBJECT"

DERVISH MONASTERY NEAR CAIRO        AHMED SIRRY, THE CHIEF DERVISH

THE ROOFLINE OF CAIRO

TAHRA BEY

HIS ENTRANCED BODY IN A COFFIN BEING LOWERED TO THE BOTTOM OF A SWIMMING BATH

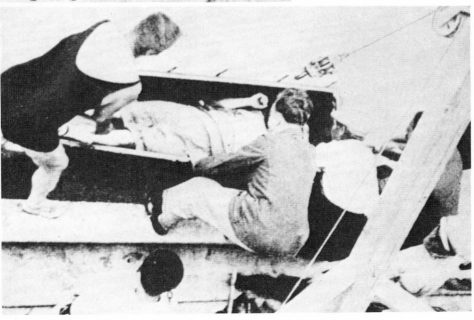

AN ANCIENT QURAN, BELONGING TO THE LATE SULTAN OF TURKEY, NOW IN THE POSSESSION OF MADAME DAHABY, OF CAIRO

SHEIKH EL MARAGHY, SPIRITUAL HEAD OF ISLAM

THE EL AZHAR MOSQUE-UNIVERSITY

HIEROGLYPHIC
WALL-CARVINGS

THE TEMPLE
OF DENDERAH

THE DENDERAH
ZODIAC

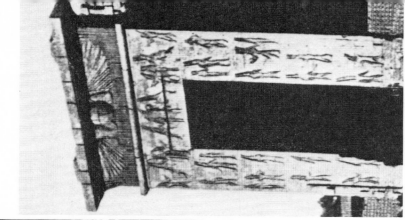

TEMPLE PYLON: KARNAK

KING SETI I: A WALL-CARVING

ENTRANCE DOORWAY OF THE INITIATION-
TEMPLE OF OSIRIS: KARNAK

SHEIK ABU SHRUMP
(*left, front row*), WITH
OTHER NOTABLES

KURNA,
THE SHEIKH'S
VILLAGE

THE VILLAGE
OF KARNAK

SHEIKH MOUSSA FINDING AND CAPTURING A SNAKE

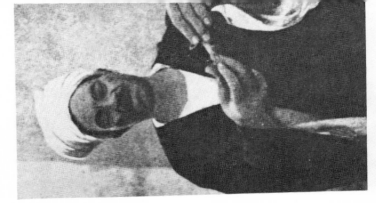

MOUSSA HOLDING A LIVE SCORPION

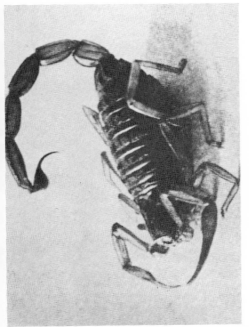

A SCORPION

SHEIKH MOUSSA

CLOSE-UP OF A SNAKE'S HEAD

MY "MAGIC TALISMAN"

SHEIKH MOUSSA AT WORK

(*Above*) SNAKE "ASLEEP" WITH MAGIC TALISMAN PLACED
UPON ITS HEAD

(*Below*) A SNAKE HISSING AT THE AUTHOR

"RA-MAK-HOTEP"
—HIS EYES

ROCK-CUT
ENTRANCE
TO A TOMB

THE VALLEY OF THE TOMBS OF THE KINGS

later be ravaged by the merciless brigand of time, but the hard, stone-carved beauty of these pictures seemed to defy all such theft. What were the secrets of those ancient paint-grinders, whose bright vermilions and clear blues retain their freshness, and why can we not imitate them to-day? The liveliness of the tints was matched by the fine drawing and splendid chiselling of those craftsmen who had once stood and worked where I then stood and thought, and who had pictured on white stone the mysterious life of vanished Egypt. Everywhere one saw representations of the king worshipping the high gods and receiving their blessings in return. In this singular temple, not wholly dedicated to a special deity as usual, several of the gods of ancient Egypt's pantheon received homage. Each had his shrine, each his wall-painting or graven figure included in some religious scene, although Osiris remained supreme among them all. Seven vaulted rooms, formed of large blocks of stone each extending from one architrave to the other, honoured Horus and Isis, Ptah and Harakht, among others.

Isis, great veiled Mother of Wisdom, prefigured in all her maternal tenderness, stretched out her arm and touched the shoulder of the devout Pharaoh. Nearby floated her sacred boat, a lotus-ornamented, elaborate shrine built into its centre; while the friendly waters and obedient winds were ready to bear it away to those paradisaical realms which are the habitats of gods, goddesses, and such humans as these deities descend to bless. Fools, seeing such a picture, wonder how the ancients could be so stupid as to believe these things, these deities who have disappeared completely to-day, and the sacred barques which bore the favoured to heaven. True, the boats were but symbols, part of a sacred language which the élite of the ancient world well understood, but which the modern world scarcely grasps; but the deities themselves were far from fictions. There is room in God's infinite universe for other and higher beings than man, and even though they took various names and forms, at various times, these deities did not change their innate character. I think, with Plutarch, that:

"Not different gods amongst different people, Barbarian or Grecian; but like the sun, moon, sky, earth, sea, are the common property of all men but yet are called by different names by different nations."

If, apparently, they have retreated from our vision to-day, their work cannot come to an end. The retreat can be only to realms less tangible to our physical senses, but we are none the less within their sphere of influence.  They still watch the world which has been entrusted to their care; they still control the trends of human evolution, even though they no longer descend into visible earthly forms.  I believe in the gods—as the ancient Egyptians believed in them—as a group of superhuman beings who watch over the evolution of the universe and the welfare of mankind, who direct the hidden destinies of peoples and guide their major affairs; finally, who are leading everyone and everything towards an ultimate perfection.

These seven consecrated chapels in the temple witnessed the burning of fire and the sprinkling of water, the offering of incense and the postures of prayer; ceremonies which became idolatrous or spiritual according to the understanding and intent of those partaking in them.  The man who thought these physical acts were sufficient substitute for inner virtues, thereby became an idolater; the man who made them symbolic remembrances of the devotion and sacrifices he would give to his Creator in his daily life, thereby became strengthened in true religion; while the priest, who used all these things as part of a system of magic which had descended to him by tradition, inherited a great responsibility, for he could call down devilish or angelic forces upon his congregation.

The masses were never allowed to penetrate to these seven inner sanctuaries whose vanished altars once shone with gold— indeed in most Egyptian temples the capacious interior court- yards were as much as they dared enter.  Such was the exclusive character of this religion wherein priestly exclusiveness played the central part.  I thought of the freedom of mosque and church, and I understand again why the priests, who had over- reached themselves in their efforts to gain and maintain power, finally lost every shred of their influence.  "Freely ye have received; freely ye should give," was a sentence which did not apply to their days.  They took and gave with the utmost reserve and caution.

¶

How strange were the mutations of time, I thought, for the sarcophagus of the man who built this place, the empty alabaster mummy-case of the Pharaoh Seti, lay over three thousand miles away in a little museum established in Lincoln's Inn

Fields, among the lawyers and estate agents of London. Had he caused it to be buried a hundred feet deeper, it might have escaped its stormy transport around the Bay of Biscay.

I looked up at ceilings painted sky-blue and dotted with multitudes of stars, and at thick roofs broken here and there by time, to admit precise oblongs of sky. Nowhere in the world does the sky turn to such an intense blue as in Egypt, I reflected again. I entered a dusty corridor and studied the famous Tablet of Abydos, that hieroglyph list of all the kings of Egypt down to Seti's time which has helped archæologists to fix their knowledge of the country's history. There was Seti himself, together with his young son Rameses, depicted in the act of offering homage to their seventy-six ancestors. The Pharaoh's royal head, strong features, and proud stiff bearing show well in profile. As my feet trod the fine soft sand which covered the temple floor in places, I studied other wall-reliefs, pictures bordered by royal cartouches or by straight lines of beautiful hieroglyph inscriptions cut deep into the stone.

There was hawk-headed, man-bodied Horus, sitting with erect back on a raised cubical throne, and holding in both hands the threefold sceptre of Egypt—the Flail Whip, the Shepherd's Crook and the Anubis Staff. Three symbolical tokens of true rulership. The whip showed mastery of the body, the crook indicated control of the feelings and the jackal-headed staff mastery of thought. The solid cube throne indicated this complete mastery of the earthly nature. Its squareness was a sign that the initiate should always act "on the square"; from which the modern Freemasonic phrase "for honourable conduct" arose; Freemasonry has an ancestry more long-trailed than most Masons think. "O, square thyself for use; a stone that may fit in the wall is not left in the ways," runs a very old Persian inscription, of Masonic interest. Along the base of the throne there ran a line of handled crosses, the celebrated "key to the Mysteries" of the Egyptians and other races, symbols of life to the Egyptologist; but, in a deeper reading, symbols of initiation into the undying higher life of the spirit.

The great aim set before the Egyptian initiates was Self-control. Hence we see the calm, imperturbable expression on the faces so often figured in portraits. Before Horus stood his devotee; the King who, with outstretched hands, sacrificially poured water on blooming lotuses standing in pots. The lotus was the sacred flower of Egypt, as of other ancient lands, and in the opened form beautifully symbolized the awakened spirit of man. The King thus perpetuated in this carving his devoted care for the growth and development of his spiritual nature. This king wore a triangular girdled apron covering the sexual organs, a garment which had precisely the same symbolism that the Freemasons' apron possesses to-day. Thus the aproned figure of the Pharaoh, going through a ritual in the temple before his divine Master, has its modern counterpart in the twentieth-century Freemason going through a ritual in the Lodge before his Worshipful Master. Abydos, as the first seat of the Osirian religion, was also the first Grand Lodge of the inner secret rites of that religion; that is of the "Mysteries," progenitors of early Freemasonry.

I threaded my way between bulging pillars, and listened to the sparrows twittering incessantly in the old roofs. I left the temple and, turning west, passed through a doorway into a sloping subterranean passage, whose walls were covered with texts and figures taken from Egypt's chief scripture: *The Book of the Dead.* This led into some excavated rooms, supposed by archæologists to have been erected as Seti's cenotaph.

The whole structure, most archaic in appearance, was dug out of more than forty feet of debris. The central room was saddle-roofed and shaped like a colossal sarcophagus. The roof was delicately sculptured with carvings showing Shu, god of the air, lifting a dead Pharaoh from the earth and protecting him with his arms. I felt at once that some hidden symbolism lay in this picture. The whole building was most remarkable. It was built of huge stones. A water-filled moat entirely surrounded the crypt and isolated the central nave. That this moat is connected with the Nile by some secret underground canal, is more than probable. Herodotus has described a very similar place said to have existed underneath the Great Pyramid, but no one has yet been able to verify what he was told by the priests. This mysterious crypt at Abydos, practically unique among excavated underground chambers, may indeed have been reconstructed by Seti to serve as his cenotaph; but I had a definite feeling that it had originally served some higher purpose. What was that purpose? I dismissed the question for the time being.

I returned to sit on an old flagstone in the shade of the pillared court. Here at Abydos, said the old traditions, the man-

god Osiris himself had been secretly buried in the royal
necropolis of Thinis, the bygone city which had once occupied
this site.  King Neferhotep placed on record the fact that he had
found Abydos a jumbled mass of ruined masonry when he took
up the sceptre of the Pharaohs, and he told how he had searched
in the priestly library of Heliopolis for archives relating to the
temple of Osiris which had anciently stood here; how after
studying those archives, he was able to reconstruct the lost
rites.  His successors made further use of these documents to
rebuild the ruins into fine structures and add to them more
buildings.  These temples stood amid the houses of the city of
Thinis.  Time had devoured them all, however.

In those earliest days of early Egypt the Mysteries of Osiris
were a celebrated feature of the religion and Abydos was the
first of all places in the land for this celebration.  It was this
which had made it one of the holiest spots and I knew it was
the spiritual fragrance of that ancient atmosphere whose vibrations I had contacted—not that of the formalistic rites which
were daily enacted in this beautiful, but later, structure of King
Seti.  For the earliest history of Abydos was bound up with
the history of Osiris himself, and takes the calendar back into
that dateless epoch where the years melt away, the prehistoric
epoch of Egyptian origin, the uncharted era before the rise
of the Pharaohs.  Those were the days when the gods had not
vanished from the ken of man; when "the demi-gods," as the
Egyptian historians called them, ruled the people.  How wonderful, I mused, that by some mysterious process of psychically
relayed vibrations the sublime atmosphere of prehistoric
Abydos still lived on here and could be picked up again by a
sensitive human receiving set.

Here, at Abydos, had been established the first and chief
sanctuary of Osiris in all Egypt; but who was Osiris? Historical
legend replies with a fantastic incredible myth of someone who
was murdered, his scattered pieces being afterwards put together.

I sank the plummet of mind into this problem and waited
for an answer. . . .

And out of the silence of the Past came this reply: One of
the great ones of Atlantis foresaw the need of preparing a new
habitat for his younger spiritual kith and kin and took them
eastwards to what is now Egypt.  He had attained that superhuman stage of being which marked the demi-gods, and so he
was not only a worldly ruler of his people but also as a god to

them.   He brought these finer souls out of the doomed continent, although it was then at the zenith of its civilization, for
the gods begin to prepare new lands long before the old ones
have departed.

Before Atlantis fell, groups of the better minds emigrated.
Those who belonged to the Western Empires moved to Central
and South America: those who belonged to the Eastern
Empires of Atlantis went to Africa, there to lay the basis of
Egypt's greatness.

They sailed in their curvilinear craft with prows pointed
towards the little-known east, and made settlements at various
places and at different times on the Euro-African shores; but
the party under Osiris's immediate direction was taken to prehistoric Egypt, on whose shores they halted before presently
sailing up the Nile, passing the three Pyramids and the Sphinx;
products of the first Atlantean outflow, until Osiris bade them
stop, not far from the present site of Abydos.   They found
Northern Egypt already inhabited by an aboriginal population
who accepted them peaceably, and who even let them, because
of their superior culture, gradually impose their influence and
rule upon themselves.   Thus was born the Lower Egyptian
civilization, and before Osiris left his people he had instituted
his religious Mysteries and had left them as a long-enduring
legacy to perpetuate his name, work and teaching.   Thus, these
men and women, these prehistoric Egyptians, were cultured
and civilized before London arose from the swamps.   Long
after Osiris passed, and when, his religion needed revivifying
and codifying, there appeared another great Teacher; a
"demi-god," named Thoth, who established a second centre
of the Osirian Mysteries at Sais.   All this had occurred among
the aboriginal communities of prehistoric Egypt.

Then how had the legend of Osiris's murder started?

I could not get the answer straightway, and decided to let it
await another meditation.

I began to make my exit across the uneven flagstones, whose
original surfaces had long since worn away.   Once they had
been covered with lovely mosaic, but, now, not a tiny pebble
was left upon this time-broken flooring.   I caught my final
glimpses of those beautiful pillars, whose bulging tops had held
up great carved stone roof-beams for so many centuries, and
were still gallantly supporting them.   This ended my wandering
through this sanctuary of antiquity.

I left the court and passed out of the precincts of the temple into the bright flood of noon sunshine. I picked my way among the stones and dust, the bits of rock and heaps of sand, the broken blocks and shapeless fragments, among patches of green bramble and spiky camel-thorns, until I could find a vantage-point whence to take a last look upon the deserted building.

It rose up in its white simplicity, with twelve shattered square pillars to guard its frontal line; a plain, narrow doorway giving entry to it. How different, and how grand, it must have looked in its heyday! Architecture in Egypt was a hieratic art. Religion was the thread upon which its craftsmen and artists slipped the beads of their beautiful work.

"The palace within it is much embellished with fine gold true and fresh from the workings. When it is seen, hearts exult and all people make obeisance. Its nobility is that which gives it splendour. Its gates, exceeding great, are of pine of the forest," boasted Seti in an inscribed decree describing his own achievement, "their bodies are gilded with fine gold and bound with bronze at their back parts. The great pylon-towers are of stone of Anu, the head-pieces of granite, their beauties reach Ra in his horizon."

Such was Abydos—reputed burying-place of the god Osiris, in reality the first centre of Mystery initiation "burials" in Egypt.

And the larks still sang enchantingly among the broken roofs of this last successor to Osiris's first sanctuary as I descended to the village with my private dream of the Past.

I had found a place I loved, and I knew that its intangible spell, laid on me as by an invisible hand, would draw me back again and yet again. Such places held me, in fact and in memory, enslaved in a servitude from which I sought no escape.

If I can catch a few immortal moments out of the fleeting hours, then only am I made aware that I have not lived in vain. At Abydos, I had caught such moments.

# CHAPTER XI

THE answer which I sought to the mystery of Osiris's legendary murder came to me at last, when I had travelled farther up the Nile and devoted myself to a study of the best-preserved large temple to be found in Egypt, that of the goddess Hathor at Denderah, which the soft warm sand had completely covered and preserved for much more than a thousand years. I had climbed up an extraordinarily narrow and worn stairway on the northern side. I stopped now and then to examine, by the light of my torch, the sculptured scenes which appeared on the walls all the length of this staircase. They depicted the most important ritual-procession of the temple—that of the New Year—moving onwards with the Pharaoh himself at its head. Priests, hierophants of the Mysteries, and standard-bearers took their carved way upon these walls as they must have taken their living way up these steps. I stepped out of the gloom with them into the brilliant sunlight, and walked across gigantic roofing-stones to a small temple which stood, secluded and alone, in a corner of the roof-terrace. It was supported by Hathor-headed columns.

I penetrated inside, and recognized the place as a sanctuary where the Osirian Mysteries were performed as late as Ptolemaic times. Its walls were decorated with chiselled reliefs showing Orisis extended on a couch, surrounded by various attendants and incense braziers. Hieroglyphs and pictures told the whole story of Osiris's death and resurrection, and inscriptions gave the apportioned prayers for the twelve hours of the night.

I sat down on the floor, that was really part of the temple roof itself, and gave myself up to renewed meditation upon the old legend. And when I had dangled my plummet long enough and deep enough there flashed across my mind the real truth, whose distorted fragments had come down through the centuries in the form of this fantastic tale of Osiris's dismemberment and subsequent piecing together.

The key came to me with the sudden remembrance of my personal experience inside the King's Chamber of the Great Pyramid, when out of the blackness of night there had arisen the vision of two High Priests, one of whom had entranced my body and led my conscious spirit out of its grip. My sleeping body had lain practically in a coma, enlivened only by the most imperceptible unconscious breathing, while the really vital element of it had escaped. I was as a dead man whose soul had quitted his body. Yet, at the end of my experience, I returned to the flesh and the aspect of death had vanished. Was this not a veritable resurrection; a return to this terrene existence of ours after a glimpse of the other state? Was this not a conscious existence after death?

I got up and re-examined the wall-pictures to confirm the illumination I had received. The outstretched Osiris lay apparently dead, a seemingly embalmed body in a mummy-wrapping, yet everything pointed to a preparation for a ceremony that would benefit a living man and not a dead one. Yes; there was the entranced body of the candidate, there were the attendant priests, and there the censers to render the entrancement more easy.

There were the night-prayers, too. For these initiations always took place with the onset of darkness. The candidate was entranced for periods of varying length—the more advanced the degree for which he had entered, the longer and deeper was his entrancement—and priests watched over him during such hours of the night as had been allotted to him.

Such was the scene which had been enacted in the rituals of Mysteries since immemorial antiquity. And its meaning? The murder of Osiris was none other than the apparent murder of every candidate who wished to partake of the Mysteries of Osiris; that is, become united with the spirit of Osiris, founder of those Mysteries.

In the oldest temples there was always a twofold plan in the architectural arrangement, and every temple had two divisions: (1) for ordinary religion, (2) for the secret Mysteries. The latter was reserved completely and placed in a special part of the sanctuary.

The candidate was plunged by hypnotic means, involving the use of powerful fumigants as well as mesmeric passes the length of his body, combined with the use of a magically impregnated rod, into a death-like trance wherein he was deprived of every semblance of life. Whilst the body remained inert, the soul retained its hold by a magnetic thread, visible to the clairvoyant initiator, so that the vital functions were preserved despite the complete suspension of animation. The whole purpose and purport of the initiation was to teach the candidate that "There is no death!" And he was taught this lesson in the clearest and most practical way possible, i.e. by being made to experience within himself the actual process of dying and mysteriously entering into another world of being. So deep was his trance that he was placed inside a painted and inscribed mummy-case whose lid was closed and sealed. To all intents and purposes, he had actually been murdered!

But when the allotted time of entrancement had elapsed, the case was opened and he was re-awakened by appropriate methods. Thus the symbolic scattered pieces of Osiris's body were put together again and he was brought back to life. This fabled resurrection of Osiris was simply the real resurrection of the Osirian candidate!

The chapel in which I stood had been the scene of many such "murders" and "resurrections." Once it had been appropriately furnished with a couch and all the appurtenances for initiation. When the candidate had passed through the trance-state and was ready for re-awakening he was carried to a point where the first rays of the rising sun would fall full upon his sleeping face.

It was a fact that in the earlier days many of the Egyptian priests of the superior ranks, and all of the High Priests, were well versed in the mysteries of hypnotism and mesmerism, and could cause those upon whom they experimented to fall into cataleptic conditions so profound that the rigor mortis of death seemed to ensue. The High Priests could do even more than this, more than modern hypnotists; for *they knew how to keep the candidate's mind awake even when his body was entranced* and to provide him with a series of supernormal experiences which he did not fail to remember on his return to normal consciousness.

In this manner they were able to impress upon him an understanding of the nature of man's soul, and, by temporarily forcing his own soul out of his body, a perception of the existence of another world of being; the so-called spirit world, for which the symbolism of his painted mummy-coffin provided fit analogy. Thus the Egyptians graved on the lids of sarcophagi, or painted on the cases of mummies, or vignetted in the texts of their sacred scriptures, a curious little bird-man flying up from, or resting upon the mummy itself. It was a human-headed bird, with human arms, and was often represented as extending to the mummy's nostrils with one hand the hieroglyphic figure of a swelling sail, the breath; and in the other a round-handled cross, or life. Whether here or written on papyrus scroll, or graven on granite stone, the symbolism of these strange hieroglyphs teaches the same doctrine of a spirit world's existence. When the Egyptian *Book of the Dead* speaks of the deceased, it really refers to the living-dead—men entranced as profoundly as in death, with bodies still and motionless, with souls loosed into another world. It refers to Initiation. In some mysterious manner this other world interpenetrates our own, and these spirits may be very close to us mortals. Nothing is lost in nature, the scientists themselves tell us, and when a man disappears from this world, leaving a senseless inert body behind, it may well be that he reappears in the ether, invisible to us, but visible to etheric beings.

Although this process of initiation bore all the outward semblance of expert hypnotism, it was something that went far beyond the entrancement methods of our modern experimenters, who tap the subconscious mind of man but who cannot make their subjects conscious of still profounder planes of existence.

In the popular mind, Osiris was one who had suffered martyrdom and died and then risen again from the grave. Thus his name became for his people the very synonym of survival after death, and his conquest of mortality made them hope for a similar conquest after their own deaths.

The common belief was in the immortality of the soul and in a life beyond the grave; and that, in the transition to this new life, the gods would judge the soul and record the measure of its good and evil deeds in the past. The wicked would receive fit punishment, while the good would go to the realm of the blessed and unite with Osiris. These notions served the masses well enough and gave the toiling peasant's mind as much as it could conveniently hold. There was little use in bewildering it with profound philosophy and subtle psychological explanations. All these popular myths, legends and fables were to be understood as partly symbolical and partly historical, as hiding an inner rational meaning, and an inner truth which was alone real. And to keep this teaching alive, the temple-priests not only employed ritual but also gave dramatic symbolic representations in public, at certain dates, which kept the story of Osiris before the populace. A very few of these performances came within the category of the Mysteries, in the sense of giving an easily understood, popular version of them; they corresponded to the Mystery Play of ancient Greece, and the Passion Play of medieval and modern Europe, such as the Christ-drama which is still performed at Ober-Ammergau in Bavaria. The real Mysteries, however, must not be confused with them and were never performed publicly and were much more than play-acting. The public performances were symbolical and sacred, but did not reveal any hidden secrets to the audience; hence the ancient popular spectacle of the Death and Resurrection of Osiris must not be thought of as the inner mysteries

The popular, personal celebrations and external ceremonies were held for the mass of people, whom they suited admirably; but there was a more philosophic doctrine and secret practice for the intelligentsia. The spiritually educated and instructed Egyptians, the nobility and the high-born, knew that and, when so inclined, sought admission to them.

The temples had special and isolated buildings for the Mysteries, which were performed by a small and selected number of priests, called hierophants; and these secret rites were carried on by the side of, and outside, the daily ceremonies for the worship of the gods. The Egyptians, themselves, called these rites the "Mysteries."

The supernormal character of the Greater Mysteries, with which the ritual dramas had little to do, was hinted at by various initiates, as when once one of them declared: "Thanks to the Mysteries, death for mortals is not an evil but a good." This could only mean that he had actually become a corpse and yet had received a great benefit from the experience. The hieroglyphic texts speak of such a one as "twice-born," and he was permitted to add to his name the words "he who has renewed his life," so that on some tomb-inscriptions archæologists still discover these phrases descriptive of the spiritual status of the defunct person.

What were the greatest secrets that the successful candidates learned in the Mysteries?

That depended on the degree through which they passed, but all their experiences could roughly be condensed into two results, which formed the core of the revelations they received.

In the earlier degrees, the candidates were made acquainted

with the human soul, pictured as a little bird-man in the system of hieroglyphs; they solved the mystery of death. They learned that it was really disappearance from one state of being, only to reappear in another; that it affected the fleshly body, but did not destroy the mind and the self. They learned, too, that the soul not only survived the destruction of its mortal envelope but progressed onwards to higher spheres.

In the advanced degrees, they were made acquainted with the divine soul; they were brought into personal communion with the Creator; they stood face to face with the Divine. They were first instructed in the true explanation of the Fall of Man from his original spiritual state. They were told the inner history of Atlantis, a history so intimately associated with the history of the Fall. Then they were lifted up, sphere beyond sphere, until they found themselves in the same highly spiritual consciousness as Man had enjoyed at the beginning. Thus, while yet on their pilgrimage in time, they had gathered the spoils of eternity.

¶

It will not be amiss if at this point in my record of travel and impressions, I interpose some descriptive lines upon the various ancient institutions of the Mysteries from a pen other than my own—the pen of a man who lived in classic times and who had, himself, been initiated into the lesser degrees, at least. He was bound by oath not to reveal in detail what he had experienced, so we must not look for more than general explanations and elusive hints. The excerpt, which is the fullest known admission by an initiate, comes from Apuleius, an initiate of the first degree of the Mysteries of Isis; his autobiographical writings of one, "Lucius," and they show how the latter knocked at the temple door in his eagerness for the secret knowledge.

The Egyptian Mysteries were for long kept sealed to foreigners, and it was only in late times that a few were admitted and initiated. Those who were so initiated almost always kept their vows of secrecy. The regulations covering entrance were strict and severe.

"And daily my desire to be admitted to the Mysteries increased ever more and more, and again and again I visited the high priest with the most urgent entreaty that he would at length initiate me into the secrets of the night that is holy to the goddess. But he, being a man of steadfast character and famous for all his observation of the strict laws of the faith, with kindly and gentle words, such as parents use to check the precocious desires of their children, put off my insistence and soothed the great trouble of my spirit by holding forth consolatory hope of greater bliss. For he said that the day of each man's initiation was fixed by the ordinance of the goddess, and that the priest destined for her service was likewise chosen by her providence.

"He bade me, like others, await all these ordinances with reverent patience, warning me that it was my duty to beware with all my soul of over-eagerness and petulance, to avoid both these faults, and neither to delay when summoned nor to hasten unbidden.

"For the gates of hell and the power of life are in the hands of the goddess, and the very act of dedication is regarded as a voluntary death and an imperilling of life, inasmuch as the goddess is wont to select those whose term of life is near its close and who stand on the threshold of the night, and are moreover men to whom the mighty Mysteries of the goddess may safely be committed. These men the goddess by her providence brings to new birth and places once more at the start of a new race of life. Therefore thou too must await the command of heaven.

"Nor did the saving grace of the great goddess play me false, or torture me by long deferment, but in the dark of night, in commands wherein was no darkness, she clearly warned me that the day of my long desire was come, whereon she would grant the fulfilment of my most earnest prayers.

"By these and other gracious admonitions the supreme goddess gladdened my spirit, so that ere yet it was clear day I shook sleep from off me and hastened straightway to the priest's lodging. I met him even as he came forth from his bedchamber and saluted him. I had resolved to demand with yet greater persistence than my wont that I should be appointed to the service of the mysteries as being now my due. But he, as soon as he beheld me, anticipated me and said: 'Lucius, happy and blessed art thou, whom the august deity deigns to favour with such goodwill.

" 'The day so long besought by thine unwearied prayers is come, on which by the divine commands of the goddess of many names thou shalt be admitted by my hands to the most holy secrets of the mysteries.'

"Then, placing his right hand in mine, the kindly old man led me to the very doors of the great shrine, and after celebrating with solemn rite the service of the opening of the gates and performing the morning sacrifice, he brought forth from the hidden places of the shrine certain books with titles written in undecipherable letters.

"He then led me back to the temple and, the day being more than half spent, set me at the feet of the goddess herself, and after that he had confided certain secrets to me, things too holy for utterance, openly before all present bade me for ten consecutive days to abstain from all pleasures of the table, to eat no living thing, and to drink no wine.

"All these precepts I observed with reverent abstinence, and at last the day came for my dedication to the goddess. The sun was sloping westward and bringing on the evening, when lo! on all sides crowds of the holy initiates flocked round me, each, after the ancient rite, honouring me with diverse gifts. Lastly, all the uninitiate were excluded, a linen robe that no man had yet worn was cast about me, the priest caught me by the hand and led me to the very heart of the holy place.

"Perchance, eager reader, thou burnest to know what then was said, what done. I would tell thee, were it lawful for me to tell, and thou shouldst know all, were it lawful for thee to hear. But both tongue and ear would be infected with like guilt did I gratify such rash curiosity. Yet since, perchance, it is pious craving that vexes thee, I will not torment thee by prolongation of thine anguish. Hear, then, and believe, for what I tell is true. I drew nigh to the confines of death, I trod the threshold of Proserpine, I was borne through all the elements and returned to earth again. I saw the sun gleaming with bright splendour at dead of night, I approached the gods above, and the gods below, and worshipped them face to face. Behold, I have told thee things of which, though thou hast heard them, thou must yet know naught."

A year later, Lucius was initiated into the Mysteries of Osiris, which were higher.

Among the few other foreigners who were permitted to receive the Egyptian initiation were Plato, Pythagoras, Thales, Lycurgus, Solon, Iamblichus, Plutarch and Herodotus. The last-named, in his writings, alludes to them with extreme reserve, describing in detail the symbolic dramas and public festivals which were always associated in the public mind with the Mysteries, and which were merely of a ceremonial nature, but refusing to divulge the inner secret rites, of which he remarks: "On these Mysteries, which are really without exception known to me, I must guard my lips in religious silence."

Let us turn next to the pages of Plutarch, the biographer.

"When you shall hear of the fables the Egyptians tell about the gods—their wanderings, cutting to pieces and other mishaps —you should not suppose that any of them happened or was done in the manner related. Nations have established and do employ symbols, some obscure, some more intelligible, in order to lead the understanding into things divine. In the same way must you hear the stories about the gods, and receive them from such as interpret myths, in a reverent and philosophic spirit.

"*At the moment of death the soul experiences the same impressions as those who are initiated into the great Mysteries.*

"Those common and trivial stories of people who identify the legends concerning these deities with the seasonable changes of the atmosphere, or with the growth, sowings and ploughings of the grain, and who say that Osiris is then buried when the sown grain is hidden in the ground, and that he comes to life again when there is a beginning of sprouting; let men take good heed and fear lest they unwittingly degrade and resolve divine beings into winds and currents, sowings and ploughings and affections of the earth, and changes of the seasons.

"The Mysteries were intended also to preserve the meaning of valuable passages in history."

This is but a hint, all that Plutarch feels he may divulge, but its full meaning is that the inner history of Atlantis and its fall was told to the initiate.

He gives the psychological purpose of the Mysteries in his treatise *De Iside et Osiride*, wherein he says:

"While we are here below, encumbered by bodily affections, we can have no intercourse with God, save as in philosophic thought we may faintly touch him as in a dream. But when our souls are released (by the Mysteries) and have passed into the region of the pure, invisible and changeless, this God will be their guide and king who depend on him and gaze with insatiable longing on the beauty which may not be spoken of by the lips of man."

He refers to the goal of the Mysteries of Isis as follows: "By these means they may be the better prepared for the attainment of the knowledge of the First and Supreme Mind, whom the Goddess exhorts them to search after. For this reason is her temple called Iseion, alluding to that knowledge of the eternal and self-existent Being which may thus be obtained, if it be properly approached."

So much for Grecian Plutarch. What has Syrian Iamblichus to say on those Mysteries of Egypt into which he was initiated?

"The essence and perfection of all good are comprehended in the gods, and the first and ancient power of them is with us priests. A knowledge of the gods is accompanied with a conversion to, and knowledge of, ourselves. I say therefore that the more divine part of man, which was formerly united to the gods by being aware of their existence, afterwards entered into another state and became fettered with the bonds of necessity and fate. Hence it is requisite to consider how he may be loosed from these bonds. There is, therefore, no other dissolution of them than the knowledge of the gods. This is the aim of the Egyptians in the priestly lifting of the soul to divinity."

Another initiate was Proclus. Let him speak too:

"In all initiations and Mysteries, the gods exhibit many forms of themselves, and sometimes indeed an unfigured light of themselves is held forth to the view; sometimes this light is figured according to human form, and sometimes it proceeds into a different shape. Some of the figures are not gods, and excite alarm."

What was the testimony of the noble philosopher Plato?

"In consequence of this divine initiation we became spectators of single and blessed visions, resident in a pure light; and were ourselves made immaculate and liberated from this surrounding garment which we call the body and to which we are now bound like an oyster to its shell." He asserted, too, that the ultimate aim of the Mysteries was to lead men back to the principles from which the race originally fell.

Homer, who had been initiated, could write in the Odyssey the following invitation to his readers:

"Haste, let us fly and all our sails expand,
    To gain our dear, our long-lost native land."

Which was the poet's way of expressing Plato's thought.

L

Another initiate of reputed foreign lineage was Moses; actually he was only half Hebrew, as one of his parents was Egyptian. "Moses was instructed in all the wisdom of the Egyptians," says the New Testament. What this sentence means —if it is to be taken literally—is that the *profoundest* wisdom of the Egyptians had been opened to him. Such could be nothing else than the knowledge imparted in the Mysteries.

Further, the same scripture declares that "Moses put a veil upon his face." We may receive some hint of the nature of this veil when we read further, that "until this very day at the reading of the Old Testament the same veil remaineth unlifted" (Corinthians, 2nd Epistle). This indicates that it was no veil made of cloth, but a veil upon matter communicated by words, i.e. upon knowledge. Therefore, the veil worn by Moses was really the pledge of silence and secrecy which he had taken during his initiation into the Mysteries.

This wisdom which Moses possessed, he learnt in the famous temple school at the city of On, named Heliopolis by the Greeks when they conquered Egypt (and called On in the Bible); a bygone city which once stood on a site a few miles north of Cairo. A sacred way stretched from the foot of the plateau upon which rested the Pyramids, across the plain to the sacred city of Heliopolis. Both the latter and Memphis—another vanished city within sight of the Pyramids—looked to the Great Pyramid as their highest shrine of the Mysteries. Heliopolis has gone, and the temple with it: the broken mud-brick walls of the town and the shattered pillars of the temples now lie a dozen feet below the sand and soil; all save the red granite obelisk which stood at its porch. That obelisk still stands— the same obelisk that Moses saw and passed and repassed many times—and it remains the oldest standing obelisk now left in the country. Other students who were attracted, like moths to the lamp of wisdom, to knock at the doors of this temple were Plato, the philosopher, and Herodotus, the historian. They, too, saw this obelisk, which stands in pathetic solitude to-day, a tall, bewildered monolith up to whose very base the peasants now till their fields.

It is brother to that other rugged obelisk which was set up by Thothmes III, in front of the Temple of the Sun at Heliopolis, and which now overlooks the Thames on the Embankment at London; which, under the name of Cleopatra's Needle, still remains to remind the hurrying world of England's metropolis of a remote, antique and powerful civilization of the past.

This soaring obelisk stood like a sentinel guarding the entrance to the temple, while the inscriptions upon its sides proclaimed the story of the building, in deeply cut hieroglyphs. The obelisk was something more than a stone shaft set up to carry a certain engraved inscription; it was also a sacred symbol, and its top always terminated in a small pyramid.

Heliopolis was a great centre of learning, sacred and secular, with thirteen thousand priest-students and teachers; with a huge population and a pre-eminent library that later helped to form the famous Alexandrian one.

The young Moses paced on his ceremonial walks around the temples or pored over his rolls of papyri: spent there many an hour in deep thought and solitary meditation.

Exceptionally serious, even as a child, Moses progressed so well in his studies and character that he passed through all the initiation degrees with honours, reaching the rare and culminating degree of Adept.    He was then fit to become a hierophant, in his turn.    And it was in the same Mystery school where he had studied—in the school attached to the Great Temple of Heliopolis, the City of the Sun—that he attained to this distinction.  He received candidates into the secret rites of Osiris, highest of the rites of the Mysteries.

In those days he bore another name, an Egyptian one, such as befitted his half-Egyptian parentage. His original name was Osarsiph. (This is no flight of imagination on the writer's part; I am taking his name, and the name of his temple, along with one or two other facts, from the ancient Egyptian records of the priest Manetho: the rest I have discovered by private research.)

When the great change came in his life, when he accepted the mission which both destiny and the gods had confided to him, he signalized the event by altering his name to an Israelite one.    All instructed Egyptians believed in the power of names. A name possessed magical value for them.  And so Osarsiph took on the name of Moses.

The Pharaoh of his time was a man of hard unspiritual character.    He was stubborn and cruel.    His treatment of the Israelites was such that the persecution aroused Moses' sympathies and stirred the strain of Hebrew blood that flowed in his veins.   He succeeded in freeing the Hebrew tribes from their servitude and captivity and took them out of the valley of Goshen, along the old historic highway which, from times immemorial, was the road between Africa and Asia, the same road along which Napoleon was one day to ride his horse, to be nearly drowned when he reached its end at Suez.

Some of Moses' later history may be found in the Bible, sadly mixed up with mere hearsay.

In the old Testament we find a series of books called the Pentateuch, which are attributed to Moses. They contain the essence of such wisdom as Moses ostensibly wished to communicate to his people, coupled with more or less historical facts about the creation of the world and the early races of man.

Now Moses, as an Adept, knew and used the sacred writing of the initiates, i.e. the hieroglyphs in their *third* or secret spiritual meaning. When he completed the Pentateuch, he wrote the text in Egyptian hieroglyphs. Access to these texts was available to his initiated priests, who understood hieroglyphs. But when the Israelites had settled down in Palestine and centuries had rolled over their heads, the knowledge of the meaning of hieroglyphs had grown vague. Little by little the priesthood became less and less familiar with the characters and could only decipher them with difficulty. This is not surprising when we remember that, even in Egypt itself, by the fourth century A.D. the art of interpreting hieroglyphs had been completely lost. When, nearly a thousand years after the great exodus of the Israelites from Egypt, the elders of Israel put together that collection of books which we now call the Old Testament, the difficulties which faced them in trying to translate Moses' writings into Hebrew were immense. For Moses wrote as an Adept, but these elders, however learned, were not Adepts. Misunderstandings occurred most frequently; symbolic expressions were taken as literal facts; hieroglyphic pictures were taken as pictures of existent things; and figurative phrases were grievously misinterpreted. A single instance will suffice; the six days of creation meant, in Moses' mind, six vast periods of time symbolically termed days for reasons which every initiate knew. But the scholars who translated him literally, really thought he meant days of twenty-four hours only.

Therefore, those early books of the Bible yield peculiar notions when read literally—peculiar because mere everyday science is rightly correcting those books on points of fact—but they yield extremely fruitful knowledge when read by the light of an understanding of what was taught in the Egyptian Mystery Temples.

Moses, then, must be claimed as one of the most notable figures who emerged from the dead trance of initiation.

# CHAPTER XII

## THE ANCIENT MYSTERIES

THOSE who were initiated into the *Ancient Mysteries* took a solemn oath never to reveal what had passed within the sacred walls. It must be remembered, in any case, that every year only a comparatively few were initiated into the Mysteries, consequently the number of persons who knew their secrets was never at any time large. Therefore, any complete and connected exposure of what actually constituted the Mysteries has never been given to the world by any ancient writer, so faithfully has this oath been kept. Nevertheless, brief allusions, comments by classical authors, occasional phrases and carven inscriptions have been discovered, sufficient to afford a few fleeting glimpses into the nature of these obscure institutions of antiquity. And those glimpses assure us that the purpose of the Mysteries, in their earlier and unspoiled state, was assuredly a high one, a blending of religious, philosophical and moral aims. "Farewell, thou who hast experienced what thou hadst never yet experienced, from a man thou hast become a god," was a parting phrase which the Orphic initiate of the highest degrees heard.

It was open to any man to knock at the doors of the Mystery Temples, but whether he could obtain admittance was another matter. In the words of Pythagoras, when turning away unsuitable applicants from his own Academy at Croton, "not every kind of wood is suitable for the making of Mercury."

The first stage of initiation—that which proved survival—brought with it a terrible and frightening experience as a prelude to the pleasanter awakening in the soul-body.

In some of the elementary initiations, but not all, there was a time when mechanical means were used to make the candidate believe that he was falling into a dangerous pit, or being over-whelmed by a tide of rushing water, or being attacked by wild animals. Thus his resourcefulness and courage were tested.

But the most frightful test was when, in the more advanced degree, he had to face appalling creatures of the nether world during a time when he was made temporarily clairvoyant.

"The mind is affected and agitated in death just as it is in initiation into the Grand Mysteries; the first stage is nothing but errors and uncertainties, labourings, wanderings and darkness. And now, arrived on the verge of death and initiation, everything wears a dreadful aspect; it is all horrors, trembling and affrightment. But this scene once over, a miraculous and divine light displays itself . . . perfect and initiated they are free, crowned, triumphant, they walk in the regions of the blessed." This passage was preserved by Stobæus from an ancient record, and confirms the experience of all other initiates.

The ancient papyri picture the candidate being led to this stage by Anubis, jackal-headed god, Master of the Mysteries: it is Anubis who conducts him across the threshold of the unseen world, into the presence of terrifying apparitions.

The knowledge taught in these schools of initiation was passed down directly from the primitive revelation of the truth to the first civilizations, and it had to be protected so as to retain its purity. Thus, one may understand why these secrets were carefully concealed and jealously guarded from the profane.

The condition into which the initiate-candidate was plunged must not be confused with ordinary sleep. It was a trance state which freed his conscious self; it was a magical sleep wherein he remained paradoxically awake, but to another world.

Moreover, to confuse such a sublime experience with the mental handiwork of the modern hypnotist would be a grave error. The latter plunges his subject into a strange condition which neither fully understands, whereas the hierophant of the Mysteries was in the possession of a secret traditional knowledge which enabled him to exercise his power as one fully armed with complete understanding. The hypnotist taps the subconscious mentality of his entranced subject down to a certain level, without himself sharing the change of condition, whereas the hierophant watched and controlled every such change by his own percipient powers. Above all, the hypnotist is only able to elucidate from his subject such matters as concern our material world and life, or to perform abnormal feats with the material body. The hierophant went deeper, and could lead the mind of the candidate step by step through an experience involving the spiritual worlds—a feat beyond the power of any modern hypnotist to achieve.

I had watched every kind of hypnotic phenomena performed in Eastern and Western countries, and I knew that, marvellous as some of them undoubtedly were, they belonged to a lower order. They were not sacred processes. They were of scientific interest but not of deeper spiritual value. Though they carried one out of the gross depths of materialism by proving the existence of mysterious subconscious forces in man's being, they could not carry one upwards into conscious discovery of the soul as a living, immortal and independent thing.

I had been able to reconstruct, both from my own experience within the Pyramid and from the evidences of wall carvings in the temples, the mysterious drama of the innermost secret rite of Osiris. That august rite was nothing more or less than a process which combined hypnotic, magical and *spiritual* forces in an attempt to detach the candidate's soul from the heavy bondage of his fleshly body for a few hours, and sometimes for a few days, that he might ever after live with the memory of this epoch-making experience and conduct himself accordingly. The survival of the soul after death, accepted by most men through faith in their religion, he was thenceforth able to accept, strengthened in his conviction by the evidence of personal knowledge.

What this meant to him could only be appreciated by those who underwent a similar experience. Even in modern times some men have involuntarily, and unexpectedly, passed through a *part* of this experience. I know of one case, an ex-Air Force officer, who was put under an anæsthetic for a surgical operation during the war. The drug had a curious effect. It made him quite unconscious of any pain in his body, yet it did not send him to sleep. He found himself, instead, hovering in the air over the operating table and watched the whole process as calmly as he might have watched an operation upon someone else's body! The experience made an extraordinary change in his character; for, he turned from a materialist into a believer in the existence of the soul, and henceforth lived with a new hope and purpose.

Who were these hierophants, whose power could bring about in a man such an amazing transformation?

These venerable custodians of a higher learning were perforce always few in number. They embraced at one time all the High Priests of Egypt, as well as certain superior members of the priesthood. Their knowledge was guarded with the utmost secrecy and kept so exclusive that Egypt's name became synonymous in classical times with mystery.

In the Egyptian galleries of the Museum of the Louvre at Paris, there is a tomb of Ptah-Mer, High Priest of Memphis, which bears an inscription, as epitaph, containing the following words: "He penetrated in the Mysteries of every sanctuary; nothing was hidden from him. *He covered with a veil everything which he had seen.*" The hierophants were compelled to maintain this extraordinary reserve for reasons of their own, yet the necessity of excluding the sceptic and the scoffer from experiments fraught with so much danger to the candidate's life is obvious, while the inadvisability of casting pearls before swine is equally obvious. However, it was more than likely that most men were not sufficiently ready or prepared to enter into such an experience, which might easily bring them madness or death, and so it was made the privilege of a few. Many knocked at the doors of the Mystery Temples in vain, while others who applied were put through a graduated series of tests which broke their nerve or diminished their desire for initiation. Thus by a process of elimination—and exclusive selection—the Mysteries became the most exclusive institution of antique times, and the secrets revealed behind their well-guarded doors were always imparted under solemn oath that they would never be divulged. Every man who emerged through those doors belonged ever after to a secret society which moved and worked with higher purpose and profounder knowledge among the profane masses. "It is said that those who have participated in the Mysteries become more spiritual, more just and better in every way," wrote Diodorus, a visitor from Sicily.

Nor were these initiations limited to Egypt. The ancient civilizations inherited these Mysteries from a remote antiquity and they constituted part of a primitive revelation from the gods to the human race. Almost every people of pre-Christian times possessed its institution and tradition of the Mysteries. The Romans, the Celts, the Druids of Britain, the Greeks, the Cretans, the Syrians, the Hindus, the Persians, the Mayas and the American Indians, among others, had corresponding temples and rites with a system of graduated illuminations for the initiates. Aristotle did not hesitate to declare that he considered the welfare of Greece secured by the Eleusinian Mysteries.

Socrates remarked that "those who are acquainted with the Mysteries insure to themselves very pleasing hopes against the hour of death." Among the ancients who have confessed or hinted that they had been initiated into the Mysteries, we may list the names of Aristides the orator, Menippus of Babylon, Sophocles the playwright, Æschylus the poet, Solon the law-giver, Cicero, Heraclitus of Ephesus, Pindar and Pythagoras.

Even to-day, in the advanced degrees of the discipline of Ju-jitsu, in Japan, degrees which are known only to a rare few because they deal with secrets which are fit only for a few, the pupil is taken through a course of the spiritual Mysteries. He is compelled to go through a ceremony of initiation which requires that he be strangled by a master. The actual deed of strangulation takes only a minute to perform; after which the candidate lies upon a couch, in effect dead. During this condition his spirit is freed from his body and receives an experience of other regions beyond our own. Then, when the allotted period of death is over, his master revives him by means of a mysterious practice whose untranslatable name is called "kwappo". He who emerges from this marvellous experience, henceforth become an initiate. Even to-day Freemasonry carries a remnant and relic of these institutions; in Egypt lies its root. Members of the Craft refer to Pythagoras as an example of ancient initiation; do they remember that he was initiated in Egypt? Those who framed the degrees of Masonry adopted some of the significant symbols of the Egyptian Mysteries.

That the inevitable degeneration of mankind brought about the disappearance or withdrawal of true hierophants, and their substitution by unillumined men, thus causing the degradation of the Mysteries into baneful caricatures of their former selves; that evil men who sought the powers of black magic ultimately conquered these institutions in Egypt and elsewhere; that what were originally sacred, exclusive and devoted to keeping alight a flame of spiritual knowledge, pure institutions, became offensive and degraded instruments of corrupt powers; these things are historical and they led to the merited disappearance of antiquity's brightest jewels.

Yet if their secrets have perished with them, the wisdom which in their brighter days they bestowed upon men is evidenced by the illustrious list of names of men who sought and found, or were proffered and accepted, the sublime experience of such initiation.

Many a papyrus text and wall-inscription proves how intensely the early Egyptians revered the Osirian rite, and shows with what awe the masses regarded those who were permitted to penetrate the secluded shrines and dedicated crypts where the most sacred and innermost phases of that rite were performed. For there existed an exalted and final degree of initiation where the souls of men were not merely freed temporarily from their bodies in a condition of simulated death, in order to prove the truth of survival, after the great change, but where they were actually carried up to the loftiest spheres of being, to the realm of the Creator Himself. In this marvellous experience the finite mind of man was drawn into contact with the infinite mind of his superior divinity. He was able for a brief while to enter into silent, spell-bound communion with the Father of All, and this fleeting contact of incomparable ecstasy was enough to change his entire attitude towards life. He had partaken of the holiest food that exists in life. He had discovered the ineffable ray of Deity which was his true innermost self, and of which the soul-body which survives death was merely the intangible vesture. He was, in verity and fact, born again in the highest sense. He who had thus been initiated became a perfect Adept, and the hieroglyphic texts speak of him as one who could expect the favour of the gods during life and the state of paradise after death.

Such an experience came with an entrancement which, although outwardly similar, was inwardly completely different from the hypnotic entrancements of the earlier degrees of initiation. No hypnotic power could ever confer it, no magical ceremony could ever evoke it. Only the supreme hierophants, themselves at one with their divinities, their wills blent with his, could by their astonishing divine force arouse the candidate to consciousness of his superior nature. This was the noblest and most impressive revelation then possible to Egyptian man, and still possible, albeit through other ways, to modern man.

§

The experience of initiation was a miniature duplicate of the experience which was destined to become that of the whole human race, through the processes of evolution—the sole difference being that, as the former was a forced hurried growth, an artificial process like entrancement was employed, whereas with the latter both psychic and spiritual development would proceed naturally.

Thus the experience repictured within the soul the entire drama of human evolution, the ineluctable fate of human beings.

The principle which lay at the back of it was that a man's normal worldly nature could be temporarily paralysed by a profound lethargic sleep, and his usually unnoticed psychic or spiritual nature awakened by processes known only to the hierophant. A man who was artificially plunged into such a coma would seem to an observer as one really physically dead; in fact, in the symbolical language of the Mysteries, he would be said to have "descended into the tomb" or to be "buried in the tomb." Thus deprived of his bodily vitality, and with the force of his personal passions and desires temporarily lulled, the candidate would truly be dead to all earthly things, while his consciousness, his soul-being, would temporarily separate itself from the flesh. Only in such a state was it possible for a man to perceive the spirit-world as it was perceived by the spirits themselves, to see visions of the gods and angels, to be taken through infinite space, to know his innermost self and, ultimately, to know the *true* God.

Such a man could justly say that he had been dead and resurrected, that he had both symbolically and literally slept in the tomb and passed through the miracle of resuscitation, awakening to discover a new understanding of the significance of death and to bear a diviner life within his breast. The imprint of his hierophant, who had brought all this about, was upon him and, ever after, the two would be invisibly connected by the closest, deepest tie. The doctrine of the immortality of the soul was more than a mere doctrine now; it was a proved fact, which had been completely demonstrated to him. When he awakened to the light of day, the initiate could truly say of himself that he had returned to the world completely transformed and spiritually reborn. He had passed through hell and heaven, and knew some of the secrets of both. If he was pledged to maintain those secrets inviolate, he was also pledged to live henceforth and to conduct himself on a basis of the real existence of those worlds. He moved among men with absolute certitude of immortality, and although he kept the sources of that certitude to himself, he could not help, even unconsciously, communicating some faith in that certitude to his fellow beings. He renewed their hopes and confirmed their faith by the mysterious subconscious telepathy which always passes between men. He no longer believed in death; he believed only in Life—eternal, self-existent, ever-conscious Life. He believed what his hierophant had unveiled to him in the guarded recesses of the temple—that the soul existed, and that it was a ray from the central sun, God, for him. The story of Osiris had acquired a personal meaning. In finding himself reborn he also found Osiris, who was existent within him as his own undying self.

This was the true teaching of Egypt's oldest sacred text, *The Book of the Dead*, which, however, in its present known form is a mixture of papyri referring both to the dead and the seemingly dead—the initiated—and is hence somewhat confusing. That it belonged, in its earliest, original and untampered form, to the Mysteries, is evidenced partly by the passage: "This is a book of exceeding great mystery. Let not the eye of any (profane) man see it—that were an abomination. Conceal its existence. 'The Book of the Master of the Hidden Temple' is its name."

Hence, in *The Book of the Dead,* the deceased person (really the initiate) repeatedly prefaced his own name with the name of Osiris. In the earliest versions of that ancient text, the deceased says of himself: "I am Osiris. I have come forth as thou, I live as the gods!" thereby vindicating the present interpretation of the dead Osiris really being the seemingly dead entranced initiate.

Thus the triumphant initiate, in the picturesquely vignetted papyrus of Nu, further exclaims:

"I, even I, am Osiris. I have become glorious. I have sat in the birth chamber of Osiris, and I was born with him, and I renew my youth along with him. I have opened the mouth of the gods. I sit upon the place where he sitteth."

And, in other papyri of this ancient *Book*:

"I raise myself to venerated God, the Master of the Great House."

Such was the instruction received in the Mysteries, an institution so celebrated in antiquity, so disregarded in modernity.

¶

We may understand, therefore, the real purport of ancient religions when we understand that their heroes also typify the human soul, and that their adventures typify the experiences of that soul in its quest of the heavenly kingdom.

Osiris thus becomes a figure of the divine element in man, and a symbolic history of that element—its descent into material worlds and its re-ascent towards spiritual consciousness.

His fabled dismemberment into fourteen or forty-two pieces symbolized the present spiritual dismemberment of the human being into a creature whose one-time harmony has been broken up.   His reason has been wrenched apart from his feelings, his flesh from his spirit, and confusion and cross-purposes pull him hither and thither.   So, too, the story of Isis collecting the fragments of the body of Osiris and restoring them to life, symbolized the restoration—in the Mysteries then, and by evolution later—of man's warring nature to perfect harmony: such harmony as where spirit and body work with one accord, and reason parallels the direction of feeling.   It was the return to primal unity.

The highest doctrine of the Egyptians, that which was the theoretical basis of the loftiest degrees of initiation, was that the soul of man must eventually return to the divine Being from which it was first rayed out, and they termed this return "becoming Osiris."   They held man even here on earth to be potentially an Osiris.   In their secret manual of initiation, the *Book of the Dead,* the released soul of the candidate is directed to protect itself, in its long and dangerous travels through the underworld, not only by the use of amulets, but by boldly proclaiming, "I am Osiris."

"O blind soul! Arm thyself with the torch of the Mysteries and in the earthly night, thou shalt discover thy luminous Double, thy celestial Self.   Follow this divine guide and he will be thy Genius.   For he holds the key to thy existence, past and future," says the same sacred Scripture.

Initiation, therefore, was to enter into a new vision of life, a spiritual vision which the human race lost in the far past when it fell from "paradise" into matter.   The Mysteries were a means of interior re-ascent, leading grade by grade to a perfect state of illumination.   They unveiled, at first, those mysterious worlds which lie beyond the threshold of physical matter, and then they unveiled the greatest mystery of all—man's own divinity. They showed the candidate infernal worlds to test his character and determination, as well as to instruct him; and afterwards unfolded to him heavenly worlds to encourage and bless him. And if they made use of the process of entrancement, this is not to say that no other way existed or exists. It was their way; but the kingdom can be found by other ways, and even without the use of trance.

Which of us can echo the noble words of the Roman philosopher-initiate who said: "Where we are, death is not; where death is, we are not. It is the last, best boon of nature; for it frees man from all his cares. It is, at the worst, the close of a banquet we have enjoyed."

Our attitude towards death provides also a significant hint as to our attitude towards life. The Mysteries changed a man's attitude towards death and consequently altered his conduct of life. They demonstrated that Death is but the obverse of the Coin of Life.

Scientific, psychical and psychological research is changing the Western world's attitude towards matters which were once dismissed as fanciful nonsense. Such research is lifting the ideas of the ancients out of the undeserved contempt in which they have lain while younger notions sprang to lusty manhood. We are beginning to detect sanity in the apparent insanity of the ancients. We are beginning to discover that their knowledge of the powers and properties of the human mind was in some directions superior to ours. The apparition of immaterial forces has startled our agnostic age. Our best scientists and foremost thinkers are joining the ranks of those who believe there is a psychic basis to life. What they think to-day, the masses will think to-morrow. We have begun—and perhaps rightly—as complete sceptics; we shall end as complete believers: such is my positive prediction. We shall rescue belief in the soul from the cold air of modern doubt. The first great message of the ancient Mysteries—"*There is no death,*" although always susceptible of personal experiential proof by a mere few, is destined to be broadcast to the whole world.

The idea of survival does not necessarily imply that we shall all scramble out of our coffins at some uncertain future date. To confuse ourselves with the fleshly houses wherein we reside is hardly creditable to our intelligence. The word resurrection has so often carried a false, purely material connotation, both in the medieval European and the uninitiate Egyptian mind, that we have to rediscover the laws that govern the secret constitution of man. The best minds among the ancients— the initiates of the Mysteries—were well versed in those laws, but, whereas their lips were sealed and their truths kept in the gloom of temple crypts, no such inhibition is expressly laid upon us to-day.

Such were the Mysteries, the most glorious of the vanished institutions of antiquity. For a day arrived, in the degradation and fall of Egypt—as in the degradation and fall of all the other ancient nations—when the prediction of her own early Prophet Hermes came literally true:

> *"O Egypt, Egypt! the land which was the seat of divinity shall be deprived of the presence of the gods. There shall not remain more of thy religion than tales, than words inscribed on stone and telling of thy lost piety. A day will come, alas, when the sacred hieroglyphs will become but idols. The world will mistake the symbols of wisdom for gods and accuse great Egypt of having worshipped hell-monsters."*

A day did come when control of the Mysteries began to fall into the wrong hands; into the hands of evil, selfish men, ambitious to misuse the influence of this mighty institution— before whom proud Pharaohs sometimes bent—for their own personal ends. Many priests became focuses for virulent evil, practising the appalling rites and dark incantations of black magic; while even some High Priests—the presumed ministers of the gods to man—became devils in human form, evoking the most awful presences from the underworld for the worst of reasons. Sorcery replaced spirituality in the high places. Amid the spiritual gloom and chaos which fell upon the land, the Mysteries soon lost their true character and high purpose. Worthy candidates became hard to find—fewer and fewer in number with the passing of time. An hour arrived when the qualified hierophants, as by some strange Nemesis, began to die off quickly and all but ceased as a body to exist. They passed without preparing a sufficient number of successors to continue their line. Unworthy men took their places. Unable properly to fulfil their allotted part in the world, the few who remained suffered their ordained fate. Preparing for the end, they sadly but calmly closed their secret books, abandoned their underground crypts and temple chambers, took a last regretful look at their ancient abodes, and departed.

They went calmly, I wrote. For far-off on the horizon of Egypt's destiny, they had sighted Nature's inevitable preparation for a reaction. They had seen a wisp of light that was destined to penetrate their country's sky and spread itself widely for a time. They had seen the star of the Christ—he who would throw the basic truth of the Mystery teaching open to the whole world, without reserve and without seclusion.

"The Mystery which hath been hidden from ages and generations," as one of Christ's Apostles declared, would be revealed to the unprivileged masses and the common folk. But what the antique institutions communicated to the elect few by a difficult process, would be communicated to all the people by the simple power of faith. Jesus had too much love in his heart to provide for a few alone, he wanted to save the many. He showed them a way which required nothing more than sufficient faith in his words; he offered them no mysterious occult process of initiation. Yet it was a way which could give those who accepted it as great a certitude of immortality as could the Mysteries.

For the Open Path of Jesus taught humility and invoked the help of a higher Power, a Power ever ready to confer complete certitude merely by bestowing Its presence upon the hearts of those who allowed Its entry. Trust in his teachings, coupled with sufficient humility to forgo the usurpation of the intellect, was all that Jesus demanded. He proffered in return the amplest of rewards—the conscious presence of the Father. In that presence, as he knew, all doubts would melt away and man himself would grasp the truth of immortality without having to undergo the experience of entrancement. Man would know this because the Father's Mind would have suffused his own intellect, and in that ineffable suffusion simple faith would be transformed into divine intuition.

¶

So the heavy doors of the Egyptian Mysteries were closed for the last time, and never again did the feet of hopeful candidates pass up the sacred step that led towards the temple entrance, or down the sloping tunnel to the temple crypt. But history moves in cycles, that which has been shall be again;

M

gloom and chaos are once more upon us, while the innate urge of man to re-establish communication with the higher worlds troubles him anew. Wherefore it is the writer's hope that conditions may be found, circumstances may be propitious, and the right persons forthcoming to plant a *modern* version, entirely altered to suit our changed epoch, of those Mysteries once more in each of the five continents of our world.

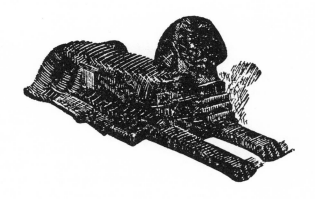

# CHAPTER XIII

**B**EFORE I left the small Mystery chapel which rested on the roof of the temple of Denderah, I turned my attention to a remarkable astronomical zodiac which had been carved into the ceiling. I knew that it was but a copy and that the original had been cut out and carried off to Paris more than a century ago, but it was an absolutely faithful copy.

The great round figure was closely packed with effigies—animal, human and divine—set within a globe and encircled by the twelve well-known signs of the zodiac. And, to complete this wondrous symbolism, the forms of twelve different gods and goddesses, some standing and others kneeling, were distributed around the globe with their upraised arms, and flattened palms ceaselessly assisting it to revolve. Thus the whole universe with its unending movement was faithfully, if emblematically, represented by this graphic piece of carving, a memorial of the round worlds which move so rhythmically through our sky, and which must leave the most sceptical of sensitive minds with a sense of wonder at the sublime Intelligence who patterned this universe.

If the Denderah zodiac is to be interpreted correctly, it must be read as a description of the heavens during a certain epoch of the past; what was that epoch is another matter. This is not the place to enter into abstruse and unfamiliar astronomical explanations. Suffice it, that the arrangement of constellations shown does not coincide with the arrangement we see in the sky to-day.

The marked position of the spring equinox upon the zodiac of the temple of Denderah differs from its present-day position in the sky, involving the sun's entrance into a constellation of the stars bearing another name.

How did this wide change arise? The reply is that because

of the motion of the earth, the axis of our globe points succes-
sively at different Pole Stars. That really means that our own
sun travels around a parent sun. This almost imperceptible
backward movement of the Equinox—so vast in number of
years and so slow in actual motion—also changes the positions
of the rising and setting of certain stars in relation to certain
constellations. We know, by means of the measured average
motion of those stars, how many tens of thousands of years
have elapsed since their first position. This interval of time is
called the Great Precession, or else "the precession of the
equinoxes." For the intersection of the equator with the
ecliptic, marking the spring equinox, is slowly displaced in
the heavens owing to this precession.

Put in another way, it means that the stars are slipping back
in an opposite direction to the order of the twelve signs of the
zodiac, a minute fraction of space each year. This grand movement of the heavens, this slow shifting of our universe, forms
a cosmic clock with the entire sky as its dial, from which
we may read backwards and forwards and by which we may
note the revolutions of the globes for thousands of years.

By an examination of an ancient map of the heavens it is
possible for an astronomer to deduce the period when the map
was made. Those who probe the distant past can sometimes
find clues of immense importance in such a map. When the
learned men whom Napoleon brought with him to Egypt
discovered this zodiac at Denderah, they became enthusiastic
over it, believing that it would provide them with a key to the
age of Egypt's civilization. For the Denderah zodiac placed
the spring equinox far from its present position. When, much
later, it was discovered that the temple had only been built in
Græco-Roman times and that the zodiac had been mingled
with a Greek one, the whole thing was thrust aside and henceforth ignored.

The suggestion that this zodiac is entirely Greek is erroneous.
Is it thought that the Egyptians, therefore, had no zodiac, of
their own? Did the priesthood study astrology and astronomy
for countless years without having a zodiac, before the first
Greek boat touched the long line of Egypt's low sandy shore,
a map of the twelve constellations of the sky, to guide them?
How did this priesthood, which venerated astrology so much
as to make it a part of their religion, practise their system without
a zodiac? No, if there was any branch of knowledge upon

which those priests prided themselves, it was the astronomical one.

The explanation is that the Egyptians copied part of their zodiac from one which had previously existed at Denderah, whose temple had been built and rebuilt more than twice. A unique astronomical record of this character would have been copied and recopied to ensure its preservation. And this was done with other ancient records, too, which were first slowly forgotten and later disappeared with the disappearance of the record-keepers, i.e. the ancient priesthood.

Archæologists working in Mesopotamia have dug up ancient Chaldean brick tablets upon which the astronomers of Chaldea had noted that spring began when the sun entered the constellation of the Bull. As, during the Christian era, at least, spring begins when the sun enters Aries, i.e. about March 21st, the implication is that such a tremendous change of climate, dates the Chaldean civilization as one of immense antiquity, an antiquity which the Chaldeans themselves claimed. Similarly, by its markings of the position of the equinox, the Denderah zodiac points to some epoch of antiquity which stretches back, not by centuries, but by hundreds of centuries! It thus dates early Egypt's civilization. For the position indicates that more than three and a half "Great Years" have been passed on the cosmic dial; that the sun has revolved around its parent sun no less than three and a half times.

As careful checking of astronomical statistics has ascertained that the average rate of the precession of the equinoxes is about 50.2 seconds per year, we can calculate backwards and work our way around the whole circle of the heavens until we reach the point indicated by the Denderah zodiac position. There are 360 degrees in the grand circle of the zodiac and at the rate of precession 25,800 solar years would make one "Great Year."

Each complete revolution, therefore, takes no less than 25,800 years, and short calculation reveals that at least 90,000 years have passed since the date marked on the zodiac of the temple of Denderah.

Ninety thousand years! Is such a figure really incredible, really impossible? The Egyptian priest-astronomers did not think so; for Herodotus, the Greek historian, tells us that they informed him that their people considered their race to be the most ancient of mankind, and that they had kept in their sacred colleges and temples their own records extending back to 12,000 years before the time of his visit.  Herodotus, we know, was unusually careful of his facts, and rightly earned the title of "the Father of History."  And they had further told him that "the sun had twice risen where he now sets and twice set where he now rises."  The implication of this extraordinary statement is that the poles of our earth had completely changed over from their former positions, involving immense shifts of land and water.  Such shifts we know, from geological research, really have occurred; but their dates carry us back to periods tremendously distant.

One result of these changes would be that the climate at the poles had formerly been tropical, instead of arctic.  There is no dispute to-day, for instance, that the whole of Northern Europe, including the British Isles, was once covered with an immense sea of ice many hundreds of feet in thickness which filled up all the valleys, and from which only the peaks of mountains and lofty hills emerged.  Such a condition of the planet could only have been caused by gigantic astronomical changes.  The statement of the Egyptian priests is, therefore, vindicated.

Now they possessed no science of geology as we know it to-day; they possessed only their ancient records, carved on stone obelisks, inscribed on clay tablets, cut into metal plates, or written with a reed on papyri.  There was also a traditional secret doctrine and history which was communicated only in the Mysteries, and then verbally, thus being handed down from mouth to ear for uncounted centuries.

How could the priests, unacquainted with geology, know of such convulsive planetary changes except from these records which they possessed?  This knowledge vindicates their claim to the existence of such records; it likewise accounts for the existence of original zodiacs from which that at the temple of Dendarah was partly copied.

Ninety thousand years does not stand out as an impossible figure in the light of these facts.  It does not mean that Egyptian culture necessarily existed on Egyptian soil at that time: the people and their culture may have existed upon some other continent and only later migrated to Africa—that is a point outside the scope of my present argument—but why should we be afraid to yield to the fact that they did exist?

Our histories of Egypt begin with the first dynasty, but we must remember that the country had been peopled for a long time prior to the first records we have. The history of that earliest race of Egyptians and the names of their kings, are unknown—to Egyptologists. The early history of Egypt is bound up with the last history of Atlantis. The Egyptian priests, who were also the astronomers, derived their zodiac from Atlantis. That is why the zodiac of Denderah can display the passage of vaster revolutions of the stars than the zodiacs of our historic era can yet display.

We greet each newly discovered vestige of that early civilization with exclamations of surprise. At a time when, according to modern ideas of "progress," we might reasonably expect these people to be crude, primitive and barbarous, we find them to be cultured, refined and religious.

We commonly take it for granted that the farther we go backwards in our enquiry into the past history of the human race, the nearer we approach to a condition of savagery. The truth is, that even in some of the remote prehistoric periods we find both savages and civilized cultured men existing coevally upon this planet; that science, which has already sketched out an age of the world that stupefies man's limited imagination, has not yet collected sufficient data with which to sketch out an accurate picture of prehistoric ages and of the life of man during those ages. But it is moving forward and one day it will obtain that picture. Let us not, therefore, too hastily deny the Egyptian priests their temple records of 90,000 years, and grudgingly grant them five or six thousand years at most, as so many do. For the age of our planet offers a constant and silent rebuke to men who think so meanly of our ancestry, whilst the age of the universe should shame them into acceptance rather than denial. For out in the infinite depths of the sky there exist strange cemeteries of the heavens where dead stars and cold globes, which once bore all the pomp and pageantry of bygone civilizations, now approach the grim hour of their final dissolution.

¶

I walked out upon the roof once more and stood behind the low parapet which crested the walls. An unbroken panorama of cultivated fields opened out around the temple and then disappeared into shining, curved desert sand-drifts. Peasants were stooping to their little patches of ground busy with their immemorial work, in the manner and with the tools of their forefathers of Biblical times. Their oxen ploddingly and patiently turned the selfsame creaking water-wheel that the oxen of their forefathers had turned. Their camels snarlingly bore the same great loads that had towered upon the backs of beasts of burden in Pharaonic times. They had scratched and turned the rich soil of this narrow strip of land that is Egypt for countless times, yet they had never exhausted and never could exhaust its astonishing, prolific fertility. Harvests grew and were gathered in these peaceful emerald plains, these opulent flat fields of Nile mud, with an ease hardly to be matched in any other country of the world. Unfailingly there came every year that welcome benediction of the Nile's rise, when the much-travelled waters changed as by magic from blue to brown and steadily lapped their way upwards, depositing the priceless gift of freshly vitalized mud over the baked lands. Yes, the old Nile was as a mother to its fortunate children who lived along its banks, and who somewhat pathetically trusted their aged parent to nourish them with her milk.

I gazed in the river's direction. The Nile! What magic lies in that name? Twice every day the priests of Egypt had to bathe their bodies in its waters in order to preserve their purity, and twice every night. In India the Brahmin priests do the same thing to-day, for the same purpose; save that they pour the waters of the Ganges or Godivari over themselves, and save that they do not disturb their nights. Both Egyptians and Indians had the same theory—that man picks up an invisible personal magnetism from his contact and intercourse with other persons, and that frequent washings were necessary to get rid of these acquired influences, which might so often be undesirable, if not worse.

But the Nile is more than a great ribbon of water; more than a river that stretches down half a continent: it is a living entity, an intelligent creature, which has taken up the burden of feeding millions of men, women and children, beasts and birds, alike. For countless centuries it has deposited strip after strip of mud upon the fields, making Egypt the paradox of our planet. It is the only country I know whose fields are so fertile, yet in no other land have I seen so little rain. Such is the magic action of this friendly stream, which has turned a strip of desert lying between two parallel lines of tawny heights into profitable, prolific soil. There, in the fields below this temple roof, the peasants were guiding the muddy irrigating water into narrow trenches that crossed and criss-crossed their fields.   The water was hauled and thrown from the river bank by a series of water-lifts and hundreds of channels.   I listened to a loin-clothed man, who bent over his water-lift, as Pharaoh's loin-clothed peasants had bent over the same kind of apparatus, singing in rhythm with every motion of the creaking wooden machine, which raised and poured water from a bucket most monotonously.   It was nothing more than a long, flexible pole poised on a horizontal prop and fitted with a heavy balancing weight at its lower end.   The bucket was attached by a rope to the other end.   A downward pull at the rope and the bucket sank in the water; a release and it rose, replenished, to deposit the water into a trench.   This ancient invention had proved its worth for the peasant of five thousand years ago; to-day it was proving its worth for the peasant of the twentieth century.

I crossed to the other side of the terrace and looked out upon another portion of this scene which had met the eyes of vanished priests and dead Pharaohs.

The Libyan hills rose suddenly out of the west—pink fortress walls behind the temple, affording it shelter and protection, as it were.   Here and there the sand had drifted in to form piled heaps wherever the hills had dipped or hollowed their long line. The ruddy heights seemed like vivid flames which had thrust huge tongues out of the earth and then been magically turned to stone.   Perhaps they were burning still, for a fierce heat was thrown back in my face from them as they caught the strong sun of the growing day.

Those long chains of hills stretched their way right across Egypt into distant Nubia, running parallel with the great river which Nature had set them up to guard in this mysterious fashion, placing them but a few miles away from its banks to prevent it running off into the vast desolation of the African desert, there to trickle its life away below the sands.   Was it done of set purpose, I speculated.   Without this striking arrange-ment of river and hill and source there could have been no Egypt, no land whose history receded so far into the sleeping shadows of antiquity.   And I accepted the response which came up to my thinking brain out of the profounder places of being —that the gods, whose instrument Nature was and nothing more, had certainly created this arrangement when they had prepared the way for the mighty civilization that was to rise

in fulfilment of their great purpose.   For just as every great
structure of man, just as this white temple of Denderah upon
whose roof I stood, has come into being in fulfilment of a plan
that existed within the minds of its architects, so every great
gathering of individuals into a nation was prearranged within
the minds of the gods, those divine architects, under whose
care and charge all mankind has existed and exists still.

I descended the old staircase and returned to the entrance, to
set about an examination of the interior of the main temple,
through which I had hurried in order to find the Mystery Chapel
which, above everything else, had first lured my interest.  In the
vast open vestibule, twenty-four huge white columns, whose
square capitals supported the carven but mutilated representations of the face of the goddess Hathor, and whose sides were
covered with hieroglyphs, rose to support the ponderous cornice
of the majestic portico.  Her face appeared on all four sides of
each pillar-head, and a small pylon had been inserted below the
abacus as part of her head-dress.  How sadly came the thought
that this temple, which was dedicated to Egypt's goddess of
beauty and love, to horn-head-dressed Hathor herself, should
have been so little harmed by the hand of Nature—it is perhaps
the best preserved of all the old temples to be seen to-day, and
one of the few which have remained so perfect—and so much
by the hand of man.  Almost all of those gigantic female faces
had been hacked to pieces by fanatic fury, though their long
ears and massive head-gears still remain.  For Denderah was
one of the most gorgeous temples in all Egypt of those still
used at the time the Edict of Theodosius, in A.D. 379, abolished
the ancient worship and gave the final death-blow to the already
dying religion.

His envoy, Cynegius, carried out his orders to the full.   He
shut up all the temples and places of initiation, and prohibited
any celebration of the Mysteries and ancient rites.  Christianity,
or rather the Church, had finally triumphed.  Then the intolerant
mobs swarmed into Denderah; drove away the priests and
trampled on the appurtenances of their rituals.  They overthrew
Hathor's statues, despoiled her gilded shrines and mutilated the
most prominent features of her carved face wherever it could
be conveniently reached.

In other places they did far worse, for they broke down the
walls, demolished the columns, shattered the statued giants, and
undid the work of thousands of years.  Such are the varying

fortunes of creeds, whose followers begin by suffering the horrors of martyrdom and persecution, and end by inflicting them upon others in their turn, and who must ravage the art of their predecessors in order to create an art of their own.

Proud, crowned Ptolemies once drove up to this temple in golden chariots, before a populace hushed with awe; so I reflected as I was about to enter. Crowds, too, once congregated in the deserted temple yard.

I placed myself at a point among the immensely girthed columns of the portico, where I could look up and inspect the beautiful blue ceiling which was spangled with many stars and bore the zodiacal circle as an adornment. Then across into the second hall, where the glorious African blue no longer illumined the six colossal columns that stood within it, as it had illumined their more numerous brothers in the vestibule. I penetrated farther into the vast, gloomy temple, flashing the light of my torch here and there. Now the beam was focused upon mitred figures cut deep into the sides of pillars and set within square frames or profuse hieroglyphic inscriptions, else separated by broad horizontal bands from each other; then it showed up the forms of Pharaohs and their deities on the walls, some on their thrones and some in procession. In a deeply carved relief, Ptolemy approached Isis and the young Horus, with offerings in both hands: a beautiful raised border surmounted the scene. Everywhere the faces had been scratched, partly erased or wholly mutilated. And everywhere Hathor recurs, the solid shafts of the stone pillars displaying her head, and the walls her entire form.

I sauntered slowly on, for the whole length of the principal hall—a good deal more than two hundred feet—in an atmosphere that was somewhat unpropitious to study and reflection. For dust loaded the century-imprisoned air and a heavy odour assailed one's nostrils. High up in the blackened roof, and among the pillar heads, whirred and squeaked a legion of ugly winged monsters, which were furious at my unexpected entry at a season of the year when tourists never invaded their domain. They were bats. "Intruder!" they shrieked in chorus. "Intruder! This is not the time to travel through Egypt. Take away that offensive lamp of yours, with its strong and horrifying glare; take yourself away, too. Leave us to enjoy our ancestral perches and traditional trysting-places among the gloomy Hathor-heads and black-surfaced cornices. Be off

with you!" But I stuck to my ground and dallied over my
task, examining closely the elaborate paintings, of huge scarab-
beetles and winged suns, faintly discernible amid the grime that
had gathered over the vast ceiling.    The bats behaved like
creatures suddenly demented, scurrying to and fro as though
they were in Bedlam, and wheezily voicing their annoyance
with me.    When at last I turned aside and descended through
a narrow corridor into the region beneath the building, I
heard them slowly relapse into subdued activity and saner
conduct.

If the great hall was a melancholy though interesting place,
the underground crypts in which I presently found myself were
still more melancholy.    These dark chambers were built into
the tremendously thick foundation walls and they, too, were
profusely decorated with carved half-reliefs that pictured the
grave rites which once were celebrated within these walls.

I left these tomb-like chambers and returned to the magnificent
portico.    Stout doors, sheathed in glittering gold, formerly
filled this doorway.    I began to wander around the outside of
the temple.

It was hard to believe that when it was rediscovered by
Abbas Pasha, in the middle of last century, most of this temple
lay under a hill of sand and debris, as in a grave; its glories
awaiting rescue by the excavator's pick and spade.    How
many peasants must have walked over it, little knowing and
little caring that the Past lay under their feet.

I paused to study, on the outside back wall, the famous relief
representation of Cleopatra, who had spent her money freely to
restore the place when parts of it were beginning to fall into
disrepair during her lifetime, and was rewarded by having this
wall-relief carved in her honour.    Her little son, Cæsarion,
stood beside her in the picture, his face curiously reminiscent
of that of his great father, Julius Cæsar.    His mother's face,
however, did not appear to me to be a true portrait, and the old
Egyptian coins show a better likeness.    She was the last of the
long line of Egyptian queens, this famous daughter of Ptolemy,
and when Julius Cæsar brought his invading legions across the
Mediterranean she lived with him as his mistress almost from
the day he arrived.    How curious, I pondered, that this woman
linked Egypt through Cæsar with a distant little island which
was to play so powerful a part in Egypt's own history more than
eighteen hundred years after.    How curious, too, that these

Roman soldiers brought to Britain among their cults the Egyptian-derived worship of Serapis and thus established a further, if indirect, contact between the two countries, so long ago.

On this carven wall she appeared fittingly wearing the horned disk headgear of Hathor, below which a falling mass of plaited hair was displayed. The face depicted was fat and chubby and that of a masterly woman, one accustomed to exercise a strong will and one who would by fair means or foul achieve her designs. It was her influence that had caused Julius Cæsar to play with the dream of making Alexandria the capital city of his Empire and the centre of the world. Here she was, definitely Semitic looking, with a prototype among any Jewish, Arab or Assyrian tribe; but hardly Græco-Egyptian. With her perished the native rule, I reflected, while I sat upon a splintered stone beam, as well as one of the acknowledged beauties of the ancient world, a woman who played a notable part in history. It was a startling thought that a great man's destiny—and that of a whole nation—will sometimes hang on the smile of a woman's lips.

The fronts of the temple walls were carved to the cornice with half-reliefs, and richly covered with hieroglyph inscriptions chiselled into the surface. The balanced and beautiful lines of mingled alphabetic and pictorial characters were an adornment in themselves. They pointed to the fact that in old Egypt, just as in old China and old Babylonia, the man who would learn to write must also learn to draw, and so every educated scribe and priest in that country was, to some extent, an artist also. To convey a thought of some object by means of a picture of it, was the natural outcome of primitive man's earliest attempts at writing. But the Egyptians did not start as crude savages, gradually to find their way to an elementary culture. Legend attributes the invention of the complete hieroglyphic script to the god Thoth, and thus enshrines in popular form a historic truth. For it was a man-god, an Adept, named Thoth (strictly Tehuti), who bestowed this sytem of writing, as a complete revelation to the Atlantean-descended emigrants of the colony on the Nile banks, in the days before the last flood washed away the last island of Atlantis. Thoth was the author of the *Book of the Dead*. He is partly pictured in his own system under the hieroglyph of the Ibis—that queer bird, with stilt-like legs and long beak.

The studies of comparative philology are increasingly proving that the different languages developed out of certain basic root-tongues, and that these in turn have developed out of one common, primeval, universal language. When these languages are one day tracked down to their primitive glyphs, the ultimate source will, I venture to predict, be found to have arisen in Atlantean days.

It was said by the ancients that hieroglyphs "speak, signify and hide." This meant that they possessed a threefold meaning. There was first of all their simple, ordinary phonetic value, necessary for speaking the language: beyond this value the common man was unable to go. Secondly, there was the further meaning which hieroglyphs carried to the scribe; the written meaning, or the symbolical expression in grammatical form on papyri and stone of the illiterate man's spoken words. Finally there was the esoteric meaning, the one known only to the initiated priests and kept secret by them.

"The Words of God"—such was the description or name given to the system of hieroglyphs by the Egyptians; not only because the system was believed to have been revealed to them by one of the gods, but also because the secret meaning of these strange characters was concealed from the masses. That meaning was revealed to those alone who had been initiated into the Mysteries. And no Egyptologist of to-day has done more than translate the popular meaning of hieroglyphs, although in so doing, he has done magnificently; the rest is beyond him. For "the Words of God" demand to be brought to them a spiritual and reverent consideration before they yield their innermost secret. The same applies to a comprehension of the secrets which were revealed in the initiation chamber of the Egyptian Mysteries.

Plotinus, an initiate who lived in ancient Alexandria, hinted at the symbolical nature of hieroglyphs when he wrote:

"In the rigorous quest of truth or in the exposition which they made freely to their disciples, Egyptian sages did not use written signs (which are but imitations of voice and speech) in their temples, but they drew figures and revealed the thought contained by the form of those images, in a way that each image enclosed a portion of knowledge and wisdom. It is the crystallization of a truth. Afterwards the master or pupil extracted the contents of the image, analysed it in words and found the reason why it was thus and not otherwise."

The fact is that the Egyptians, like other nations of the earliest Eastern lands, never dreamt of separating religion and secular life into watertight compartments, and therefore never dreamt of using language, writing and speech merely as a vehicle of communication. Just as they thought that names had magical powers, so they symbolized in their hieroglyphic alphabet the principles of that mysterious knowledge which was imparted behind the closed doors of the Mysteries.

He alone who had been led into the presence of the divine Osiris, the conqueror of "death," who made men and women "to be born again" (as the *Book of the Dead* designated the aim of the high grades of initiation) could explain and expound the final significance of hieroglyphs—the most perfect system of literary symbolism in the world.

Herodotus, too, himself an initiate, somewhere confirms, I believe, that hieroglyphs were entirely sacred and symbolical in their hidden meaning, and that this latter was known only to the highest degree of the order of priesthood. While Iamblichus, another ancient initiate, has written that the secret hieroglyphic language was used by the gods themselves.

I shall throw out a hint, in the form of a question, as to the principle involved in the secret meaning of hieroglyphs.

In hieroglyphs the sitting figure classifies the person as among the gods: therefore it is usually shown as part of the written name of Egyptian deities, and is displayed among the hieroglyphs written over their sketched portraits. Now, why did the Egyptians adopt a *sitting* figure and not a standing one?

Rather than risk the scorn of academic Professors of Egyptology, who would be perfectly justified in casting contempt upon a free-lance's intrusion into their sacred precinct, beyond proffering this hint, I shall leave the reader to supply his own answer.

The work of the great Egyptologists—within its own field —deserves every praise. But for them—and destiny—the inscriptional treasures which lie upon temple walls and papyrus texts would never have been translated.

The part which destiny played in this discovery is striking. Had Napoleon never invaded Egypt those walls and texts might still have remained unread. Napoleon was, in a most extraordinary manner, himself a man of destiny, and he affected the fortunes of every kingdom, every man, and every subject which he touched.    He was truly an instrument of Providence, but also an instrument of Nemesis.

His invasion opened the way to an understanding of ancient Egyptian life and thought.    It is often the unconscious work of the soldier to prepare a way for the work of the scholar, the message of the spiritual teacher, or the bales of the trader and sometimes to destroy these, too—as history unquestionably points out.

At the commencement of Greek rule over Egypt, the old tongue began to be cast aside.    The new rulers naturally tried to make Greek learning and language dominant among the educated classes.    The important Government posts were given only to those Egyptians who had mastered Greek, for instance. The ancient sacred college of Heliopolis, where great numbers of priests were trained, and where the knowledge of Egyptian was maintained, was suppressed and closed.    Save by a few individual priests, who obstinately and secretly clung to the traditional language, the Greek alphabet was practically adopted as the national alphabet of Egypt.

By the end of the third century after the opening of the Christian era, in the whole of Egypt no one could be found competent to explain the simple everyday meaning of a hiero-glyphic inscription, let alone capable of writing a new one.

Fifteen hundred years rolled past.    The art of interpreting hieroglyphs still remained as one utterly lost.    And then Napoleon's storm-tossed frigate stole, under the nose of Admiral Nelson, into Alexandria.

His army soon busied itself throwing up fortifications and digging itself in generally.    One of the first places where it established itself was the important strategic position of the Nile mouth, near the port of Rosetta.    Here a young artillery officer, Lieutenant Boussard, made the all-important discovery which ultimately provided a key to the interpretation of hiero-glyphs.    For the spades of his men, who were digging the foundations of Fort St. Julien, loosened the soil around a broken slab of black basalt which he had brought to light.    He at once perceived the importance of this now-famed "Rosetta stone," for it bore a trilingual inscription, a decree of the priests of Memphis conferring honours on Ptolemy V.    There were fifty-four lines of Greek engraved upon its surface, with parallel translations into two other scripts; the hieroglyphic and the demotic.

The stone was sent to Europe, where scholars set to work upon it; until, at length, they tracked down the hieroglyphic equivalent of the Greek alphabet. With this key in their hands, they were able to trace out the meanings of papyri and inscriptions which had puzzled the world for so many centuries.

# CHAPTER XIV

AT last I had entered the real Egypt, the old and
fascinating Egypt, the country where Nile, temple,
field, village and sky combined to create a vivid and
seductive impression of the land where Pharaohs
ruled in pomp, and flagstones daily echoed to the chants of many
priests. Here, at Luxor, 450 miles down the river from Cairo,
one slipped back and fitted into the Past without effort and
looked out upon a landscape which presented many of the
ancient scenes. It is the South, or Upper Egypt as the geo-
graphers have immemorially called it, that has kept more of
those scenes for modern observers.

Its classically famous capital, Thebes, Homer's "Hundred-
gated city," has vanished, but it has left us Karnak; once the
headquarters of the Egyptian priesthood.

To-day, Karnak is the pearl of this region. The fame of its
widespread mass of now ruined but still stately temples has
spread all over the world. It contains the largest temple still
to be seen in Egypt, the Great Hall of Amen-Ra, to which, in
olden days, all other temples in Egypt were tributary. So I
made Karnak my place of pilgrimage for days on end, moving
amid its mouldering ruins and broken pillars both by the bright
light of the sun and by the dimmer light of the moon.

Karnak, which stands out of a forest of green palms to the
north, lies two or three miles down the river from Luxor and
a little more inland. One approached it along a dusty road,
across a wide plain and under a sky of palest blue, past a Sheikh's
white cupola'd tomb and a grove of tamarisk trees, until a huge
sandstone pylon towered suddenly into view. Crested hoopoes
were everywhere in the fields, busily picking up sustenance
from the stubbled ground. On the way one noticed, here and
there and peeping out of the soil, odd, headless, half-shattered
or overturned members of a double row of small, ram-headed

sphinxs; which were once set up all the way from Luxor to Karnak, but now mostly lie buried in the wayside fields. Hundreds must originally have been erected on both sides of the three-mile road.

The magnificent twenty-yard-long entrance pylon made an attractive sight.

In the pylon form, with its tall, sloping sides and curved, overhanging architrave, architecture found a handsome and powerful expression. On the front was the carven relief portrait of the Ptolemy who had built it, exhibiting him in the act of making a sacrificial offering before the Theban gods; while four vertical, socket-footed grooves, which run the whole height of the mighty portal, indicated where wooden flagstaffs had once been fixed, to fly gay-coloured bunting on the days of temple festivals, and to ward off evil influences.

Passing inside, I found myself in the open court of the temple of hawk-headed Khonsu; that god who, in popular uninitiated parlance, was the son of Amen. The broken stumps of a double colonnade occupied the centre. The walls depicted a sacred procession of boats floating up the Nile to Luxor, and carrying the image of Amen-Ra. I penetrated into the ruined sanctuary where once was kept the sacred temple-boat of Khonsu. All the mummery that was practised within these walls meant much to the people, to the priests who sought power, and especially to the kings themselves. But it meant little to the initiated few who witnessed rite and ceremony as mere symbol and token, not as manifestations of reality.

And, next, I discovered a series of interesting low-reliefs, each in a separate border, upon the east wall of an inner chamber adjoining the sanctuary. The thing that caught my eye in the first place was a carving of my friend of the long-drawn winter night's meditation—the Sphinx!

I at once realized that I had alighted upon something important, because one might go for days without detecting the Sphinx upon a wall or pillar carving.

The first panel showed the Pharaoh Rameses IV in the presence of the goddess Ament, to whom he was offering a statuette. The latter had a flat base and supported two figures. In front squatted a child; none other than Horus, the son of Osiris. There was a large lock of hair on the side of his head: he was crowned with the symbolic sun and serpent; his left hand rested on his knee, but his right hand was raised to his face with its index finger pointing to his closed lips—thus enjoining silence.

The figure behind him was the Sphinx.

Ament held her right hand extended towards Rameses; she gripped a handled cross between her fingers, and pointed its end directly between the king's eyes.

What was the signification of this scene?

The Egyptologist would, no doubt, offer a perfectly connected and obvious reading, and one which, on its own level, would be correct enough. He would tell you that the king was simply engaged in making sacrifices to the gods—nothing more. Often these wall-scenes are nothing but pictured histories or recitals of war triumphs. Obviously this scene was nothing of the kind, but indicative of some extremely sacrosanct rite; particularly as it appeared upon a wall near the sanctuary, the holy of holies of this temple.

And, just as the system of Egyptian hieroglyphs was employed to signify an esoteric meaning known only to initiated priests, even though the same symbolical characters were used; so, too, the very figures under which the gods were represented carried a far profounder meaning to the initiate of ancient times. The inner teaching of this picture, therefore, can only be detected by one conversant with the doctrine and methods of the Mysteries.

The significance of this panel especially lay in the action of the goddess Ament. The handled cross, or cross with a circle on the top, which she pointed midway between Rameses' eyes, was called by initiated priests "the Key to the Mysteries" and represented admittance into the Mysteries themselves. Yet to the Egyptologist it merely represents life. As a key it symbolized the unlocking of the guarded door of that august institution, but as a geometrical pattern it symbolized the eternal spirit of the initiate rising triumphant out of his "crucified" material body. The circle, having neither visible beginning nor end, stood for the everlasting nature of godlike spirit; while the cross symbolized the death-like state of entrancement into which the initiate was thrown, and thus his death, his crucifixion. In certain temples he was actually tied to a wooden couch, which was shaped like a cross.

The point midway between the eyebrows is roughly the position of a gland in the brain—the pineal gland—by whose complicated function doctors are still puzzled. In the first stages of initiation, this gland was stimulated into certain activity by the hierophant, an activity which temporarily enabled the candidate to see psychic visions of spirit-creatures congregating for the time being in his vicinity. The method resorted to for this purpose was partly mesmeric, but partly dependent on certain powerful incenses.

When, therefore, Ament pointed her cross between the Pharaoh's eyes, she thereby indicated that he would be given admittance to the Mysteries and that his clairvoyant vision would there be temporarily unfolded. But he was prohibited from revealing to others what he saw and experienced during his initiation. This was indicated by the first figure on the statuette of the child Horus, "Horus of the horizon," really the god Hormakhu—the god traditionally associated with the Sphinx—whose finger, pointing to his closed lips, strictly admonished such secrecy. Similar images stood near the sanctuaries and Mystery-chambers of all the temples, each pressing a finger to the lips in symbolic injunction to preserve silence concerning the divine Mysteries.

Ament herself was a feminine Amen, "the hidden one."

The act of the king in holding the statuette in an attitude of offering emphasized that he was ready to make the sacrifice of his speech and to preserve continual silence.

Upon the flat base of the statuette and behind this figure of Hormakhu was couched the carven figure of the Sphinx. Why?

The Sphinx, like the entranced initiate who completely lost the power of speech during his initiation, is always silent. Throughout its long life it has never spoken an audible word to man. The Sphinx has ever known how to keep its secrets. What were those ancient secrets?

They were the secrets of initiation.

The Sphinx guarded the mightiest temple of initiation in the ancient world—the Great Pyramid.

For the ceremonial approach to the latter was always from the Nile bank, and everyone coming from the river to enter it would have to pass the Sphinx first.

The Sphinx, in its own silence, symbolized both the silence and secrecy of initiation.

Thus, the Pharaoh had been warned to expect the greatest mystic revelation which could be given to man.

Three more panels completed this interesting series of Mystery pictures, to which any tripper and tourist may have access to-day but to which, in ancient times, approach was forbidden except to a privileged few. They described the results of the king's approach to the Mysteries.

The second panel represented him standing between adult hawk-headed Horus and ibis-faced Thoth. Each god held a vase over Rameses' head, but instead of a stream of water, each poured a stream of handled crosses over and around him.

Now Thoth was the god of both wisdom and secret learning. Here he bestowed, through initiation, that mysterious blended knowledge of psychical forces and spiritual wisdom for which Egypt was so famed in early times. He was also Lord of the Moon. Hence all magical and religious ceremonies of secret importance, and especially all initiations into the Mysteries, were conducted at night, and at those phases of the moon which marked its greatest influence; that is, new and full moon.

The adult, hawk-faced Horus was the sun-god. His part of this scene was emblematical of the fact that initiation, although begun at night, terminated at day, with the arrival of dawn. When the rays of the morning sun lit up the top of the candidate's head, the hierophant addressed certain "words of power" to him, and he awoke.

The third panel revealed Rameses, now the wise initiate, being led forward by two other gods, who grasped his hands in welcome and displayed the ansated cross before his face, indicating his fellowship with them by virtue of his attainment. in the last scene the king was depicted offering a statuette to the god Amen-Ra. The statuette was a seated god with a feather stuck on its head—the god of Truth. The Pharaoh had now attained to Wisdom, would henceforth be "true of voice," would make the sacrifice of his life upon the altar of truth; that is would conform, both in his thought and act, obediently to the spiritual laws governing human life, just unveiled to him by his initiation.

Thus these chiselled pictures unfolded to me a glimpse of the secret inner life of an instructed Pharaoh, and something of the meaning of Egypt's celebrated but exclusive Mysteries.

And then I was attracted westwards to a beautiful little temple where some among these initiated few had learnt their wisdom. It was a shrine of the Osirian Mysteries, and to me perhaps one of the most important places in all Karnak itself, small though it was. There, on the entrance jambs, I saw carvings showing the Ptolemy who had erected it being taken into the presence of divine Osiris himself. Across the threshold, I found myself in an oblong portico whose coloured and much-inscribed roof was supported by two handsome, reeded and flowered columns, each of which was surmounted by Hathor's staring face. In the east wall were two small windows with stone gratings, but the dim light which infiltrated through them was no longer needed; for three large blocks had disappeared from the stone roof, and through this hole came light a-plenty.

Beyond this was a small vestibule whose walls were covered with bold bas-reliefs and vertical lines of hieroglyphs. And—a rare sight in the ruinous condition of most other temples still standing—three perfectly preserved doorways led out of the end and side walls of this tiny vestibule. Each lintel was topped by an architrave formed of a line of more than twenty stately cobras. The serpents were not mere half-reliefs chiselled into the surface of the wall, but solid sculptures; their heads were raised and their hoods outstretched. The familiar emblem of the winged sun rested on a shelf below each line, the whole forming a massive adornment nearly one yard high.

These royal cobra adornments indicated, to my mind, that the three chambers to which the doorways gave access possessed considerable importance in the temple plan. I passed through the doorway at the farther end (the doors themselves no longer exist, although the top and bottom sockets into which the posts were fitted can clearly be seen) and reached a little shrine whose sides depicted the king at worship as well as the standard of the goddess Hathor. Below this yawned a large gap in the stone flooring, which was revealed under torchlight as the broken entrance to an underground crypt. I again examined the two side chambers there and found holes in the corners, which led down to the same crypt, as well as to an underground passage. Indeed, the entire place was honeycombed with subterranean vaults and corridors; on the right of the portico, I discovered two other floor-gaps, opening above narrow passages whose dust was entirely untrodden.

Exploration revealed that one of these passages actually traversed the ground until it reached the temple of Khonsu itself.

The entire floor of the temple was so thickly covered with dust that one must infer the pile to have formed through many centuries. I examined the ancient stone floor for human tracks, but, apart from the imprint of naked feet, evidently those of the

Arab watchman from the nearby temple of Khonsu, I could discover no sign of the tread of shoes. All over the floor the dust lay thickly heaped and the only other disturbances in its surface were the numerous graceful patterns threaded from one hole to another by one or two tiny snakes, whose tracks were clearly visible. I speculated how long it was since tourist or traveller had disturbed the solitary silence of this shrine. I knew that one guide-book dismissed this temple with the comment that it was hardly worth a visit. I knew, too, that no visitors were welcomed or expected, for the Government Department of Antiquities had fitted a locked wooden gate across the entrance. I had been unable to obtain entrance before getting the Arab custodian of the main temple to produce a key from his bunch, to accompany me to this little shrine of Osiris and unlock this gate. Why? Was it because of these dangerous gaps in the floor?

What was the meaning of these mysterious crypts and melancholy corridors? I remembered the curious, moat-bordered crypt, dug out of forty feet of debris, which had puzzled me at Abydos.

¶

As I pondered upon the point, the tomb-like place seemed to light up before my eyes, and I saw anew the celebration of the ancient rite which dramatized the death and resurrection of Osiris—that rite which I had observed carved in stone on the walls of the little Mystery Temple that stood upon the roof-terrace of Denderah—that rite which I had seen in vision, and experienced in person, during the night I spent in the gloomy King's Chamber of the Great Pyramid—that rite which Atlantean Osiris had left as his legacy to the High Priests of ancient Egypt.

Why were such dismal and dark places favoured for these mysterious initiations?

The answer is threefold: to ensure complete safety and secrecy for what was, after all, both a privileged and dangerous experiment: to ensure the easier entrancement of the candidate by blotting out sight of his surroundings and thus preventing distraction of his attention from the interior state he was about to enter: and, finally, to provide a perfect symbolism—so dear to the heart of the ancients—of the condition of spiritual darkness and ignorance in which the hierophants found their candidate at the beginning of his initiation; for upon awakening he would open his eyes to the rays of the sun in another place, whither he would be carried towards the end of this experience in spiritual illumination. After a lengthy initiation, begun at night and finished with the dawn of day, the newly-made initiate had stepped out of materialistic ignorance (darkness) into spiritual perception (light).

The secret rites of the Mysteries were practised in underground crypts, or in reserved chambers set close to the holy shrine, or in little temples built on the roofs; never elsewhere. All these places were forbidden territory to the populace, who dared not approach them under the direst penalties. The hierophants who had undertaken to initiate a candidate likewise undertook a heavy responsibility. His life or death was in their hands. For an unexpected intruder to interrupt the sacred rite of initiation meant his death, no less than an unexpected intrusion upon a delicate surgical operation, in our time, might mean the death of the unfortunate patient. And what, after all, was initiation but a kind of psychic surgical operation, a separation of the psychic from the physical part of man? Hence, all the initiatory chambers were placed out of reach and were always well guarded. Those which lay near the shrine of a great temple would have to be approached through complete blackness, for as one left the doorway the light receded, to disappear altogether when the threshold of the holy shrine was reached. Once the candidate was thoroughly entranced, his body was left in this protective darkness until the close of his initiation, when he was carried out to the light.

Those chambers which were underground vaults were used in the same manner, every light being extinguished after entrancement, so that the crypts became both symbolical and literal graves.

¶

I dropped down a hole and explored a dark vault where the priests had once practised their most secret rites, and then I emerged with relief into the friendly sunlight and fresh air.

I passed between the enormous portals of the fine temple of Amen-Ra in my onward journey through the dimmed glories of Karnak. These portals were fit for the passage of giants rather than of puny mortals. They towered up like precipices above my head. The Egyptian taste for exaggerated size sometimes rose to stunning dimensions, as in the case of the Great Pyramid near Cairo and the pylon walls under whose shadow I stood. They were almost fifty feet thick, thicker than any fortress walls need be. Well, indeed, was the profane outer world kept from polluting the sacred precincts of this temple, which the ancients proudly called "the throne of the world." Alas! it was now but a broken throne, and when I emerged in the large forecourt, there I found a wide mass of mutilated masonry relieved from its desolation by some unfallen pillars. I walked slowly across this quadrangle, treading on rough earth and growing weeds, where once had been a beautiful mosaic pavement that extended for hundreds of feet in length.

This space traversed, I arrived at a high doorway, covered with coloured half-reliefs and standing between the shattered remnants of another pylon, which was now but a tumbled mass of hot fallen stones and quite bereft of its former outline. Yet that doorway must once have risen a hundred feet above the ground. Gone were the seven steps which the builders had placed before the entrance, seven symbolical graduations of man's progress from the lower world of everyday existence to the highest sphere of spiritual attainment. For the Egyptians —as many of the ancients—understood well the mysterious numbering which underlies the whole constructed universe; they knew that the seventh day or grade brought Rest, the highest peace for man, no less than for other created beings and things. I had found this sevenfold numbering in all their temples throughout the land, while it had appeared in clear and startling expression within the Grand Gallery of the Great Pyramid. Therefore they had fittingly placed those steps, which time and man have all but torn from the ground, at the very entrance to the vestibule of Karnak's grandest and most impressive feature, the Great Hypostyle Hall of the Temple of Amen-Ra.

I entered, and a bewildering perspective of sixteen serried ranks of columns opened out before me. The sun's rays fell upon a scene without parallel in my memory. Nearly every one of the hundred and thirty upright pillars thrust a strong, horizontal shadow across the unpaved ground. The white stone shafts stood up like an army of giant soldiers. Their girth, too, was incredible—averaging apiece thirty feet round. It was monstrous, this grandiose scale of architecture, this three hundred feet broad forest of colossal stone trees: it was Egyptian!

And the Pharaoh who had created most of this Hall was Seti, he who had also created that temple at Abydos where I had felt such unutterable peace. Here one could not resist the impression of strength, of power, which was conveyed to one from the vanished epoch of the builders of this Hall. Seti had not lived, could not live, to finish his colossal creation, and so the great Rameses took up the incompleted task, turning the rocks of Assuan into enormous graven pillars, and poising thirty-ton decorated architraves upon their tops, without using cement or metal ties to fix them. The effect of all this was to turn the mind to a more extended outlook, to lift one out of the petty round of pitifully meagre activities, to inspire one with grand ambitions and lofty aspirations, and to provoke a yearning for a far wider scope for one's energies. One wanted, in fine, to be like Rameses himself and plan and build such mighty temples of prodigious height, then set around them ample model cities where men could live by the light of noble ideas and nobler ideals.

Once, this Hall of many prayers had been roofed and pavemented; now it was open to the blue depths of the sky, while its floor was a mingled mass of earth, sand, weeds and stones. When that vast roof was in place, the interior of the Hall must have been dim indeed, for the only light would have been grudgingly given by stone-grated clerestory windows above the central avenue. But the mighty roof had fallen into a hundred pieces, of which little remained.

One did not want to criticize those ancient architects, yet the fact rose clear to the eye that the bulging strong pillars had been set far too close together. A better arrangement would have provided longer, less interrupted, views. But perhaps the ancients cared more for their symbolism and less for their perspectives.

Every pillar was lavishly carved and capped by heavy bud or by bell-shaped calyx. The beautifully rounded surfaces of the shafts were covered with coloured pictures and inscribed hieroglyphs, and the same decorations were on the architraves and the walls too. They were carven with the histories of Egypt's gods and kings, or painted in colours that remained undiminished. I recognized the painted figures and oblong cartouches—King Seti worshipping in the presence of the god Thoth under the sacred tree of Heliopolis, driving the Hittites before his victorious chariot, securing tall cedar trees in distant Lebanon for the flagstaffs of his temples, and returning triumphantly to his own beloved land. There were many other figures; some half nude, others full robed, but all bearing those strangely intense, remote faces which were characteristic of this people. On the southern wall, graven on a stele and let into the brick, hieroglyphs gave record of history's first official treaty; that between Rameses the Great, "the valiant, the son of Seti I, the great ruler of Egypt," and the Hittite King Khetesar, "the son of Meresar, the great chief of Kheta," as the text called him: concluding with the pleasant words: "the good treaty of peace and of brotherhood, setting peace between them for ever."

I moved away to a narrow uncovered court where a single solid obelisk thrust a pointing pyramidal finger towards heaven and flung a purple shadow to the ground. It bore the royal cartouche of Thothmes I, who had erected it, and its shaft was covered with three vertical lines of inscriptions. "Horus, Beloved of Truth, King of Upper and Lower Egypt, Amen. He made it as his monument for his father Amen-Ra—the Leader of the Two Lands, raising for him two obelisks, even very great ones, at the double façade," read part of one of them. Always that grand adoration of the gods.

Farther on, amid the shattered remains of a colonnade, rose another obelisk, taller and more impressive still, like a snake-tongue of flame out of the ground. For almost a hundred feet it spired its way into the sky—the second highest obelisk still existent in the world. This erect monolith of shining pink granite bore on its base the proud boast that its top had been encased in a mixture of gold and silver, so that it could be seen from a very great distance, and that the entire enterprise of quarrying and transporting the granite from Syene for this and its now vanished fellow-obelisk had taken not more than seven months. It was erected by a woman who was in some ways the Queen Elizabeth, and more, of Egypt; the vigorous Queen Hatshepsu. She sometimes dressed like a man and always showed a strong masculinity in her rule, this long-nosed, strong-jawed lady who flung up lofty obelisks and massive temples, sent out pioneering expeditions, and wielded the sceptre of the Pharaohs no less powerfully because of her sex; whose veil she had cast aside, with all that it stood for, upon the death of her husband.

Read her haughty dedication of this obelisk, cut in hieroglyphic characters upon the four sides of the lower part:

"I was sitting in my palace, I was thinking of my Creator, when my heart urged me to make for Him two obelisks whose points reached unto the sky, in the noble hall of columns which is between the two great pylons of Thothmes I.

"When they see my monument in after years, let them exclaim: 'This it is that was made by me.' This was made under my order, this mountain fashioned of gold. I rule over this land like the son of Isis; I am powerful even as the son of Nu when the sun reposes in the Morning Boat and remains in the Evening Boat. It shall exist for ever, like unto the North Star. Of a truth these are two huge obelisks brightened by My Majesty with gold for the sake of my Father, Amen, and out of love, in order to perpetuate his name, that they might stand erect in the Temple precinct for ever. They are of one solid block of granite, without any joint or division in them."

§

I went to the great gate that once led to the Temple of Mut, constructed by the second of the Ptolemies, but now leads to palm-fringed fields. Its lovely outline and embellished surfaces held my gaze again and again. Above its lintel the sculptured, winged sun played, according to ancient thought, a protective part in warding off the entry of evil influences.

I rested in a red rectangular room upon the wall of which was inscribed the name of Philip of Macedon, whose coin, perfectly preserved by the kindly earth, I had found only the other day some ten miles away.

And so I picked my way among the ruined courtyards and broken sanctuaries of Karnak; among grey, roofless walls covered with sculptured reliefs and pink granite shrines bereft of their statued gods and goddesses, and around piles of broken masonry. I stepped pensively across a bare, undulating tract, site of a building which had been scattered to the ground and removed, to come upon an assembly of mutilated Sphinxes and idols with lioness heads. I walked with care through the spiky green bramble which grew thickly in the ruined hall of Thothmes III, and then stood in meditation under the low architrave of the half-gone shrine at its far end. What kings had oft proudly walked upon this track and inscribed their victories upon pillar and wall, and yet where were they now? Thothmes, Amenhotep, Seti, Rameses, Tutankhamen, Ptolemy —the bearded faces of these men who had ruled Egypt and swayed its life thousands of years ago, passed in procession before my gaze and faded away into the air. Was pride worth while, I asked myself, when every achievement and every accomplishment was destined to be blown away like dust? Was it not better to walk one's path in this world quietly, humbly, and to remember that one held all things only by the grace of a higher power?

The day was nearly gone, and had begun to yield itself to dusk like a serpent to its charmer, by the time I had finished my perambulation of this broken city of temples.

There was once a king of the twenty-second dynasty who built a wall of mud bricks to girdle all the temples of Karnak, and when it was complete its circuit was not less than one mile and a half. Karnak was a saga in stone, an epic of majestic effort and inevitable destruction, a ruined yet immortal glory!

I lingered on while the marvellous but swift sunset, like a dazzling angel whose quivering halo was coloured in every hue from gold to red, hovered over the scene, and ended this visit. The vast picture of ruin and field and desert suffused with so many tints, overwhelmed me into ecstatic absorption.

Again and again I returned to Karnak, letting the days slip by in mingled dalliance and research while adding to my store of unforgettable memories and unusual facts. Karnak's glamour slipped over you, like an approaching river-mist, almost imperceptibly until the time came when you awoke to find that it surrounded you. Men without subtle intelligence and fine feeling can see nothing more in these half-broken temples than a heap of bricks, stones, dust and mortar. Pity them! Let us rise from contemplation of these majestic ruins with souls impressed and awed, conscious of the beauty and dignity which they retain even in their present state of pathetic dilapidation.

I was fortunate in having the whole ground to myself; so that I could move untroubled and undisturbed by others, in a silence that reigned supreme and absolute, broken only at odd times by the drowsy hum of bees and the pleasant twittering of sparrows. For it was midsummer, and all the crowds of perspiring tourists had deserted Luxor and long since fled before the advancing wave of terrific heat and swarms of re-emerging insect and animal life, which appears in Southern Egypt at this season. Flies, mosquitoes, scorpions and snakes, not to mention other forms of life, reappeared in a temperature which devitalized humans but seemed to revitalize obnoxious creatures and insects. But the compensations of solitude, in one's studies, were ample enough to make sufficient amends for these things, whilst the heat never seemed to take the sharpness off the edge of my intellectual interests. Indeed, I found that one could make friends with the sun; it was partly a matter of mental attitude. The moment you thought the sun was going to hurt or weaken you, doors were opened to admit such hurt. Active faith in inner resources always called them up into tangible existence.

For me the advantage of my solitary tenure of Karnak was enormous. I could surrender myself to its stillness with recurring profit.

The capacity for solitude is not encouraged in this jazzy epoch. The taste for silence is not fostered by this Machine Age. But, I believe in the necessity of a little withdrawal every day, a short period of silent solitary meditation. Thus one can renew the tired heart and inspire the fatigued mind. Life resembles a roaring cauldron nowadays, and men are drawn into it. With each day that passes, they become less intimate with themselves and more intimate with the cauldron.

Recourse to regular meditation yields abundant fruits from the obvious spiritual deepening. It bestows steadiness in the hour of decision, courage to live one's own life independently of mass opinion, and stability amid the hectic tempo of to-day.

The worst of modern life is when it weakens the powers of deep thought; in the insane haste of a town like New York man cannot sit down to remember that the inner life is being paralysed; he can only remember that he is in a hurry. Nature, however, is in no hurry—she took many million years to make this puny figure hurrying down Broadway—and she can well await the coming of that time when, with a calmer life and quieter activity, he will emerge from self-inflicted disaster and agonies to gaze into the deep well of divine thought which was buried beneath the noisy surface of himself and his environment.

Our physical senses own us; it is time we began to own our

senses. In the sacred ship of the soul, we ride into seas where the bodily senses dare not follow.

We can understand the doctrines of the Seers, and grasp the truths enunciated in their books and sayings, often by referring the latter to the life of meditation, and not only to the active life in the everyday world.

# CHAPTER XV

**M**OST fascinating were my midnight visits and especially the one which happened under a full moon. The nights of Egypt placed her ancient temples under a mysterious light that fittingly revealed what should be revealed and hid the rest in a gloom that suited those temples well.

I had taken various methods of approaching Karnak by night, all equally charming. I had floated swiftly in a boat with a huge sail, under a strong breeze, down the Nile; I had ridden slowly in the saddle, on a plodding beast; and I had driven up the old highway, in a more or less comfortable horse-trap. But on this night of the full moon I could find no better method of approach than to walk the few miles as the old priests walked, even in the days of the pomp and pageantry of old Egypt. The silver sheen glittered over the white dust that lay so thick upon the road on whose edge I walked. Now and then bats dipped down through the air and darted off again shrieking. But otherwise a great stillness had fallen upon the land, not to be broken until I reached the village of Karnak itself, where shadowy robed figures passed me in the night—sometimes with dancing lanterns in their hands—and where the yellow gleams of lamp-light shone through unglazed windows. My feet silently trod the soft, sandy dust which covered the route; yet those keen-eared peasants seemed to know, as by a sixth sense, that a stranger was moving at night through their village, for they came in ones and twos to their doors to look at me, or peered quizzically out of their windows. The thing was inexplicable and, in the unreal world created by a full moon, weird in the extreme. Their movements set a dog or two barking half-heartedly, but I put both them and myself at ease with a muttered greeting though I never stopped. I understood them well, these simple, pleasant folk, who took the minor troubles of life with an airy philosophy of *"Maleesh!"* (Never mind!) which was really captivating.

And presently the huge silvery pylon of Ptolemy stood at the end of my path, like a spectral sentinel of the great temple; its square top towered up into the indigo sky.

It was not ready to receive me, however, for a barred grille had been placed across it. I woke the sleeping watchman who jumped, startled, out of his narrow cot; then stood rubbing his sleepy eyes in the bright glare of my electric torch. After he had unlocked the small modern gate, I paid him well for thus disturbing his rest, and he let me pass in to wander alone. I crossed the Forecourt and sat down for a few minutes among the mass of tumbled sandstone blocks which once formed the lofty pylon dividing the Forecourt from the Great Hypostyle Hall, and meditated on the fallen grandeur of this monument to Amen-Ra. Soon I was moving amid the stately columns and majestic ruins of the Great Hall itself. The moonlight dappled the shafts that rose up by my side and flung their deep black shadows on the ground, so that carven hieroglyphs appeared at one moment in gleaming relief, and the next as suddenly disappeared into the night. I switched off the light of my own torch, save where I was uncertain of my path, that it might not play the rival to the mellower illumination of the moon, which turned the entire temple into a place met with in dreams alone. The Obelisk of Queen Hatshepsu suddenly confronted me: it looked like a splendid silver needle.

And as I went slowly onwards through the faintly relieved darkness into the covered sanctuaries that lay beyond the impressive colonnades of the Hypostyle Hall, there came a dim sense that my solitude was no longer solitude. Yet these stupendous halls and smaller shrines had not been crowded with worshippers for fifteen hundred years at least; the mutilated stone gods had silently suffered their long desertion for no less a time; and I knew of no one in modern Egypt who could be accused of having reverted to the ancient faith. Why, then, did I *feel* the companionship of living people all around me in this time-worn place, which was as silent as the grave itself? I let my torch play its beam around me; it merely rested in turn on stone ruins and broken floors, or flashed chiselled pictures and inscribed hieroglyphs into fleeting life, but revealed never a sign of human forms.

I could not rid myself of this oppressive feeling as I walked farther on, a lonely visitor at the dead of night. The night always brings its own terrors with it, and always accentuates one's slightest dread, yet I had learned to love and accept these soft Egyptian nights which haunted me with their supernal loveliness. But here these mouldering temples of Karnak took on a half-sinister outline in the queer wan light, and I was conscious of an uneasy reaction to both the hour and the environment. Why was I thus affected?

I followed the ancient paved road which led to the northern ruins and straight to the exquisite little Temple of Ptah. I crossed the small pillared court and, having passed through another gateway, I penetrated the threshold of the sanctuary itself. A vivid shaft of moonlight lit up one of the strangest statues in this place, that of the goddess Sekhmet. She dwelt alone in this gloomy room, a forlorn figure of a woman with the head of a lioness. Her fierce, sullen face fitted well the role assigned to her in Egyptian mythology, that of a punitive destroyer of mankind. With what terror she must have inspired her victims, who could look for no mercy from her!

I sat down upon a granite plinth and watched the silvery rays dance upon the dilapidated walls. Somewhere, far off, there rose the faint howl of a prowling jackal. As I sat, still and passive, the eerie sense of invisible company crept anew over my heart, chilling it with the fear which uncertainty always brings.

Did the ghosts of those proud-faced priests and their throngs of devout worshippers still haunt this ancient place and murmur their prayers to Ptah, he who held a symbolled sceptre of power and stability? Did the spirits of vanished priests and departed kings flit to and fro across their ancient haunts, like living shadows without substance?

I remembered involuntarily the curious story told me by a friend in Cairo, an English official in the service of the Egyptian Government. He had met a young man who was connected with the aristocracy, and had come out from England to Egypt for a few weeks as an ordinary tourist. He was a happy-go-lucky fellow with no interest beyond material things. When he got to Luxor, he went out one afternoon to Karnak, where he took a camera snap of the Great Hall in the Temple of Amen-Ra. After the negative was developed and printed, he was astonished to discover on it the figure of a tall Egyptian priest standing with his back against one of the pillars, his arms folded on his breast.

This incident made so powerful an impression on the young man's mind that his whole character was changed and he became a devoted student of things psychic and spiritual.

I could not tear myself away from the stone seat, but sat in wondering reflection and uneasy speculation in the silent society of these stone divinities.

A half-hour passed in this way, and then I must have fallen into some kind of reverie.

A shroud seemed to fall from before my eyes, my attention concentrated itself on a point midway between my eyebrows; after which an unearthly light enveloped me.

Within that light I saw a brown-skinned masculine figure with raised shoulders, standing sideways near me. And as I gazed upon him, he turned and confronted me.

I trembled with the shock of recognition.

For that figure was myself.

He bore precisely the same face that I bear to-day, but the dress was that of ancient Egypt. He was neither prince nor commoner, but a priest of a certain rank. I knew that at once by his head-dress and robe.

The light spread out rapidly around him, and far beyond— spread until it took in a vivid scene about an altar. Then the figure of my vision bestirred himself and strode slowly towards that altar, and when he reached it, prayed . . . and prayed . . . and prayed. . . .

And whilst he walked, I went with him; and when he prayed, I prayed with him, too—not as a companion *but as himself*. I was both spectator and actor in this paradoxical vision. I found that he was grieved at heart, sorrowful over the condition of his country, sad at the decadence which had descended upon his ancient land. Most of all, he was unhappy about the evil hands into which the leadership of his religion had fallen. Again and again, in his prayers, he begged the old gods to save the truth for his people. But at the end of his petitions his heart was as heavy as lead. For no response came and he knew that Egypt's doom was irrevocable. He turned away with downcast face; sad, sad, sad.

The light melted back into darkness; the priestly figure disappeared, and the altar with him; I found myself in solitary meditation near the Temple of Ptah once more. My own heart, too, was sad, sad, sad.

Was this merely some dream suggested by the environment?

Was it but the riotous hallucination of a meditative mind?
Was it the emergence of a latent idea derived from my interest
in the Past?

Was it the clairvoyant vision of a spirit-priest who had really
been there?

Or was it an ancestral reminiscence of a former existence of
mine in Egypt?

For me, knowing my own intensely stirred feelings, during
and after the time of the vision, there was but a single possible
reply.

A wise man will not leap swiftly to conclusions, for Truth
is an elusive lady who, says ancient report, lives at the bottom
of an extremely deep well.

Yet I accepted, I had to accept, an affirmative answer to the
last question.

Einstein has upset the conservative views of time which once
prevailed. He has demonstrated mathematically that someone
able to take a four-dimensional glimpse of things will have a
very different sense of past and present from that which man
ordinarily enjoys. This may help one to understand the
possibility that Nature keeps a perfect memory of the past, in
which are perpetuated the pictures of vanished centuries. I
could well comprehend how in these sensitive moments of
meditation, a man might involuntarily and mysteriously touch
this memory.

¶

Another night found me driving out at eleven in the evening
to a rendezvous in the small village of Naga Tahtani, some
distance beyond Karnak. Luxor and Karnak had been left
behind when I took the road beside the banks of the Nile for a
good stretch and then turned off, at a sharp right angle, for
twenty minutes or so.

In an open space that marked the centre of the village—it
corresponded to the English village green, but here it was only
an unpaved sandy square—I found more than two hundred
men squatting in the dust. Not a single woman was present.
They were dressed in long Arab robes and white turbans and
seemed a simple, primitive type of people.

On a raised verandah of whitewashed, plastered earth sat

four notables, four venerable men of superior rank and mentality; they were sheikhs, to judge by their faces and dress, and
with their flowing silken robes made picturesque figures.  All
were aged, grey-haired men.  That worn-out hero of flapper
novels, the handsome young desert sheikh who kidnaps beautiful
English damsels, may be found in England perhaps, but he is
certainly nowhere here in Egypt.

Sheikh Abu Shrump, the only man I knew in the whole
assembly, was among them.  He welcomed me cordially and
introduced me to the Chief of Karnak, to another sheikh, who
both touched their foreheads and breasts in urbane acknowledg-
ment, and then to the Chief of the village and surrounding district; his name was Sheikh Mekki Gahba, and it was outside his
house that the verandah had been raised.  He immediately pressed
me to have the inevitable coffee; which offer, fortunately, I was
able to change into milkless tea.

I took my place upon one of the cushions which lay on the
platform next to my friend, Sheikh Abu Shrump, who lived in
the village of Kurna on the other side of the Nile, and who was
the most famous and respected holy man in the region of Luxor
for twenty miles around.

He was a pious follower of the Prophet—despite his reputation
as one who controlled the genii and made powerful talismans—
and gloried in the fact that he had made the Pilgrimage to Mecca.
He wore a flat green turban around his head.  His heavy moustache, side-whiskers, and short beard had turned white.  His
dark-skinned face was genial but grave, pleasant but dignified.
His eyes were noticeably large and in repose gave one an impression of profundity.  A long, loose-fitting, brown robe of
thick material fell to his ankles.  Upon the fourth finger of his
right hand he wore an enormous silver ring, whose surface
bore an Arabic inscription.

The Omdeh (Mayor) of Luxor had brought me the invitation
to attend this gathering and insisted on my acceptance.  We
had met in the street, one sultry afternoon, and he had given
me the Arabic greeting: "May your day be happy," when
Sheikh Abu Shrump had dismounted from his gorgeously
caparisoned donkey to pay a promised visit and to take tea
with me.  A few days later the Mayor had called, bearing a
joint invitation from himself and the Sheikh to attend a midnight
assembly of the Dervishes of Karnak-Luxor district.

I had found my way to this queer meeting, the only European

SHEIKH ABU SHRUMP'S ARABIC TALISMAN

among them, and I tried to forget the conspicuous shape of my London-made clothes.

He explained that this meeting was the first which had been held for many years in the region, while Sheikh Abu Shrump pointed out that such a Dervish assembly was always dated according to certain phases of the moon; that it was always held on a night of the new or full moon, as these nights were considered to be particularly sacred.

"This is not going to be a noisy shouting assembly," the Sheikh added. "We are all quiet people who have gathered together out of love for Allah."

I looked around. A tall flagpole had been planted in the centre of the open space and from its top fluttered a rose-coloured pennant which was embroidered with gilt Arabic lettering. Row after row of squatting Bedouins and villagers was grouped around the pole, in the form of a perfect circle. In an adjoining field I had passed a varied assortment of tethered beasts belonging to the richer of these men, some of whom had ridden, I was told, from villages as far as twenty miles off. None was permitted to be present except those who had been invited.

The scene presented under the star-dotted blue African sky was charming. Over two hundred white-turbaned heads formed a great circle on the ground and bobbled up and down below me. Some were the heads of old, white-haired men; others those of mere boys. Heavily fronded palm trees, whose leaves rasped together in a night breeze and whose black shadows were printed across the court, fringed two sides of the open place, while a few square buildings bordered the other sides. Masses of tropical creepers surrounded the buildings. Beyond lay darkness, the fields, the hills, the Nile and the desert. The light of the moon and stars was assisted by a single powerful lamp, which was suspended on the verandah above our heads.

With the coming of midnight, one of the Dervishes stood up and sang out a verse of the holy *Quran* in a clear and melodious voice. He had no sooner ended the last word than it drew in response a long-drawn chant of "There is no God but Allah" from two hundred throats.

A boy, who seemed no more than six years old, although that meant a good deal more maturity in the East than in Europe, advanced to the centre of the throng, took up his stand next to the flagstaff, and sang from memory and at the top of his silvery voice further verses from the *Quran*. Next came a bearded old man who walked slowly throughout the whole length of each row of sitters, carrying a brass bowl of burning charcoal upon which some handfuls of incense had been thrown. The fragrant clouds of smoke were wafted across the open court to our verandah.

Then three men faced each other around the flagstaff and commenced a long religious chant which went on for fifteen to twenty minutes. One felt the intense devout fervour of their hearts expressing itself in the solemn tones of their voices. Then they dropped to the ground and a fourth man arose to take up the chant. He chose for his words a favourite Dervish song which came from his lips with almost melancholy passion. Its poetic Arabic lines were expressive of that burning longing for Allah which the true Dervish is supposed to feel. By the time he had finished, the words had become plaintive cries wrung from his heart; cries for the conscious presence of Allah, his Creator.

"My union seems most distant," he sang:
"Will my Beloved e'er meet mine eye?
  Alas! Did not Thy distance
Draw my tears, I would not sigh.

"By dreary nights I am broken,
Absence makes my hope expire,
  My tears, like pearls, are dropping
And my heart is wrapped in fire.
  Whose is like unto my condition?
Scarcely remedy know I,
  Alas! Did not Thy distance
Draw my tears, I would not sigh.

"O First, and sole Eternal!
Show thy favour yet to me.
  Thy slave, Ahmad El-Bakree,
Hath no lord excepting Thee.
  By the Greatness of our Prophet
Do thou not his wish deny.
  Alas! Did not Thy distance
Draw my tears, I would not sigh."

When he sat down I saw that most of the others were out-wardly affected by the burning longing that was the theme of his song, but the grave Sheikh beside me remained imperturbable and impassive.

And then the entire assembly rose and the first three singers, together with the boy, moved with the utmost slowness inside the serried circles. As they took each slow pace they rolled their heads in unison, now downwards, now to the right and now to the left, repeating the long-drawn "Allah—Allah-ah-ah!" so many times that I could not count them. They wrung a sweet, melancholy melody out of that single word. Their bodies swayed from side to side in monotonous and exact rhythm. The two hundred men stood perfectly still, watching and listening for more than half an hour whilst the Dervishes circled amongst them with a perfect rhythm that never once abated. When at last the singers took their rest, their patient audience sank down to the dust once more. That the latter was enjoying the scene was a thing beyond doubt.

Now followed an interval when tiny cups of coffee were served to all the persons present, while the Mayor thoughtfully ordered little glasses of scented *kerkadi* for me, a hot drink made from the flowers of a plant which grows in the Sudan. It is infused just like tea but has a somewhat acrid taste.

Sheikh Abu Shrump made no attempt to explain the night's function to me. We merely looked at each other from time to time; he knew that he could count upon my sympathy, whilst I knew the happiness he was feeling at the nocturnal invocation of Allah's presence. The thought came to me that somewhere in Europe and America, in the pleasure-haunts of great cities, thousands of other assemblies were listening to song and music, to jazz. But they were listening to song that was without God; they were enjoying themselves, true, getting some fun out of life, yet . . . ?

I told the aged Sheikh of my thought, and for answer he simply quoted a verse from the *Quran*:

"In your own selves are signs for men of firm faith, will ye not behold them? Think within thine own self on God, with lowliness and reverence and silence, at evening and at morn; and be not one of the heedless. To those only who lend an ear will He make an answer."

Here we sat, in this pool of yellow light, surrounded by a circle of darkness, attempting to turn our hearts towards adoration of the Supreme Power. We named the Nameless,

Allah; but who, melting into this tender adoration, could honestly circumscribe it with any name?

I looked up, hushed. There were the scintillating planets, which hung in space in this clear sky, and drew one's gaze upward. Each possessed the subtle, intangible beauty of a great poem; each evoked a troubling reminder that I was but a transient passenger on the surface of this planet, which was itself mantled in mystery as the night.

I looked down again. God-hunger was printed on every one of those earnest faces below me.

Once more the Dervishes began their slow chant: "There is no Deity but Allah!" bowing the head and body twice with each repetition of the phrase. They sang softly at first until, after a quarter of an hour, they quickened the rhythm of their chant and movements, deepening as well the tone of their voices. That which had formerly been a measured song became ultimately a series of sharp, forcible ejaculations. As time passed on they grew more and more excited and their words resembled hoarse exclamations, uttered as they rolled their heads in unison with their voices, crossed their hands upon their breasts, and swayed their bodies. Yet, never at any time, or in any way, did they earn the title of "howling Dervishes." That high degree of ecstatic fervour which they had reached was never in any way offensive, and stopped suddenly immediately it had swelled and accelerated to its rapturous crescendo.

There was dead, divine silence, most impressive by contrast with the volume of sound heard before. Thereafter they rested.

Coffee and tea were once more served, and for the remainder of the night the meeting continued along gentler lines. The Dervishes chanted in subdued voices, sometimes reinforced by the audience, whose two hundred throats repeated the name of Allah at certain moments, sending up a melodious, throbbing offering of song to the heavens.

When, at long last, the first rays of the liberating dawn broke into our circle, the Dervishes fell silent. There was a final meditation—"On and in Allah" they called it—in which the whole assembly took part, before the meeting broke up, under the rosy dawn-light that lay in thin streamers across the sky.

A couple of days later Sheikh Abu Shrump came as my guest to tea. He brought a small square piece of paper which had been folded many times so as to form a packet. He told me that it was a talisman inscribed with verses from the *Quran* and with certain magical symbols and spells. He said, furthermore, that the paper had been prepared at the Dervish meeting the other night, along with some other sheets, where it had received the impress, or magnetic influence, of the higher forces then evoked. It was also inscribed with my name (in Arabic). The "magic paper," as the old Sheikh called it, should be carried in my pocket on any occasion when I desired any particular enterprise to be successful, or in any place where hostile forces were to be feared.

He warned me, however, very frankly if somewhat naïvely, not to wear the talisman should I engage myself in intimate relations with a woman, as then it would be temporarily deprived of some of its power.

Although I had never asked for this strange gift, I accepted it as a matter of course, hoping for the best.

Abu Shrump lived in the village of Kurna, which is the nearest village to the bleak desolate Valley of the Tombs of the Kings, and he had, as the most distinguished personage in the place, received so many visits from Mr. Howard Carter during the many years when the latter had been excavating in the neighbourhood, that the two had become great friends.

In illustration of the efficacy of the second power of his "magic paper," the Sheikh told me that the excavated tombs had often been the haunt of frightful genii of a most evil character, who had been sealed up for ages within those tombs; and that he, Abu Shrump, had deliberately extended his protective power over his friend, Howard Carter, in order to protect the latter against the hostile genii. The fact that such a long trail of deaths or disasters had followed in the wake of other members of the archæological expedition connected with the opening of King Tutankhamen's tomb, but had avoided Mr. Carter, was a point he impressed upon me.

Among the other activities of Sheikh Abu Shrump was the practice of healing. One day I watched a demonstration. A man came to him with rheumatic pains in the left thigh. He gently stroked the latter for a minute, recited a prayer from the *Quran* for another minute or two, and then told his patient that the pain would soon go. I took the trouble to follow up the history of this case and found that there was certainly a diminution of the pain, although it was difficult for me to ascertain whether this was a permanent relief or a temporary one.

The Sheikh told me that he had learned the secrets—such as they were—of the Dervish's art from his grandfather, and that these secrets had descended by traditional communication from the lifetime of Muhammed himself. "Blessed be His name!" added the old man reverently.

# CHAPTER XVI

"*EX Oriente Lux!*" ("Out of the East—Light!") runs the old phrase. The ardent researches of talented scholars and the fascinating discoveries of inquisitive travellers have combined to give ample testimony to the truth of that phrase. We Westerners are rightly proud of our achievements in "face-lifting" this world of ours, but we get a little disturbed sometimes when we hear of a half-naked fakir performing a feat which we can neither match nor understand. The thing keeps on occurring sufficiently often to remind us that there are ancient secrets and hoary wisdom in the lands which lie both east and west of Suez, and that the inhabitants of those colourful lands are not all such stupid, benighted heathens some of us think they are.

I am driven to these reflections when I remember my adventures with Sheikh Moussa, that man who, in the empire of the snakes, ruled as a king. I had met snake-charmers a-plenty in different parts of the East, as anyone may still meet them to-day, but I had been initiated by certain members of their fraternity into the cunning tricks and disillusioning secrets of their art, and thereafter lost my respect for all of them except a few. Knowing how they achieved their effects with harmless, fangless reptiles deprived one of the pleasure of sharing the wonderment of their gaping audiences, whether native or European.

But Sheikh Moussa did not belong to their tribe. He prided himself on being a real magician—in the ancient sense of that ill-used word—and on tackling, in the name of the Prophet, all manner of serpents by means of nothing less than a straightforward use of old-fashioned magical power. He never failed to justify this pride.

What Westerner can go out into the desert and poke among the stones and sand for a snake, and then grip it with his hand as one would grip a walking-stick? What Westerner can permit himself to be bitten by a newly caught cobra and watch, with a smile, the blood stream down his wounded arm? What Westerner can enter a house and unfailingly track down any reptile hitherto undetectable, that may be hidden in some hole, nook or furnishing?

I have watched the Sheikh do all these things, and more, and thus exercise a subtle dominion over the subtlest of creatures. With all our tremendous advance in scientific knowledge we either cannot or dare not attempt to do these things which this Oriental did with insouciant impunity.

I had seen in India a charmer who walked into a village, carrying two small sacks on his shoulder. He showed the villagers that one contained a few rats and the other poison-fanged snakes. He put his hand into the latter sack and took out a pair of the serpents; he let them bite him on the arm and throat several times. Then he lifted out a rat and put it on the ground. Bewildered for a moment, it looked around, and in that moment the snakes struck at it and bit it on the head. A minute later the unfortunate rat lay dead, killed by the venom in the snake's jaws.

The Sheikh's name was the Arabic form of Moses, and it was a curious coincidence that he should bear the cognomen of the great patriarch who astonished a Pharaoh and his court by catching the tail of a snake and turning it into a rod—so far as the story in the Book of Exodus can be taken literally.

Moussa lived in the little town of Luxor, where I tracked him down with hardly any more effort than that which he used to track down his cobras and vipers. For he is not only the best-known charmer of snakes in the entire region, but because Luxor is a favourite resort of tourists, he may be said to be the best known in the world, for those tourists return home to spread his fame to distant parts of the earth.

He was not the kind of snake-charmer who gathered a small crowd around himself in a dusty street and then put a fangless cobra through its paces to the tune of a reed-pipe. Therefore hundreds of tourists have visited Luxor without becoming aware of his existence, but several of the old habitués, who come season after season, who get to know the place and its inhabitants, sooner or later alight upon him.

Moussa's profession was really that of unofficial snake-catcher to the native population of the town, just as even now one finds men holding the post of official rat-catcher to some municipality in Europe. Whenever the presence of a snake was suspected in any Luxor household, or whenever one was observed to make a flitting appearance in room or garden, the startled householder would run off at once to fetch Sheikh Moussa; the latter would infallibly detect the reptile's hiding-place—whether it was in a fissure in the wall, among the beams of the roof, or in a hole in the garden—and then order the creature to emerge. As a rule it obeyed, but if it refused he would thrust his hand into the suspected refuge and grasp the reptile by its throat. After that, he would put the snake into his round basket and carry it off. When a farmer saw snakes too frequently in the field where his cattle were pasturing, he would send for Moussa and thus rid himself of the danger. Similarly, too, before the few hotels opened their closed doors in November or December to the tourists once more, their managers would send for Moussa and have him make a thorough inspection of their premises, an inspection which sometimes developed into a thrilling snake-hunt, for snakes are fond of moving in and settling down in deserted buildings. When Moussa left the hotels, one could guarantee on oath that not a single snake was left behind—such was the efficacy of his work.

When we first sat face to face—Sheikh Moussa el Hawi and I—a crowd of forty-odd persons had congregated outside whilst he partook of some tea and fruit which I offered him. They had observed him walking slowly down the street, with his round basket and stick, the appurtenances of his profession, and they had rightly guessed that he was about to embark on active service. As the terrific heats of midsummer had fallen upon the town, the crowd of idlers and loungers who could or would do nothing, scented some excitement, some break in their monotonous, semi-lethargic state, and they had proceeded to follow him through the dusty lanes which led to my domicile. They waited patiently outside the door for the re-emergence of their whilom entertainer.

While Moussa sat in the creaking cane chair I studied his appearance. He was short in stature. He wore a flat turban made up of many folds of white linen. A triangular piece of white shirt showed on his chest, the apex pointing downwards, under a long, heavy, dark brown, coarse-textured goats'-hair robe of the type that Bedouin Arabs wear over a flowing white robe.

He was no more than about forty-eight, I judged, although his face and forehead were somewhat lined. A bristling stubble of a week's growth of hair on his chin, a ragged untrimmed moustache and a bulbous nose were what I noticed first; but the eyes, which were heavy-lidded and slightly watery, made no particular impression on me. The expression around his mouth was good-tempered and pleasant. He was obviously a simple, unintellectual man, with simple tastes, however expert he might be in his own peculiar profession.

Two large silver rings adorned his right hand, and two more his left. I knew, from the inscriptions engraved upon them, that he wore three of them for some mysterious protective power he believed they carried. While the fourth was a seal-ring, engraved with his name and an expression of trust in Allah. I was aware that, as Muhammed disapproved of gold, his devout followers often favoured silver rings even when they could afford gold.

Tea over, we set to work. Moussa offered to catch a snake in any spot I chose, so that it should not be said that he had previously hidden it in a prepared place. He added that he did not mind where I took him to hunt.

I selected a large garden belonging to a rambling old house, which had been disused for a dozen years or more in consequence of a wrangle among relatives as to who was the real heir to this once desirable property. Since the death of its owner it had stood untenanted, the while numerous claimants paid lawyers and attended courts in an effort to get what they probably had no right to. Meanwhile thieves had stolen all the furniture, the roof and floors had been stripped, the cracked and dilapidated walls would probably fall to pieces, and by the time the wrangle ended there might well be no house to occupy. At any rate, I knew that the place would have long since been turned into a free, if unfurnished, hostel for snakes, scorpions, rats and other creatures less contentious than human beings. The garden stretched away to the River Nile and was as forsaken as a wilderness; it was in a ruinous enough condition to attract all the snakes in Luxor. Moussa appeared to be quite gratified with my choice, and so we all marched away to the scene of his coming exploits. The crowd of forty-odd tattered hangers-on got so stirred by the prospect that, as they too marched, they actually shouted once or twice, despite the enervating heat, the nearest Arabic equivalent to "Hurrah, Sheikh Moussa!"

P

¶

When we reached the garden, Moussa insisted on satisfying any lingering doubts in my mind—although I had none but rather felt him to be patently honest—by divesting himself of his brown outer robe and white under robe, leaving himself standing in nothing else than a shirt and a pair of socks! The object of this unexpected exhibition was to prove that he did not carry snakes concealed in the folds of his robes or, maybe, twined around his legs! I assured him at once that the proof was ample, and he re-clothed himself.

Moussa went slowly over to a debris-strewn area of the garden, carrying a three-feet-long strong palm-stick in his right hand; he then suddenly stopped, and struck the stones a few gentle blows. At the same time he made a clucking noise with his tongue, and broke into a high-pitched unbroken recital of certain phrases of the *Quran*, mingled with magical incantations and adjurations to a scorpion to come forth.

"There is a scorpion under this stone," he explained, pointing to a rugged piece of rock. "I have smelled it!"

No scorpions emerged, so Moussa recommenced his adjurations and spells, this time in a stronger voice which was full of the tone of emphatic command. He was successful, for a large scorpion yielded to his exhortations and immediately crawled out from under the stone and then stopped. Moussa bent down and picked it up with his unprotected fingers. He brought it close to me and held it aloft in the air that I might examine it carefully. It was a yellowish-green creature, about three inches long. The sting—that dangerous, yet tiny weapon, stuck on to the end of its tail—was perfect and undestroyed. In the minute yellow bladder attached to it was enough poison, perhaps, to give anyone a painful death. And although the dreadful sting was raised threateningly in the air, the scorpion never once thrust it into Moussa's flesh.

"Are you satisfied?" asked the charmer. "You see, it is very big but does not bite me. No scorpion may bite me, for I have forbidden it to do so!"

He placed it on the back of his left hand.

The poisonous insect moved its sting several times, as by natural instinct, to attack him, but each time stopped dead short when the point was within a quarter of an inch of its captor's skin.

Then, as a further exhibition of his power over the scorpion, Moussa placed it on the ground. It moved across the rubble and debris as though about to escape, when the Sheikh suddenly commanded it to stand still. And stop it did!

He picked it up again and carried it over to his wicker-work basket. The latter was a large, queer-shaped, round vessel, possessing the outline of a gigantic ink-bottle. He raised the well-fitting lid, put the scorpion inside, and shut down the basket.

We went off in search of bigger game. Moussa assured me that he would be able to detect the whereabouts of a snake merely by his own sense of smell, an explanation that did not seem very convincing to me. However, he stopped again in a part of the garden nearer the Nile, shouted a brief command and struck his palm-stick upon the roots of a tree. Thereupon he began, in the same high-pitched monotone, a sonorous series of recurring phrases calling upon the serpent to come out of its hole, and adjuring it, by Allah, by His Prophet and by King Solomon, not to resist his will. His manner was very intense and concentrated. Occasionally he again struck the roots of the tree.

Two minutes passed in this way, but no snake showed itself. Moussa appeared to become a little angry and excited at this disobedience to his command. The perspiration streamed down his face in large drops and his lips actually trembled. Thrashing the tree with his stick, "By the life of the Prophet! I swear that it is there!" he said to me. Muttering to himself, he bent over the ground for a moment and then shouted: "Everyone stand away!   Big cobra coming!"

The crowd of spectators scattered in a trice to safe distance, whilst I retreated backwards a yard or two, keeping my eyes steadily fixed upon every movement that he made. He curled up the right sleeve of his brown robe, peered closely at the ground over which he was stooping, uttered his magical spells with redoubled force and bravely thrust his hand into the depths of a narrow hole among the roots. I could not see the snake from where I stood, but evidently it had retreated deeper into its refuge. Because, with a look of much annoyance on his face, Moussa withdrew his arm, rolled up his sleeve still farther and once more plunged his arm into the black opening of the hole; this time, almost up to his shoulder-blade. In a moment his hand was out again, a squirming, struggling serpent held tight in his grasp. He had forcibly pulled it out, as though it were nothing more than a piece of harmless rope, instead of a living medium of crawling death.

He flung it flat upon the ground, let it coil for a moment, and immediately caught it by the tail. The snake twisted one way and another, displaying a surprising agility, but could not escape from his grip. He next picked it up by the throat, just behind the head, and again held it aloft, inviting me to come closer and examine the victim of his art. The reptile's body swayed to and fro; it hissed loudly and continuously, in a fit of fury at its capture; its forked tongue shot out and back at lightning speed, but Moussa's grasp was like iron. When it found there was no escape, the infuriated cobra calmed down a little, apparently biding its time. At this point Moussa uttered a strong adjuration and let the snake slip from his grasp. It slid this way and that in the dust, whereat Moussa's hand touched the tail again as a protective measure.

It had the familiar pattern of its kind, and in its livery of green and yellowish grey looked very colourful.

I approached a pace or two closer and studied it with interest. Its hood, bearing those curious marks which look like a pair of spectacles, marks that identify its species, remained expanded, and a slightly sickly odour emanated from the scaled body. The creature was about five feet long and two and a half inches thick. Its sinister little eyes stared malevolently and unwinkingly at the Sheikh. The latter half-chanted a fresh spell, into which he put all his power of command and resolution. Pointing his forefinger at the snake he bade it lay its head in his hand, at the same time forbidding it to bite him. The snake hissed, seemingly resisting him, and darted out its forked tongue; but slowly, extremely slowly, all the time staring at its captor with its beady eyes, it moved forward and at last yielded to what seemed inevitable.

The cobra ceased its hissing and softly placed its head inside the flattened, upturned palm of the charmer! There it rested, as a child might rest its tired head upon its mother's lap, limp and quiescent.

It was a sight that I had never witnessed before and certainly a weird one. I watched with bated breath.

I wanted to test the genuineness of this charmer's feat, and of his snakes, to prove whether they were really venomous. I obtained a large tablespoon and asked Moussa to thrust it into the red little mouth, which he did. As those jaws closed on the spoon, the snake's venom spat down the curved fangs repeatedly, issuing in amber-coloured fluid. Soon that silver spoon was partly filled with a quantity of poison, of the consistency of glycerine, and like treacle in appearance; which amazed me when I recalled that a drop or two would be sufficient to kill a man.

As a last feat Sheikh Moussa took hold of its body and, with a single movement, flung the snake around his neck, as though it were a lady's fur. It now appeared to be thoroughly tamed, accepting its undignified position without making any visible objection.

The man lifted the lid of his basket and held the snake's head immediately over the open top. With a single word he commanded the creature to go in. Without any delay it slid down into the wickerwork depths, until the whole of its long, smooth-ringed body had disappeared. Then something happened—undoubtedly a meeting with the large scorpion which already lay at the bottom of the basket—for the cobra suddenly writhed and twisted backwards out of the basket and attempted to make its escape. A sharp word from Moussa, a moment's hesitation, and it re-entered its rounded prison. Its captor shut down the lid, which he fastened tightly.

What would happen inside that basket? I pictured the virulent scorpion and the deadly snake engaged in mortal combat and I wondered which would be the victor. Or would they rest, side by side, in peace?

Moussa turned a tired but triumphant face in my direction. His demonstration was over.

We were now surrounded by an enormous group of spectators who had gradually crept closer and closer as the danger diminished and their courage increased. The original audience of forty had now swelled to double that number, for news travels in the East with a speed that defies understanding. With one accord the crowd of men—of all classes from beggars to effendis, boys and girls, standing and lolling in various attitudes—gave a tremendous ovation to the victorious snake-charmer.

"Praised be Sheikh Moussa!" yelled the quaint chorus three times.

¶

Two days later, when I returned from a brief trip up the Nile to visit an old lady hermit-fakir who lived alone in a hut on an island, I found the Sheikh sitting on crossed legs upon the verandah, patiently awaiting my arrival. He greeted me with a smile, as I took off my sun-helmet and invited him to come in and have some tea. He thanked me but refused, saying he would enter only for a chat.

An hour afterwards, as a result of that chat, the snake-charmer had accepted me as his pupil. "You are not only my first European pupil—you are but the second pupil I have ever had."

I understood the allusion too well. His first pupil had been his youngest son, whom he had trained for several months to succeed him and take up the same profession after his father's death. One day, after the boy had learnt the secret lore, Moussa sent him out into the desert alone—the first time that he had not accompanied the boy—saying: "Now your training is concluded. Go out and catch your first snake by yourself."

The boy never returned, and when the father went to seek for him, he found him dead.

He lay doubled up, his features and body showing the violent death-throes that accompany the agonizing results of a fatal snake-bite.

His father's explanation was that a snake-charmer was not only made, but born, i.e. he must have an innate tendency to the work. The boy had not this tendency, but the father had selected him for reasons of convenience. However, he said that he had three other sons, and when, through old age, he could no longer carry on, or when he sensed the approach of death, he then would initiate one of them to take his place.

Moussa made me understand that I was not a professional but an honorary pupil, and I had to promise that I would not take up the work of snake-charming for pecuniary profit. The reason why he did not make very clear, but I gathered that he had obtained his own initiation under certain pledges not to reveal the secrets imparted to him, except to a member of his own family whom he was to select and train as his successor. Apparently this was intended to keep the knowledge within the family, thereby placing the latter in an exceptional, profitable and influential position. Moussa explained that his own teacher, therefore, had been his father, Sheikh Mahmed; and that the latter, in turn, had been trained by his grandfather.

Of the last-mentioned gentleman, Moussa told me another anecdote, in illustration of the importance of exercising some control over one's temper when dealing with snakes. He had been engaged, at the end of the summer season, to clear a large building of snakes, and had had a successful "bag" of all the reptiles in the place—except one. The latter was a small but vicious specimen of viper. The snake had encamped inside a hole in the kitchen, from which it obstinately refused to emerge. Again and again the charmer called it forth but without response. At last, he lost his temper and, instead of uttering a fresh invocation to meet the necessity, shouted: "If I cannot charm you to come out—then I will catch you, anyway!" With that Moussa's grandfather plunged his hand into the hole, and tried to grasp the viper. He succeeded and dragged it out, but in doing so got his thumb bitten. As the sharp fangs closed upon his skin, they injected their deadly poison into the flesh. When the venom spread along his hand and arm, the latter swelled out into a huge lump and turned quite black. Within a few hours the unfortunate man died. After a lifetime of immunity during the practice of his calling, he had suddenly been deprived of it. That was a risk of this profession, said the Sheikh; but it was all Allah's will.

It was apparent that snake-charming in Egypt was hardly a vocation to attract numerous recruits, as I had heard of other fatalities. Yet in India I had heard of few charmers being killed. Nevertheless, among the uninitiated populace of India no less than twenty-six thousand had fallen victims to the fatal bites of venomous serpents during the past year—most of the latter snakes being cobras.

Moussa proposed to impart to me a knowledge that would turn away the bite of the most venomous serpent. He bared his right arm above the elbow and showed me a cord bracelet of seven small sewn leather talisman-cases, each about an inch and a quarter square. They made a gaudy display with their various colours, an effect which was enhanced by the coloured woollen skeins of thread whereby they were attached. He explained that each of those flat tiny bags contained a paper inscribed with certain verses of the *Quran* together with some magical spells.

"I always wear these as an extra protection against dangerous snakes," he informed me. "These talismans have been made by the doctrines of magic. It is necessary that you should have one too, and therefore I shall prepare it. Soon I shall bring the written paper first and show you its power."

I asked him a few questions about his feats of the other day.

"What happens to the snakes you catch, Sheikh Moussa?"

"I keep them until they die. I am forbidden to kill them, as then I would lose my power over them."

"But, in that case, you must have a whole Zoological Gardens snake section in your house!" I exclaimed.

He laughed.

"Oh, no! I catch three kinds of snakes. The small ones fight with the scorpions in my baskets and are generally killed. As it is the scorpions who do the killing, I receive no blame!"

I thought this an extremely specious kind of logic and wondered whether or not it would appeal to the avenging angel of the serpent kingdom.

Moussa explained that he could not take the trouble and responsibility of letting the snakes loose again; moreover, once he let them go, they would never return. Nevertheless, there were a few cases where he let snakes loose in the desert.

"Within three or four days, the bad snakes who are wicked and bad-tempered usually turn round in their fury and bite themselves and so commit suicide. The good snakes who are large, I let die a natural death from starvation. So in neither of these two cases do I kill them."

"What is the power whereby you charm the snakes to come out of their holes? Is it a kind of hypnotism?"

"Not exactly. By the honour of Islam, I can only say that it is a power which is passed down from master to disciple at initiation. To utter the invocations alone will not be sufficient to conquer the snakes. The talismans, prayers and commands are all necessary and great helps, as is also the secret invocation which is communicated to the disciple for mental use only, but the principal power to charm the snakes comes from this force which is given over to the pupil by his teacher. Just as a new clergyman in the Christian Church is supposed to receive a certain grace when the bishop lays his hands upon his head in the ceremony of appointment, so the disciple receives the power over snakes which is invisibly passed into him. It is this force which really enables him to control the snakes."

Then the Sheikh told me that he was really a member of a certain Dervish order which specialized in the handling of venomous serpents, and that this order was the only real tribe of magicians using mystic powers to control snakes. These Dervishes had been numerous in Egypt up to a century or so ago, but they had now almost disappeared from modern Egypt. The common snake-charmer had never been initiated into this Dervish order and was consequently dependent upon working with harmless snakes or upon the use of certain substances which protected the skin, or some other inferior method.

Moussa explained that he proposed to transmit a certain degree of that mystic power to me, sufficient to render me immune from the bite of the deadliest serpents and most dangerous scorpions. This, together with the words of certain invocations, both public and secret, which he would communicate to me, as also the promised gift of a written talisman, would constitute my initiation into his Dervish order. I must, however, carry out his detailed instructions which would be given me during the training; I was also to continue to respect the name of Allah and His Prophet, Muhammed. This I agreed to do.

An extraordinary requirement—but one common enough in all initiations by Yogis and fakirs of the Orient—was that, for seven days before the power was transmitted, the disciple had to seclude himself and live only on a little bread and water. He should also devote the week to prayer and meditation, detaching himself from all worldly concerns and interests for the period.

The Sheikh claimed that this secret power, with the secret invocation, had been traditionally passed down since the days of King Solomon, for whom Moussa appeared to have an exaggerated reverence. In the latter respect, he was not alone; for I had discovered that most Egyptian fakirs seemed to regard Solomon as having been himself the first and greatest of fakirs, a supreme master of occult wisdom, and indeed a magician with unlimited powers.

§

In due time the preliminaries were complete; the Sheikh communicated a secret Arabic "Word of Power," which, so he asserted, would influence the serpents if mentally pronounced by any trained person; he also brought me the promised talisman. It was a sheet of paper covered with Arabic writing, mostly magical spells and verses from the *Quran*. He further brought the leather case in which he wished me to enclose it after I had used the paper for a couple of days;

he himself would sew up this case. The latter was a pretty object of red sheepskin leather, one side being branded with criss-cross diagonal lines. A long skein of twisted scarlet, green, and yellow woollen threads ran through one edge of the case to serve as a loop wherewith to keep it attached to one's clothing.

"This talisman will only be useful when you use it, as I have written your name on it," Moussa observed, "and it will be valueless to anyone else. After I have sewn it up, always wear it under your shirt close to the skin, and take care not to lose it; because, if you do, you will never find it again. Meanwhile, carry the paper folded up into a small piece."

Without any fuss or ceremony, other than a laying-on of hands and a lengthy chanted invocation, the final transmission of the mystic power was accomplished. Thenceforth I should be immune against scorpion and snake, he claimed. The initiation had yet to have its value tested; although Moussa admitted that the immunity would last for no more than two years, after which time I should have to seek him out again, if I desired to obtain a renewal of the transmitted power.

# CHAPTER XVII

## I BECOME A SNAKE-CHARMING DERVISH

I PLAYED a sort of overture to my real tuition in charming, by memorizing the Rifa-ee invocations and then handling various kinds of quite harmless snakes. Nevertheless, the latter were quite able and willing to bite me. The sensation of being bitten was exceedingly unpleasant, being something like having an angler's hook ripped through one's skin. However, the wounds were really superficial and free from any trace of venom. The next step was to handle poisonous snakes whose fangs had been extracted. These wretched reptiles, too, were fond of biting a mere novice like myself, until a time arrived when my incantations really seemed to work and when I developed so much confidence that I felt my own will being successfully imposed upon that of the snakes. This matter of courageous faith, concentrated thoughts and incessant will-power, I soon discovered to play quite an important part in rendering the creatures more tractable.

I continued my training by crossing the Nile, and going out into the desert with the Sheikh, hunting for venomous, full-fanged snakes. He captured a couple of them, one being a large cobra with a beautifully coloured green skin streaked with yellow, and the other a smaller thin reptile with a diamond-shaped head and a pattern of diamonds all along its back. We brought them back, safely covered up in his basket, triumphantly to Luxor.

We took up a position in an open part of the garden. Moussa suddenly raised the lid and dipped his hand into the basket, exclaiming:

"Now begins your first lesson. Hold this snake!"

The cobra was outstretched towards me, its head turning to and fro.

I was startled at this sudden command. Never before had I deliberately approached an unguarded snake at close range, much less even attempted to hold one. I hesitated.

"Have no fear!" the Sheikh said, reassuringly.

Instantly I realized that this experience was a test. The wheels of my brain revolved at express speed. Again I hesitated—and who would not hesitate before grasping a deadly, newly-caught cobra, which can bestow death with most horrible agonies. And then I felt, as by some telepathic interplay of thought between myself and my teacher, that to accept fear of the snake at this crucial moment might mean failure to pass the test and, perhaps, the dismissal of my dream of becoming a snake-charmer. I knew that the situation called for an instant decision, whether of acceptance or refusal; obviously the former if I wished to continue this mysterious traffic with the serpent tribe.

"All right!" I said mentally. "Death now or later—*maleesh!* (never mind!") I put out my hand and grasped the round ringed body of the cobra. Instead of experiencing a cold clammy touch, I was surprised to discover that the contact yielded a not unpleasant sensation.

The serpent jerked its head up to look at its new captor. Our eyes met. It stopped its movement and remained in a fixed attitude of watchfulness, as still as a fixed rod.

Again that natural and inevitable feeling of fear passed through me, but it endured no longer than a flash of lightning; I returned instantly to my resolution to go through with the whole thing until the finish, cost what it might, a resolution to which I clung thenceforth with implacable determination.

Moussa looked at me and smiled enthusiastically.

"You see, now you have become its master," he announced proudly.

Whether the snake fully accepted the situation it was too early for me to determine. The serpent species has not earned a reputation for treachery and cunning for nothing; I did not assume that a first victory meant the winning of a war. A novice at the game, I lacked the complete inner certitude so much to be admired in the character of a man like my master.

The cobra began to sway flexibly in my grasp. It twisted to and fro, still keeping its wicked-looking head and baleful eyes turned upon me, and its tiny forked tongue pointed at me. The hiss it let out sounded occasionally like heavy human breathing.

Here was an outlawed creature which did not know, could not be expected to know, the meaning of mercy; which was pitilessly at war with the world: which, like an Ishmaelite, fully understood that it lived in a class apart, the hated enemy of all the rest of the animal kingdom, and of nearly all the human race too.

The serpent brought its small face closer and closer to mine, and I surmised that my second test was at hand. I am not enamoured of life, and I doubt not that death opens another door; but I would prefer to let my vital force ebb away in a good cause. Moussa took the cobra from me and set it down on the ground. I had no wish to handle the snake any longer, to continue to hold this writhing sleek creature; but I was curiously fascinated by it, glad to have had the opportunity of studying it at such close range. It coiled in front of me now, about eighteen inches away, its head and the forepart of its body gracefully raised about the same distance into the air, and continued to watch me closely.

As I returned its gaze, I speculated on the death-dealing potencies of its tiny mouth. All the danger of a serpent lay concentrated in that menacing aperture, just as all its mystery seemed to be concentrated in those fixed lidless eyes.

The bite of an Egyptian cobra injects a poison into the body that quickly paralyses the nerves, either atrophying or destroying the nervous system. This is inevitably followed by heart failure or inability to breathe.

What arrangement had Nature made to provide snakes with such powers of life and death, I silently questioned myself. Finally I asked Moussa to let me examine the interior of the cobra's mouth. He instantly agreed and, gripping it by the neck, forced a stick into the narrow slit of a mouth and revealed its unfamiliar anatomical structure to me.

The opened mouth was a vivid red colour, which made a striking contrast against the green and dull yellow of the skin. I could not help being impressed by the highly efficient biting-mechanism which was thus displayed. The curved teeth which served as fangs were set in the very front of the jaw, one at each corner, and lay tucked up against the upper jaw. I discovered by the action of the mouth in attempting to avoid the stick, which irritatingly prodded the palate, that this pair of poison teeth was not immovably embedded in the jaw; they were worked by a certain muscle so that they could be swung forward to stand semi-erect and then slipped back into place. I could not recollect any other species with movable teeth.

The active fangs were tucked into a covering of mucous membrane and behind them there were other fangs, kept as it were, in reserve. On both sides of each fang there was a tiny bag in which the poison was secreted. The gland which fed this sac probably worked on the same principle as our own salivary glands.

Another point about the fang-tooth was its hollowness. One could trace some analogy between it and the needle of a hypodermic syringe. The cobra could drive the very sharp needle-like edges of its fangs straight into the flesh of its victim, while simultaneously squeezing the muscles of the venom sacs adjacent to its fangs, thus causing the poison to run down the tooth and be injected into the wound; much as the hypodermic needle pierces the flesh while simultaneously drawing the drug out of the barrel of the syringe.

The Sheikh now suggested that I should make my second experiment in the control of snakes by willing the creature to go to sleep, at the same time testing the efficacy of the talisman he had written out for me; as this talisman was essential to the success of my experiment.

He let the cobra go, and retreated to one side. The reptile immediately faced me and fixed those lustrous, unwavering black eyes upon my own. I first tested its watchfulness by slowly walking around it until I had paced a whole circle. The cobra moved its head and its beautifully marked body in perfect parallel unison with each step that I took. Not for one instant did that terrible pair of eyes let go of mine.

Perhaps my movement annoyed it, for it began to rear up a little higher, raising its flattened head, and hissing loudly and angrily; once more shooting forth its black, thread-like tongue and spreading out its regal hood. I had a feeling that whenever a cobra expanded its hood into the elliptical curve as perfect as that of an umbrella, it does so to terrify its victim. The dreadful spectacle-marking on the front of the upraised hood accentuates the effect.

I knew that even without actually lunging forward and biting me to endanger my life, the cobra had only to spit a little spray of the venom into my eyes—which is the usual intention of some of these snakes—to cause perpetual blindness.

I exerted my will and endeavoured to impose it upon the serpent. "Go to sleep!" I commanded mentally. Next I approached a few inches closer, holding the talisman in my right hand, and still giving my silent command. The hissing sound came to an end, the hood contracted, the swaying movement grew more languid, and the cobra lost the regal pose which it had hitherto maintained. I doubled the paper, in the form of a gabled roof, and placed it upon the cobra's head. The snake sank down almost at once, so that I had to replace the talisman. Finally, it became quite feeble and lay prone upon the ground, its sinuous body curled like a letter S in the dust.

Thereafter it never moved but remained rigid. Whether it was really asleep, or in a hypnotic trance, or watchfully but helplessly yielding to the "magic" of the talisman, I did not trouble to determine.

Thus ended my first effort at snake-charming.

§

On a few other occasions, Moussa and I went out on short expeditions to hunt members of the serpent tribe and to bring them back alive. I was unable to detect their whereabouts, but Moussa would collect them from different spots in the desert, or along the less frequented parts of the banks of the Nile, with astonishing celerity. He claimed to be able to smell them and thus track them down; a gift I never acquired, as he said a training of at least a year or two was required, for development into the complete snake-charmer equipped with every professional qualification.

Sometimes the snakes would hiss and even spit at Moussa in their anger when he called them; eventually, however, they always yielded and came sliding limply into his hands. But upon one occasion there was a mishap.

We had caught a horned viper which had given trouble from the start. When at last we tried to coax it to enter the basket, it apparently mistook a movement which the Sheikh made as one of attack—for some snakes are surprisingly nervous creatures—and hit at him in self-defence. The small mouth closed upon his right arm in a trice, and he was bitten. Blood streamed down the skin at once. The gushing red fluid increased in flow and I hastily tied a handkerchief around his wound to staunch it, preparatory to taking such further action as he advised. I hoped the Sheikh had made his last will and testament and that some relative would take care of his wife and children.

But Moussa merely smiled.

"*Maleesh!*" he murmured. "No matter! The viper cannot hurt me. This is only a tooth-bite, not a fang-bite."

I was astounded.

"No snake is permitted to bite me with its poison fangs," he added, "but sometimes I receive what is just a flesh-bite from its ordinary teeth. That has happened before and does not trouble me."

Yes, it was true—the Sheikh was impervious to the reptile bite, however poisonous it was for others. And to prove his immunity Moussa forced the snake to open its mouth and then put his fingers immediately below its poison fangs. At any moment the reptile could, if it wished, bury those fangs into the skin of his fingers and kill him. Yet the fangs did not move and finally he withdrew his hand, unharmed.

The next day there was no inflammation and his wounded arm had half-healed.

People often quoted to me later cases of extracted fangs which they had seen. Though their care for truth was praiseworthy, to connect these examples with our cobras would be to strain credulity to intolerable limits.

As for the two-year immunity which he claimed to have conferred upon me, I can say only that I handled deadly cobras and poisonous vipers several times, and even put them round my neck, yet they never once attacked me. I almost turned them into pets, so interested did I become in these mysterious creatures. Moussa warned me, however, that with reference to scorpions, the black-coloured variety were vicious and disobedient, and that my power might fail to overcome them; also that there was always a slight risk that even a snake of the same character might be encountered. He told me that I might recognize a dangerous snake should I encounter one, by first uttering the secret "Word of Power" before approaching it. If the snake ignored it and did not stop its movement, then it should be left untouched; such a snake might easily turn and kill one, as it was entirely vicious.

I received an unexpected opportunity to deal with a scorpion some time later, when I had parted from the Sheikh and was travelling still farther into Southern Egypt. I put in some time on research work at the magnificent old temple of Edfu, and took the trouble to drop down a hole in the floor of a small room near the sanctuary, as the steps had long since disappeared.

One had to walk with care in these decaying underground places because snakes were especially fond of them. They would wriggle purposely through the tight-fitting crevices in the masonry, which compressed their bodies and so scraped off the old skin when the time had come to shed it. They liked, too, the solitude, the darkness and the shady coolness of such old refuges, and, therefore, frequently teemed in them.

Crawling along an extremely narrow tunnel, which was heavily laden with the undisturbed dust of many centuries, I passed into another dingy passage and eventually arrived in a low subterranean crypt. I recognized immediately that the latter had served for initiation purposes in the cloistered rites of the ancient Mysteries. The place was pitch-dark and I relied on the beam of an electric pocket torch for illumination.

When I had finished a very thorough examination I turned back and retraced my steps into the passage. Suddenly a monstrous yellow scorpion emerged from a crevice in the stone-work and scurried towards my feet. Scorpions have quite a predilection for the underground crypts of old ruins. Owing to the broken character of the flagstones, the all-surrounding darkness, and the roof of the passage being so low, I could not move freely or quickly. I stood my ground, therefore, and pointed my first finger at the poisonous insect. In a loud voice I uttered the "Word of Power," and peremptorily commanded it to stop. Moussa had warned me that I should pronounce the invocation—as indeed all magical invocations—with the utmost mental concentration and strength I could muster.

The scorpion stopped dead still, as though suddenly confronted by some barrier!

It remained in the same spot, transfixed, and did not attempt to move forward or backward during the time I picked my way onward to safety.

For all I can tell, the unfortunate scorpion may still be on the same spot, awaiting the command of release!

On rare occasions Moussa exercised a playful habit of approaching a tree where he knew a scorpion to be hiding, and commanding it to come down. After a short or long delay, a scorpion invariably made its appearance upon the tree and actually leapt down on to the Sheikh's flat turban!

Once when I discussed the mystic power which belonged to the Rifa-ee snake-charming Dervishes and tried to get Moussa, out of his long experience, to define its precise nature, he could or would only say:

"It is only by the power of Allah that a snake yields to us. The snakes trust us as we are forbidden to kill them by our own hand. We do not betray their trust. So our invocations always contain some words from the holy *Quran*."

I am betraying no secrets if I give here the incantation which is used by the Rifa-ee Dervishes, into whose order I was initiated, because this call is the one publicly chanted, and has no doubt been heard, in its original sonorous and poetic Arabic form, by hundreds of uninitiated persons.

So far as mere expression of thought bears weight, I see no reason why the English translation should not be equally effective; although the incantation alone is hardly likely to induce a snake to emerge from its hiding place, or to place its flat head in any one's lap! The words run as follows:

"O thou snake! Come forth! I adjure thee by Allah, if thou art above or if thou art below, that ye come forth!

"None can conquer Allah, and over Him none can prevail. O! my helper in the time of need! In the name of the Holy Place and the Holy Book, I adjure thee to come forth!

"In the name of Him whose splendour has thrown open all doors, come out and submit to the covenant. I am the owner of the Word.

"In the Most Great Name of the Master of all help. I call on thee, by permission of my Sheikh and of the Master of my fraternity, Ahmad el Rifa-ee. Come forth!

"In the name of Solomon the Wise, who holds dominion over all reptiles. Hear! Allah ordereth thee. Come forth, O snake! Come forth! Peace be on thee. I shall harm thee not."

¶

After I parted from Sheikh Moussa, I could not help recurrently thinking that underneath the doctrines and practices of the Rifa-ee Dervishes there lay a remnant of some ancient serpent-worshipping cult, that went back, perhaps, to immeasurable antiquity. I knew that Moussa—good Muhammedan that he was—would strenuously deny this; indeed, I did once tackle him on the point, but he deflected the question with the response that there was no God but Allah! The more I pressed the point, the more he emphasized the supremacy of Allah, until I realized that he either could not or would not grasp my question clearly; so I had perforce to drop the subject.

Putting together what I had learnt from snake-charmers of all kinds; paralleling the evidences of serpent-worship which I had seen openly practised in India, and which I knew had been openly practised in ancient Egypt; and studying my own changed reactions to the snake tribe since the memorable day of my initiation, I was finally forced to the conclusion that my conjecture was a correct one. The more I thought over the matter, the more was the number of evidences which I could cull together in my mind that this strange knowledge was but a relic of one of the Dark Continent's earliest religions.

For I had noticed a gradual but drastic change in my personal attitude towards the reptilian world. No longer did I regard all snakes with the formidable, irrepressible loathing I had formerly felt, the horror which springs up unbidden in every normal human heart. No longer did I perceive in all of them dreaded and implacable enemies of every other living thing. No longer did I fear each one as a creeping incarnation of treachery and deceit. Instead, I had slowly but increasingly come to feel a peculiar admiration for the sheen and sinuous beauty of their bodies and the graceful air of their upreared necks; a strange fascination for their undeniable weirdness and uncanny mystery; and a subtle sense of pity for them. This change was not something that I sought, but something that had grown imperceptibly and of its own accord.

It is a striking contrast that in all Christian countries the serpent is taken as a symbol of evil alone, or of the devil himself, whereas in almost all ancient civilizations and even among most of the few remaining primitive ones to-day, as in Central Africa, it was and is recognized as being divided into two species—the divine and the evil.

All over Africa, all over India, among the Druids and in most parts of Central America where the echoes of Atlantis have lingered, serpent worship has existed as a reality. The mile-long walls of the great Aztec temple ot Mexico were decorated with sculptured serpents.

The Dravidians, who were the aboriginal black-skinned people of India, and who have now mostly been driven to the south, regard the cobra—and especially the spectacle-hooded variety—as a divine creature and hesitate to kill it, although they will kill any other snake without regret.    Some priests there actually keep fangless cobras in the temples, feed them on milk and sugar, and pamper them with ceremonial worship.    Such snakes become quite tame and quickly emerge from their holes in the temple when a reed-pipe is played to them.    When one of them dies it is wrapped up in a shroud and cremated, as if it were a human body.

Many a peasant, whether in the north, south, west, east or centre of India, finds much satisfaction in worshipping the image of a hooded cobra, or in placing food near the hole of a living one, for he regards such a creature as being the bodily vehicle of some higher power, some spirit to be reverenced and honoured.    This notion has been handed down to him through the most ancient traditions of his land, and he accepts it without question, as he accepts so many other strange notions. No other species of snake receives his worship.

In the holy of holies of many a temple, shrouded in darkness or lit by the dimmest of lamps, and across whose threshold no man of alien faith may tread, the sculptured figure of the serpent twines itself around the base of the shrine or rears its hooded head.    Turning to South Africa, Zulus who live far from towns and have not picked up the notions of civilizations, believe that in the special cases of snakes which find their way into houses and huts, the spirits of dead relatives have reincarnated.    Therefore they do not attempt to kill them, but merely attempt to get them out of the house, usually by sending for the witch-doctor, who often combines snake-charming with his many other pursuits.

Several times when looking into a cobra's eyes, I thought of this weird Zulu belief.    Despite their baffling and mysterious fixity, I received occasionally an uncanny and indescribable feeling that there was behind them an intelligence which was almost human.

Once, when I had slung a particularly thick and exceptionally large specimen of a snake around my neck for not more than a single minute, I had experienced a sudden slipping away of my mind from its earthly surroundings, and a bewildering psychic state supervened.    I felt that I was losing my physical moorings and that the inner world of spirits was opening up.    I seemed to depart from our whirling ball of land and water for some dark, ghostly, supra-mundane sphere whose atmosphere was definitely evil.    I did not relish the idea of falling into such a condition and losing my "grip" on things with creeping death so close to my face; I let the snake fall gently to the ground. Immediately, my consciousness reverted to normal and was focused once more on the familiar physical world around me. This happened only once, but it was unforgettable.

Had I sensed the snake's own state of consciousness? Did it function in two worlds at the same time? And was one of them a nether world of horrors? Who can say?

On a jungle expedition in the south of India I had unexpectedly come upon a weird sight, nothing less than a meeting of cobras. A number of the beasts were gathered round in a circle, their bodies raised majestically into the air. What were these hooded heads discussing, I wondered; what mysterious secrets were they communicating to one another? But I must confess that I fled from the sight. One cobra was unpleasant enough in those days—a crowd was more than human feelings could endure.

Among the carved and painted memorials of ancient Egypt the serpent meets the eye at every step. Upon the architrave of the giant entrance pylon to the Temple of Amen-Ra at Karnak there rises two magnificent stone cobras, poised pillars of gracefulness. Not far away the little Temple of Osiris is profusely sculptured with serried ranks of serpents. On the other side of the river, the walls of almost every royal tomb in the Valley of the Dead, where time-shrivelled mummies lie deep in the Theban hills, bear painted witness to the important place which the snake occupied in early Egyptian religion and thought. Many a representation of the public ceremonials of the temples throughout Egypt demonstrates precisely the same thing. And, finally, the shrines where the secret rites of the Mysteries were performed do not fail to add their mute testimony. Upon the summit of every obelisk and the porticoes of most temples the serpent is sculptured. Out of the perfect disk that was emblematical of the much-beloved and ever-worshipped sun, almost always a pair of serpents spread out their hooded heads.

These things had a significant connection with the psychic world and out of this connection—with its possibilities of degenerating into sorcery in evil hands—the evil reputation of the snake symbol developed, as apart from the feared physical qualities of snakes.

The Egyptians recognized this possibility and pictured an

evil serpent as well as a good one. The former was generally drawn crawling, the latter upright. They had their devil in the form of Apepi, the dark, many-folded serpent who was head of the powers of darkness, i.e. the devil.

But there was a higher symbolism which was recognized, and it was this:

The serpent offers a perfect symbol of the energizing creative Force of the Supreme Spirit who created the universe, and of the creation itself. The Pharaohs wore the figure of a hooded serpent in the front of their headdress, as a symbol of their claimed divine descent. The serpent thus stood for divinity as well as—in certain species—for the devil.

The first force that moved across the dark face of the deep at the beginning of Creation was this divine force which was typified by the good serpent. Just as a snake assumes a hundred different patterns in its movements and yet remains one, so the universe assumed unnumbered patterns (shapes or forms of things and creatures) and yet, in its essential nature, remains the one Spirit. Science has begun to endorse the last sentence, merely using another name for Spirit. Just as the snake periodically throws off its old dead skin and assumes a new one, so the forms which compose the universe die and are then, quickly or slowly, thrown back into the primal state of matter. "Dust thou art and to dust thou shalt return." . . . Yet the symbolism does not end there. The new skin of the serpent stands for the new form into which that matter will ultimately be shaped. And just as the serpent continues to live despite the death of its outer skin, so the Spirit is undying and remains immortal despite the death of its outer forms.

The serpent is self-moving; it is unassisted by hands, feet, or other external limbs. So, too, is the Creative Force entirely self-moving as it passes from form to form in its building of a whole world or of a single creature.

When the Egyptians portrayed the scaled serpent biting its own tail, thus forming a complete circle, they meant that to symbolize the created universe itself. The scales are the stars. The act of biting itself symbolizes the self-dissolution of the universe which must one day arrive, when the Spirit withdraws from Matter.

In the symbolism of the snake, there are many other meanings ranging from the divine to the devilish. There is finally the special meaning assigned it in the Mysteries.

It stood in these innermost rites for the working of the Force which freed the soul of man during initiation, a Force which slowly crept through the body of the entranced initiate almost exactly like the slow creeping of a snake.

Thus the serpent symbol rears its head over the antique world, with two distinct heads; as a devil to be fought and dreaded, and a divinity to be reverenced and worshipped; as the Creator of All Things, and as the Source of All Evil.

# CHAPTER XVIII

ALONG pink and brown ridge of hills lies against the sky some miles west of the Nile at Luxor, forming a barrier between the Libyan Desert and the cultivated river valley. Hidden among them is a dry sunburnt gorge where no vegetation grows or can grow; where the soil is either rocky stone or arid sand; and where the only living things are snakes and scorpions. Long buried in this bare valley were the royal dead of vanished Thebes, for it is the famous Valley of the Tombs of the Kings. "Were," I wrote, because many of those mummified bodies have now been extracted from their gloomy caverns and exposed in the stuffy galleries of great museums for all the world to view. And if others still elude discovery, it is not because time and trouble and money are wanting.

There was much that I desired to study in the tombs themselves; in the uncovered temples that lie within a few miles or so of the Valley; in minute fragments of Thebes that now peep above the soil; and along the edges of the Western Desert itself. To make all these frequent and short expeditions from Luxor, there is no animal equal to a good donkey as a means of transport, because it knows how to pick its surefooted way between boulders, over sharp stones and by the edge of precipices.

I had engaged a "boy" as general servant, and one of his first orders was to find a contractor who could supply me with a good beast for these short excursions. Youssef was called a boy in deference to conventional traveller's terminology, although he would never see forty again and although he possessed a wife and three children. He frequently reminded me of the existence of his family; in fact every time I pulled out my purse to settle our accounts. And when I playfully tried to put a snake around his neck, he indignantly complained that if the reptile bit him there would be no one "to give feed to my family!" Apparently, long habit of giving feed to donkeys had caused him to regard his own family as being much on the level with the donkeys in their demands for necessary sustenance. Anyway, he was well-mannered and possessed an excellent sense of humour; in short, I liked him.

He completed negotiations with the contractor and, terms being arranged, he returned in due course with a nice-looking, large-sized, well-saddled white donkey. I climbed on to the animal and it started off. All went well until we reached the river-bank, where we three were taken on to a boat and sailed for the western side of the broad grey Nile. Having disembarked, I mounted again and set off on the seven-mile journey to the Valley.

It did not take more than a quarter of an hour's riding to discover, and to confirm, the fact that the beast belied its attractive looks. When at long last we had covered nearly half the distance I complained to Youssef that either his powers of selection were not up to the high standard which they doubtless usually maintained, or else that the contractor's herd must have been extremely meagre in quality if this animal represented his best specimen. I added that it was quite a lazy creature and I regretted to have to accuse it of being fonder of sleep than of moving. Youssef threw up his hands and turned the white of his eyes to the sky. "In sha Allah!" he exclaimed, astonished. "Who are we to dare to correct the Almighty's handiwork?"

I found his question unanswerable and thereafter relapsed into eternal silence on that particular subject. We left the maize-bearing fields behind; and took little more than a glance at the twin Colossi of Memnon—a pair of giant statues whose perished faces are entirely featureless, whose deformed throne-seated bodies once rested on sentry-duty in front of the pylon of a vanished palace-temple built by Amenhotep III, and who rise fifty feet high above the wheat-field which has replaced the temple. Without noses, without eyes, without ears and without mouths, the Colossi sit as they have sat for centuries, lamenting perhaps, as the Roman visitor Petronianus has scratched on the base, the injuries inflicted upon them by the Persian invader Cambyses. Once a stone causeway stretched back for more than a thousand feet behind them, with pairs of statues and sphinxes marking the sides. All this has gone too. We turned away from the fertile vegetation of the flat Nile land and struck off at a tangent to the river, travelling towards a point where the Theban hills met. We met the usual groups of white-robed men and black-robed women on the road.

We passed a typical village of mud huts, a few low, white-washed houses, a miniature minaret set on a tiny white cupola'd mosque and the inevitable grove of palm trees planted for the sake of their pleasant shade.

I halted near the village well to let the thirsty donkey and its human passenger have a drink. The animal dipped its nose into a strange trough—no less a thing than a broken stone sarcophagus that once may have harboured a Pharaoh!

We moved on and did not stop for the half-destroyed temples of Kurna, nor the excavated mortuary tombs of the Theban nobles at Abd-el-Kurna, nor even the remarkable necropolis of Dira Abun Naga.

I wanted to make my way to the desolate little valley leading to the heights before the blazing sun was upon us. We had set out at dawn and it was not an hour too soon in this summer month. For I knew that on those rock-strewn heights every degree of temperature would be doubled, and the sun's rays thrown back and reflected anew upon me.

Bit by bit we moved westwards along the ancient road and then circled round to reach the foot of the hills, where the ground was strewn with boulders of every shape. Here we entered the first narrow defile.

At last the slow-plodding donkey, treading the dry, sandy, rock-bordered road, brought me to the entrance of the famous Valley where once-powerful Pharaohs had been carried when they lay huddled in death's grip and their earthly pomp had reached its inescapable end.

The ragged pink cliffs which stood up like sentinels on the right and left to guard the way in, looked well against the cobalt blue sky when I gazed up at them. All along the gorge stretched the high silhouette of the ridge. The heights reflected the downbeating glaring white light while the debris upon the ground reflected the intense heat. Hemmed in on both sides by precipitous limestone walls, its complete isolation and utter lack of living green growth showed how extraordinarily suitable the place was for the melancholy purpose to which it had been appropriated—the hiding of the mummies of the kings of Egypt. On the other side slept the nobles and high priests.

I continued up the valley towards the farther end where the opened tombs lay, and where both sides of the ravine had been pitted and perforated with openings for graves, a task not too easy, for each opening had had to be hewn into solid rock. My donkey put its hooves down stiffly as we wound along the dry ravine, for fallen boulders, rough stones, loose quartz and flints littered the narrowing track, and made riding more difficult. Here and there upon the towering sides was a blackened, burnt-up summit. Piles of scintillating stones and chalky chips glared blindingly in the intensely white sunlight. The heat lay heavily over everything like an inescapable fog, and visibly palpitated in the air. Not an inch of shade was available and one seemed to be heading into an enormous furnace. My lips were parched, my tongue was dry. The scene was unutterably desolate and yet there was a certain grandeur about its dreariness.

Not a sound broke the silence, not a bird lifted its song to the heat-burdened desert air; not one green plant reared itself out of the solitudes of stone and sand.

The gaunt hills culminated in a single square-shaped peak whose sloping sides were debris-covered, but even before we reached it the tombs revealed themselves. Here men had dug into the ancient hills, so storied with buried mummies and their treasures, and brought to light those things which had been put away with such care.

¶

The sides of the Valley were simply honeycombed with slanting tunnels that led into the sepulchral chambers, forming a subterranean city of the dead. To descend the flight of rock-cut steps and then enter into the gloomy sloping corridor of one of these tombs was to descend into the nether world. I flashed a beam of torchlight upon the walls. They were covered with a thin stucco that was vividly painted from floor to roof with writhing serpents, royal portraits and priestly figures raising suppliant hands to their deities, sacred barques and guardian spirits, human-headed crocodiles and funerary offerings, scarab-beetles and symbolical bats, all arranged in a series of successive scenes depicting the occupations of the deceased man and his journey in the underworld. Closely set columns of hieroglyphs were also inscribed upon the walls, their object being to assist the adventurous passage of the newly arrived soul, for they were sacred texts taken from *The Book of the Gates* and *The Book of Him who is in the Underworld*. These texts told of the nether world of spirits, of the serpent powers who guarded it, and of a bottomless hell whose blackness was complete. They told, too, how the passage of the soul should be guarded so as to escape the dreadful ordeals, what addresses should be made to the judgment gods, and how the latter should be answered.

I moved deeper and deeper into the tomb, the inclined passage yielding to a chamber, and the latter to another sloping passage, and this repeating itself until I had penetrated nearly three-hundred feet into the hill. Thousands of tons of solid rock mounted above my head. Every inch of the walls was pictured and inscribed, the whole forming a processional of ancient Egyptian life and holding up a mirror to death. In the chief chamber there was a hollow in the floor to take a heavy granite sarcophagus which rested in it. Once, this stone coffin was the last dwelling of a richly jewelled Pharaoh, but his stiff mummy, with its coverings of pitch and linen, had been removed with all the other discovered mummies, to repose in the well-lit rooms of museums and satisfy twentieth-century curiosity.

Having run the gauntlet of multitudinous painted eyes, out of the thick yet cool gloom I emerged at last into the scorching rays and intolerable glare of the late morning sun, only to traverse a few yards of stony track and plunge again into another deep and decorated tomb. Half a dozen tombs were visited in this way, during a cursory survey of long stretches of instructive figured walls that would be revisited for close detailed research on later days. Seti's impressive tomb, although cut into the rock and down into the bowels of the earth more than four-hundred feet long, did not hold me so much as that smaller one of Rameses IX, where I found sculptures and paintings that were outstanding among the Valley tombs. They were more spiritual than most of the others, bright and optimistic, lifting the mind up towards the glorious destiny of man and his unquenchable immortality, rather than depressing it.

Over the portal of the doorway was painted the great red disk of the sun, with Rameses himself worshipping it. The crude symbolism of this was, that as, in Nature, the red westering sun sinks into black night, so the soul of this king had gone down into the dark tomb with him; then, like the inevitable dawning of the same sun, his soul would rise triumphantly again to new life: that just as the sun arose unfailingly in the east each morning after its disappearance and was therefore undying, so the Pharaoh's soul would arise in the spiritual world after traversing the dark regions of the nether world—for it, too, was undying.

But for those who had passed through the initiations of the Ancient Mysteries there was a yet profounder meaning. Death had lost its terrors, for they had already "died" during life; and they knew that the soul would not merely live on after death, but that it would also live again *in the flesh*. The light of my electric torch played upon the left wall of the first passage as I advanced farther, and there I saw the representations of Rameses brought into the presence of the great gods—Osiris and Harakht and Amen-Ra. I moved on, and there was the king burning incense as an act of worship. I passed two chambers above whose doorways were hieroglyphed praisings of the sun-god, and reached another wall where a priest poured out a stream of symbolic characters as in baptism over the Pharaoh's figure—among them the handled cross, key of the Mysteries and emblem of eternal life. And the dress of Rameses had changed as a result, for he now assumed an Osiris-form himself. His soul was released and justified, and he had been truly resurrected, and he had the right to preface his own name with that of the divine Osiris.

For was not his beautiful prayer: "Behold, I am in Thy presence, O Lord of Amenteit. There is no sin in my body. I have not spoken that which is not true knowingly, nor have I done aught with a false heart. Grant Thou that I may be like unto those favoured ones who are in Thy following, and that I may be an Osiris greatly favoured of the Beautiful God, and beloved of the Lord of the World."

And Thoth, who records on his palette the result of the weighing of the heart of the deceased, and delivers the judgment of the great company of the gods, had said: "Hear ye this judgment. The heart of Osiris hath in very truth been weighed, and his soul hath stood as witness for him; it hath been found true by trial in the Great Balance. There hath not been found any wickedness in him; he hath not done harm by his deeds; and he hath not uttered evil report while he was upon earth."

And the great company of the gods had responded: "That which cometh forth from thy mouth shall be declared true.

Osiris victorious is holy and righteous. He hath not sinned, neither hath he done evil against us. It shall not be allowed to the devourer to prevail over him. Entrance into the presence of the god Osiris shall be granted unto him, together with an eternal home in the Fields of Peace."

In the third corridor the king offered a sacrificial statuette of the goddess of Truth to Ptah. Next followed a picture of his own Osirified, stretched-out mummy, and above it the rising sun, out of the radiant disk of which emerged the scarab-beetle —symbol of newly created life and token of sure resurrection of the soul.

I passed through two chambers and descended into the chief burial vault, now plundered of its treasures and bereft of its Pharaoh and his coffins. Only a painted spot indicates the place where his sarcophagus rested. Other emblems of immortality were painted on a wall of this chamber, such as the infant Horus seated in the presence of the winged sun. The vaulted ceiling carried a representation of the starred evening sky, and of the zodiacal constellations that make up the glorious panoply of the heavens.

I returned from these crowded underworlds and paradisaical overworlds to the entrance, scene after scene flickering past me in the lamplight like an unravelling cinema film. Once again the bright glare burst upon me suddenly.

These opened tombs provide a handy illustration of the foolishness of disregarding as baseless all ancient traditions. Diodorus, writing about 55 B.C., mentioned that the records of the Egyptian priests contained references to the fact that forty-seven Pharaohs were buried at Thebes. Modern Egyptologists did not disregard Diodorus's statement, but acted upon it in full faith, and this enabled them to make the discoveries in the Valley of the Kings, which in later years led to the grand climax of the finding of Tutankhamen's tomb of treasures.

But now I wanted to leave the Pharaohs who sought a spurious immortality in death through the means of embalming preparations and linen wrappings! It was late afternoon, the air was heavy with midsummer heat, my palate was parched, and I crossed the stony track in quest of Youssef and his treasured flask of life-sustaining tea. He had gone off somewhere in search of a scrap of shade. Look where I would, he was undiscoverable. Youssef had melted in the heat. But, finally, what my eyes had failed to detect, my ears were able to report. For from the doorway of an out-of-the-way tomb of one of Egypt's renowned warrior-kings, I heard the sonorous refrain of loud and recurrent snoring. I hurried over to that tomb, and beheld a prostrate, white-robed man whose face seemed enwrapped in some delicious dream.

It was Youssef!

¶

The days slipped pleasurably by while I slaked my unquenchable thirst for reasearch into the secret thoughts and sacred expectations of the vanished Theban world. I became as familiar—and sometimes as friendly—with those calm, majestic figures of the gods, and those grave preoccupied faces of their mortal adorers, as I did with the living forms of the present-day inhabitants of Thebes' successor, Luxor. And I noted the psychic signs left in the atmosphere of some of these tombs which marked the mournful declension into sorcerous practices of a once great race.

It was on one of these studious expeditions that I encountered the man whose conversations I have hesitated to record in these chapters, because the implications of some of his statements were beyond my ability to verify by personal investigation and because these statements may either astonish our prosaic century or—more likely—bring down merited ridicule upon his incognito name, and consequently upon myself for having deemed such fables worth reporting. However, I have played the pros and cons in the balance and the scale-pan of the pros has been weighted a trifle heavier than the other. Moreover, it was, and is, this man's wish that I publish these things, whose importance to our time he seemed to rate higher than my own blasé judgment could rate it.

I had put in a good day's research among the Tombs of the Kings, having started off soon after daybreak and continued till a late hour in the afternoon. To get home more quickly, I had taken the bridle-path which went over the Libyan Mountains and descended in the vicinity of the unique terraced cliff-temple of Deir el Bahri, and thus avoided, at the price of a stiff mountain climb, the considerable detour made by the ancient road around those mountains.

Here the donkey which had proved so disappointing at first, but to which I had gradually become reconciled—and indeed almost affectionate—demonstrated its real worth in picking its sure-footed way up the steep precipice. Each hoof of the once-abused animal was planted efficiently amongst the slippery debris of loose stones and crumbling rock that formed our track; I made no attempt to guide the donkey; it was unnecessary because its unerring instinct knew better than I where to plant those hooves. It was really quite powerful and was much taller than those seen in England, being about the size of a small mule.    Up and up we struggled to ascend the high peak whose towering summit overtops the entire ridge, while the terrific sun poured its relentless rays upon us both. There were long stretches of the track and a few dangerous bends where I had to dismount and let the donkey precede me for some distance, in order not to overtax its strength.    I pressed my feet into the stirrups as the donkey approached the end of its climb up the slippery gorge, to keep from falling off. When the top was gained, I slid off the panting creature's back and let it rest; I looked at the magnificent panorama which stretched itself out two thousand feet below.    The peak completely dominated the surrounding hills and level plain.    There was a striking contrast between the yellow desert and the lush green of the irrigated lands.    The brooding peace of this spectacle brought me a definite sense of spiritual comfort. What a spot in which to enter into communion with Nature! The entire scene rested in silence and I could not resist the feeling of having shaken off all ties with the world beyond.

I turned and moved a few steps—and then I noticed the stranger.

He sat—or rather squatted on crossed legs—upon a low boulder, whose top he had carefully covered with a cloth.    His head was turbaned; long, raven-black hair, tinged with grey, crept out of its white folds; it remained unmoved; and he too seemed to be gazing at the grand spectacle which Nature had unfolded at our feet.    He was a small man with small feet, and neatly dressed in a dark grey robe which was cut high at the neck.    Although the face was strengthened by a goatee beard, he gave the impression of someone aged forty or thereabouts.    Not until he turned his head at last in my direction did I observe his eyes.    As the full force of his gaze was bent upon me, I experienced an indescribable sensation of standing in the presence of an utterly unusual man.    I felt that this meeting would be recorded for ever in my memory.

Those eyes were the most striking feature of a striking face. They were large and beautiful, perfect circles of luminous colour, and the whites were so pronounced as to give almost supernatural depth to the jet-black pupils.

We looked at each other in silence for full two minutes. There was such authority and distinction in his face that I thought it almost impertinent to address him first. What his first words to me were I shall, alas! never remember, for my mind seemed to haze over even before he spoke. Some hidden gland of latent clairvoyant vision inside my head, began to stir into sudden function. I saw a radiant spoked wheel of light revolve before me and slightly above my head, at high speed. With its working there was a receding of my physical moorings, and an entry into some supernormal and ethereal state of consciousness.

Suffice to say that he did address me, when the vision of the whirling wheel died away; my mind returned to realize that I stood on the top of the loftiest peak of the Theban hills, and was surrounded by an outspread scene of desolate grandeur.

I broke the silence by greeting him with "Good afternoon" in Arabic. He responded immediately, speaking perfectly-accented English. Indeed, had I shut my eyes I could have imagined some English-born college graduate was replying, instead of this long-robed Oriental.

And, before I could think over what form my introductory words should take, I unexpectedly found myself blurting out, as though urged by an interior force:

"Sir, I feel sure that you will understand a peculiar experience which I have just had whilst standing near to you." I described my unexpected vision to him.

He gazed meditatively at me, then nodded his head.

"I do," he replied, quietly.

"I am sensitive to atmospheres, and the fact that this thing happened when your personality was brought into contact with mine makes me believe that you possess some unusual power," I continued.

Again his eyes studied me. After the pause he said:

"I deliberately wanted you to have that experience. I willed that it should silently carry to you a certain message—and it has!"

"You mean——?"

"That now you recognize the Order to which I belong."

It was true.  I had discovered in him every sign and token which identifies the high-grade Fakir or Yogi.  Even without the memory of my extraordinary experience, I had but to look into his eyes to obtain intuitive confirmation.

What attracted most attention and compelled most admiration was the size and quality of his eyes.  They were large and lustrous, strong and commanding, strangely long-fixed when they gazed at me.  As I talked to him, there crept over me an irresistible sensation of their duplex power, penetrative and hypnotic at the same time.  They read my soul and they then ruled it.  They drew from my mind some of its secrets and they compelled me to remain passive before him.

"This is indeed an unexpected pleasure," I exclaimed.  "It is astonishing to me that the only person I should meet in this wild deserted region should be one of your Order."

"You think so?" he responded.  "I am not astonished. The hour has struck for this meeting.  It is not mere chance that you are talking to me now.  I tell you that a higher power than chance has first ordained and then arranged our meeting."

I listened with mildly anticipatory thrill.  My thoughts were scurrying to and fro in an effort to take stock of the situation, while my feelings naturally slipped into the mood of veneration which a man of spiritual attainments always draws from me.

And he went on to tell me how the ways of some men cross and criss-cross at the bidding of unseen forces, and how seeming coincidences may be pre-arranged links in a chain of causes destined to have certain effects.  He told me other things, too, calmly referring to himself—without the slightest vanity but as a mere statement of an existent fact—as an Adept.

"It is a word which I prefer to any other; it was good enough for the ancients—including the Egyptians—and it is good enough for me.  In those days the Adept was known and his status accepted; to-day he is practically unknown and the mere fact of his existence scornfully disputed.  But the wheel will turn, and your century will be compelled to recognize that the law of spiritual evolution is ever at work, creating inevitably those who can freely function as spiritual beings no less than as material ones."

I felt that what he had told me was true.  He was indeed one of those mysterious men of whom Eastern tradition not infrequently speaks—those Adepts who had entered into the councils of the gods and knew the deepest spiritual secrets man could never learn.

They prefer to work in silence and secrecy rather than be hampered by the misunderstanding world, and where a public channel must be found, not seldom they send forth their disciples, who thus become foils for the criticism of the ignorant and targets for the barbed arrows of the malicious.

The other man said that he could exchange thoughts with his fellow Adepts at will and at any distance; that an Adept could temporarily use the body of another person—generally a disciple—by a process technically called "over-shadowing," during which he projects his soul into the other's body, that other being perfectly ready and willing and receptive and passive.

"I have been waiting for you here," he remarked with a slight smile. "You are writing. There is a message to be given to the world. Take it down when I shall give it to you, for it is important. Meanwhile our meeting to-day is but introductory, Mr. Paul Brunton!"

I drew back with a start. How had he ascertained my name? But, of course, the Adepts were famed for their extraordinary powers of mind-reading, even at a long distance.

"May I know your name, too?" I ventured.

He pursed his lips and looked across the panoramic landscape below the hill. I watched his noble-looking face and waited for an answer.

"Yes, you may," he rejoined at length. "But it is for your private information alone—not for your writings. I do not want my identity revealed. Call me Ra-Mak-Hotep. Yes, it is an ancient Egyptian name and your Egyptologists can doubtless offer an excellent literal interpretation of the words—but for me it means only one thing: *at peace*. Egypt is not my home. To-day, the whole world is my home. Asia, Africa, Europe and America—I know all these lands and move through them. I am an Easterner in body only, for in mind I belong to no single country and in heart I belong only to Peace."

He spoke somewhat quickly, forcibly and feelingly, yet it was quite obvious that all his feelings were under perfect control.

For more than an hour we talked of spiritual things, sitting on the hill-top under a sun whose light still glared in one's eyes and whose heat still caressed one closely. Yet I forgot these conditions in my absorbed interest in this man and his words. He told me of some matters which concerned the world, and of many others which concerned only myself. He gave me precise instructions and special exercises in connection with my own efforts to arrive at a degree of spiritual equilibrium and enlightenment beyond that which I had so far attained. He spoke frankly and critically, even sternly, of certain obstacles in my path, arising out of my personal faults. Finally, he fixed an appointment with me for the following day, near the Roman altar, inside the colonnade that stands on the Nile bank at the Temple of Luxor.

Without rising from his rocky seat, he bade me farewell, excusing himself from further conversation on account of his being extremely busy and with much to do at the moment.

I left him regretfully, loath to part from one whose conversation was so original and fascinating, and whose personality was so inspiring and uplifting.

The descent of the hill was steep and slithery; I made it on foot down the rock and rubble, holding the donkey's rein in one hand. When we reached the base I mounted the saddle and took a last look at the peak, which loomed up so portentously.

Ra-Mak-Hotep had not even begun his return journey. He was evidently still squatting on that bleak hill-top.

What could he be doing up there, to keep him "extremely busy" while sitting as immobile as a statue? Would he still be there when the shadows of dusk deepened over the pink terraces of the Libyan Hills?

# CHAPTER XIX

THE second meeting duly took place in the ruined Temple of Luxor. I sat on a long block of stone carved with hieroglyphs, while the Adept squatted on cross-legs on the same block, and faced me. My note-book was prepared and, with pen poised expectantly, I was ready to take down his message; to inscribe on the white sheets the less picturesque characters of our twentieth-century system of hieroglyphs—shorthand!

Ra-Mak-Hotep wasted no time on preliminaries but plunged straightway into the subject of his message:

"Those who broke open the tombs of ancient Egypt have released forces upon the world that have endangered it. Both the tomb robbers of long ago and the archæologists of our own days have all unwittingly opened the tombs of those who dealt in black magic. For in the final cycle of Egyptian history there was a great degeneration of the men of knowledge—the priesthood—and sorcery and the black arts were commonly practised. When the white light of truth which was formerly shining through the pure Egyptian religion became dimmed, and the noisome shadows of false, materialistic doctrines crept in to replace it, the practice of mummification arose, together with all the elaborate accompanying rituals. Yet, under the misleading and cunningly perverted teachings which supported this practice, there was an element of secret self-interest which sought to keep a long-preserved physical link with the physical world through the embalmment of the body.

"This practice originally was intended only for the Adept-Kings of Egypt's prehistoric golden age, and for the spiritually advanced High Priests who were true channels of God, that their material bodies, impregnated with their holy power, might continue to exist and serve as focuses radiating that power into the world.

"A kind of ancestor-worship also developed, under which the bodies of the dead were embalmed, merely as a formal rite to show succeeding generations what their deceased ancestors looked like. It was really a hollow imitation of the mummification which was practised in earlier epochs of Egypt to preserve holy relics of good kings and priests. For in the dark period which later descended on Egypt, when it was bereft of true spiritual light and when the hell-forces of the nether world were evoked by those with much knowledge but little compassion, the instructed men of the priestly and ruling classes caused their own bodies to be embalmed. This was done, sometimes for the purposes of black magic, sometimes out of fear of the spirit's destruction in the purgatory that awaited it after death, and sometimes out of ignorant conformity to custom. In almost every case, before such a man passed out at death, he arranged for and had his tomb prepared whilst he was alive. After the preparation of the physical tomb he invoked (or had invoked for him by a priest of sufficient knowledge) a spirit-entity, an artificial elemental creation, imperceptible to bodily senses, sometimes good but more often bad, to protect and watch his mummy and act as a guardian spirit over his tomb.

"Further to protect these embalmed bodies, the tombs were first hidden with *cunning* care and then it was generally taught to the people that any profaner of these tombs would be visited by the spirit-powers with the most dreadful punishment. This teaching was believed, and those tombs were long left in peace. But with the increasing decay of the priesthood and rulers, even the people began to lose their superstitious faith, and tomb-robberies commenced, for the sake of plundering the jewels which were buried with almost every mummy of an important personage.

"It was true that wherever the embalmed body was that of a person with some knowledge of magic, or under the protection and guidance of someone with such knowledge, spirit-powers had been invoked to protect those tombs and punish intruders. Those powers were often exceedingly evil, menacing and destructive. They existed within the closed tombs, and could continue to exist, for thousands of years. Hence your archæologists who, in all ignorance, break open such spirit-shielded graves, do so at their own peril.

"Yet if it were merely a matter which affected the safety of archæologists and their families alone, what I have to tell you would be of little importance. But it is not. It is a matter that affects the safety of the whole world.

"For among the tombs of high and low personages whom they excavate, there are those which were so protected. Every such tomb which has been unsealed lets out, like a flood, a rush of pent-up noxious evil spirit-entities upon our *physical* world. Each mummy that is taken out of such a tomb and transported to your European and American museums, carries with it the etheric link with those entities, and hence their awful influence. Those influences can bring only harm to the world, harm of various kinds, even to the point of destructively affecting the destinies of nations. You Westerners have no shield against them, and because they are invisible to you, they are none the less potent.

"When your world has come to realize that evil spirits are imprisoned in a number of those tombs, it may be too late; for by then all the tombs will have been opened, and those devilish creatures will have made their escape. Among other things they are and will be responsible for international treacheries. Ignorance of Nature's laws does not excuse man from suffering whenever he transgresses against those laws; and ignorance of the existence of evil, magical forces does not excuse your century from suffering the punishment which your unnecessary intrusions into their realms will bring upon it.

"These artificially-created elemental spirits have been released in sufficient numbers during the present century to terrorize the world from their psychic realm, which is immaterial enough to be invisible but close enough to influence the physical existences of the living. We who hold the spiritual welfare of mankind at heart, battle against these dark forces on their own levels, yet we are not permitted by Nature's laws to destroy them any more than we are permitted to destroy living men whom we know to be potent dangers to their fellow beings. Our powers are restricted to shielding persons and institutions under our especial protection.

"Those objects which are taken out of the tombs along with the mummies—such as scarabs, jewels, amulets and furniture —carry with them the influence of those tombs. If the latter were not magically linked up with evil entities, then no harm could result from their appropriation and rifling, but if they were so linked, then their unsealing may bring misfortune and disaster. But the ordinary archæologists and Egyptologists, unaware of such facts and unable to detect the difference between the two, delve into both alike. Whether it heeds it or not, let the world receive this message: *let it not meddle with tombs whose psychic nature men do not understand. Let the world stop opening these graves until it has acquired sufficient knowledge to comprehend the serious results of what it is doing.*

"Most of the kings had some degree of occult powers, whether for good or for evil purposes, for they were initiated in them by their High Priests.

"Originally, the magical powers of injuring other people was used only for self-defence or to hinder criminal persons, but with the fall of Egypt's higher ideals this knowledge was perverted for evil ends such as injuring enemies from a distance or removing those who stood in the path of the magician's (or his patron's) ambition. The knowledge was also used for the shielding of the tombs.

"Every opening of an ancient Egyptian tomb may be an unconscious intercourse with invisible forces of a dangerous character. Even through the opening of the tomb of a king who had a good soul and possessed advanced powers, injury may come to the world as punishment for thus disturbing the grave of an advanced soul. Nevertheless, the objects—such as scarabs—taken from his grave will not carry a noxious influence, but, on the contrary, a beneficent one. Yet if the object is owned by a person with evil thoughts, it will not help him; its benefits being only for those with good thoughts. Which last rule applies, however noble the soul of the departed and however lasting his spiritual influence. King Tutankhamen, for instance, was such a man. He possessed much occult knowledge and a spiritual soul. The opening of his tomb has brought suffering on the violators; and also, in untraceable ways, on the world at large. During the next few years the world will suffer and pay for such desecrations of Egypt's dead, although these material troubles will be turned to spiritual benefit.

¶

"Therefore, I repeat that foreigners who for the sake of hidden treasures, or that exaggerated curiosity which often disguises itself as scientific enquiry, seek to exploit any ancient country where magic was much understood and practised, take grave risks. There are secret tombs of the great Lamas at Lhassa, in Tibet, whose existence partly accounts for the reluctance of the Tibetans to allow foreigners to enter their country. Yet a day will come when people may be permitted to see those tombs and interfere with them, bringing consequent disasters upon themselves.

"In ancient times, Egypt was the chief centre of magical knowledge and practice. In magic, either white or black, i.e. used for good or evil purposes, Egypt excelled even India. To-day, those powerful psychic forces let loose in the past, still affect the country and its people—again either for uplifting or unfortunate results. Some of the latter, for instance, are diseases, like eczema, which are simply the consequence of evil, magical influences still persisting in the land and afflicting living Egyptians.

"Let this warning go out through your pen. Now you may understand why we have met. Even if it be scorned and ignored, my duty and yours—if you will accept it—shall have been done. Nature's laws do not pardon ignorance; but even that excuse shall have gone."

Thus ended Ra-Mak-Hotep's message. I have faithfully transcribed it and have set it down here for what it is worth.

§

We met a few more times, the Adept and I, and then I was called away to pursue my travels farther south. At each of our meetings he stored my head with information about the tenets of the mysterious fraternity to which he belonged. It was during a reference to some experiences of mine in India, where I had met a young Yogi who claimed that his Master was more than four hundred years old, that Ra-Mak-Hotep gravely announced the startling and incredible information that some Adepts who had lived and moved in ancient Egypt were still alive!

I shall not quickly forget the exclamations of astonishment with which I greeted his statement.

The pith of his assertions was that there are Adepts whose bodies lie in a comatose state in certain Egyptian tombs which have not yet been discovered, and which, he claimed, would never be discovered by the ordinary archæologist.

"The tombs of these great Adepts are too well-guarded and

will never be found by your 'diggers,' " he explained. "Those tombs are not tombs of the dead, but of the living. They contain, not mummies, but the bodies of Adepts in a unique state which the word 'trance' most nearly describes. You have discovered in India that fakirs have permitted themselves to be buried for short or long periods of time whilst keeping their bodies in an entranced state.[1] The function of their breathing organs was completely suspended during the period of burial. Up to a certain point, the Egyptian Adepts are in a similar state, but their knowledge is far more profound, and they have kept their bodies entranced, yet alive, for thousands of years.

"Moreover, there is one vital difference between them and those Hindu fakirs. The latter fall into a totally unconscious state during their burial, and remember nothing until they awaken again—unless they are Adepts, in which case they

---

[1] In my account of the Indian Yogis, *A Search in Secret India*, a reference to one of these fakirs appears on page 93. It may be of interest to supplement that reference with the following further details, which I have taken from Sir Claude Wade's official account.

The fakir was buried alive in a box which was placed in a cell three feet below the floor and with a guard comprising two companies of soldiers. Four sentries were furnished and relieved every two hours, night and day to guard the building from intrusion.

"On opening the box," wrote Sir Claude, "we saw the figure enclosed in a bag of white linen fastened by a string over the head. The servant began pouring warm water over the figure—the legs and arms of the body were shrivelled and stiff, the face full, the head reclining on the shoulder like that of a corpse. I then called to the medical gentleman who was attending me to come down and inspect the body, which he did, but could discover no pulsation in the heart, temples or arm. There was, however, a heat about the region of the brain which existed in no other part of the body. The process of resuscitation including bathing with hot water, friction, the removal of wax and cotton pledgets from the nostrils and ears, the rubbing of the eyelids with clarified butter, and, what will appear most curious to many, the application of a hot wheaten cake about an inch thick to the top of the head. After the cake had been applied for the third time, the body was violently convulsed, the nostrils became inflated, the respiration ensued, and the limbs assumed a natural fullness, but the pulsation was still faintly perceptible. The tongue was then annointed with clarified butter, the eyeballs became dilated and recovered their natural colour, and the fakir recognized those present and spoke."

I remember a very old Indian, who had witnessed a case of burying a Yogi alive for twenty-seven days. He told me that when the man had been disinterred and resuscitated, the air rushed into his lungs with a whistling noise, like that of a steam-whistle.

could never be persuaded to give a public demonstration of their powers. The Egyptian Adepts, however, remain fully conscious during their interment, and although their bodies are in coma, their spirits are free and working. In India you visited the Sage Who Never Speaks, who lives near Madras, and on the first occasion you found him in a profound trance, seemingly as though dead. Yet you must know that his mind was very much alive, because on your second visit he not only knew all about your first one, but mentioned his objection to your having attempted to take his photograph then. Such a man functions in the inner realms of being, or even on the physical realm by using an etheric body. The buried Egyptian Adepts are mentally in a similar condition while physically their bodies are, of course, much more profoundly entranced. Their spirits move and travel, their minds think in a condition of full consciousness and they have the advantage of being aware of two worlds—the material and the spirit worlds.

"Their bodies are hidden in undiscoverable tombs, which await the return of their spirits. One day the latter will re-animate those comatose bodies, which will then step forth into the outer world again. The process of re-animation will have to be performed by the right persons, who possess the necessary knowledge. Part of the ritual of awakening will consist in chanting certain secret 'Words of Power.' It may seem curious to you, but their bodies are apparently embalmed, for they lie swathed in linen and enclosed in mummy coffins. There is, however, the vital difference that they have never had their hearts cut out as was done with real mummies. All their vital organs remain intact, except that they have collapsed stomachs, due to the fact that no food has been intaken since the beginning of their entrancement. Another difference is that the living Adepts have had their faces and bodies entirely covered with a coating of wax. This coating was applied after the state of entrancement had been induced.

"Their tombs are well concealed, and their number is extremely small—naturally, for only highly advanced Adepts could enter this state and not all Adepts were willing to do so. I do not like to use the word 'trance' in their case because it gives a wrong impression, but I know no other word which can fitly be employed. Their condition is quite different, for instance, from the trance of spiritualist mediums and hypnotic subjects. There are really profound degrees of trance which modern investigators have never traced. All such conditions which they have contacted are superficial in comparison with the profound and unique condition of the entombed Egyptian Adepts. In the repose of the latter there is really much activity; they are not really in trance states, as the world understands that word.

"There is one Adept who has been in his tomb since 260 B.C.; another since more than 3000 B.C.; still another who has lain there for 10,000 years! They are all working very actively in secret for the spiritual welfare of mankind. They know what is going on in the entire world, despite the fact that their bodies are interred. They are perfect men. By that I mean that their bodies cannot be touched—not even by any insect or parasite —such is the tremendous radiation of their spiritual forces. Moreover, they are in constant telepathic communication with certain living Adepts of our time who themselves possess a functioning body. The spiritual treasures preserved by those ancient Egyptian Adepts are handed over to these living Adepts. When the time comes to awaken them, the ritual of arousal will have to be performed by one of the latter."

# Epilogue

AND after I had wandered afar throughout the whole length of this hoary land of Egypt and witnessed divers more curious things, I turned my steps homeward to my good friends, who sit in eternal meditation on the edge of the Libyan Desert.

"Tell me, O wise Sphinx!" I cried, "whither I may go to rest my tired feet, which seem to have walked enow along the dusty road of life?"

And the Sphinx made response:

"Ask thy question of the One whose lonely child I am, whose womb brought me forth to endure the sorrowful buffetings of this world. For I am Man himself, and yonder is my mother, Earth. Ask her!"

So I trod on a little farther and came to the Great Pyramid. And I went inside the dark passage and crawled down into the deep bowels of the earth, into the dismal subterranean vault itself.

And I uttered the pass-words of greeting, according to my instruction from the seventh verse of the sixty-fourth chapter of the most ancient book in all Egypt:

"Hail! Lord of the Shrine Which Standeth in the Middle of the Earth!"

Thereupon I sat down on the rocky floor and plunged my mind into its own native quietude, patiently waiting for an answer.

When at last the Great One, the Master of the Divine House, made his appearance, I begged him to lead me into the presence of She who is called "The Mistress of the Hidden Temple," who is none other than the Living Soul of Our Earth.

And the Master yielded to my strong entreaty and conducted me through a secret door into the Temple which lieth hid hereabouts. The divine Mother received me most graciously, yet remained seated at a distance, and bade me state my request.

To her I repeated my enquiry:

"Tell me, O Mistress of the Hidden Temple, whither I may go rest my tired feet, which seem to have walked enow along the dusty of life?"

*She gazed long and earnestly into my eyes before She spoke forth in answer:*

*"Seven ways are open before thee, O Seeker. Seven steps await to be mounted by the man who would enter into my secret chamber. Seven lessons must be learnt by those of thy human race who would see my face unveiled. Not till thou hast travelled all the ways, climbed all the steps, and mastered all the lessons canst thou hope to find rest for thy feet or peace for thy soul."*

*I heard her mellow voice, which seemed to speak with a myriad æons of age behind its calm tones, reverberating across the Great Hall of the Temple.*

*"What are those ways, O divine Mother?"*

*And She said:*

*"The Road that leadeth to Many Houses and the Track that Leadeth into the Desert, the Street that Groweth Red Flowers; the Ascent of High Mountains and the Descent into Dark Caves, the Path of Ever-Wandering and the Way of Sitting Still."*

*I asked:*

*"What are those seven steps?"*

*She answered:*

*"The first is Tears, the second Prayer, the third Work, the fourth Rest, the fifth Death, the sixth is Life and the last is Pity."*

*"And what of the seven lessons that man must learn, O Mother?"*

*And She made response:*

*"Pleasure is the first and easiest, Pain is the next, Hate is the third, Illusion the fourth, Truth the fifth, Love is sixth and Peace must be learnt at the end."*

*And I wondered at these things.*

*Then the Mistress of the Hidden Temple withdrew from the Great Hall and I saw that behind her there had been a great golden star, and within the star a radiant crown and two silver crescents. Below the crown there was a white cross, and around the arms of the cross were seven red roses.*

*And the wall behind was deep blue, and upon it there suddenly appeared many words, brilliant with light like set jewels. And of those words I was commanded to read those only which were at the end.*

*And those words were:*

*"For Egypt is the image of the things of heaven, and truly a temp* *of the whole world.*

*"And when Egypt shall have witnessed these things, then*

*Lord and Father who is the Supreme God, First in Power and Governor of the World, shall look into the hearts and deeds of men and, by His will, shall recall them to their ancient goodness, in order that the world itself may truly appear to be an adorable work of His hands."*

## COMMENTARY ON EPILOGUE

(as given by the Author to explain the symbolic meanings.)

*Many Houses-* In temples there are chapels, shrines, crypts, auditoriums and each serves one purpose. The many houses are to get a rounded experience, to fulfill you as a man, to build up the different sides of your nature. You must harmonize them. Each house is one side of your being—also what is outside (society is the house of others).

*Track into the Desert-* The hermit withdraws to find peace (in nature) after turning from the world (first outwardly and then inwardly) from finding satisfaction in human things (society and human nature).

*Street that Grows Red Flowers-* The astral, the passions which beset a person who has to attain self-purification. The flowers of passion are inherited from the animal nature, but we are not animals alone so we must control them. This Street is our heritage from the animal—we must claim our manhood, by controlling the animal.

*Ascent of High Mtns.-* Aspiration is essential to lift you from the level where you are. This is the longing for the higher being. You need courage to do it. Because you are lifting yourself out of the herd who are satisfied with small satisfactions, you climb alone.

*...scent of Dark Caves-* These are phases where you don't see your way at ...you are groping and surrounded by darkness. The darkness is the ...tainty—i.e., whether you are going forwards or backwards. When this ...es acute, it is the dark night of the soul, where there is great spiritual ...ss, deadness. You are inwardly dead and your aspiration calms down ...quite still. This darkness must be borne (as it too will pass).

*...f Ever Wandering-* This is the path of inability in being satisfied ...what has been achieved. Must go on seeking—the thirst for ...edge. May go through different teachings and assimilate something ...each. During this time you are a wandering scholar and seeker.

*...of Sitting Still-* In the end you must drop all aspiration, the visiting of ...rs and gurus. Must be still and let the God within lead and deliver ... You must rely on the God within.

...nding on your past history you must travel these paths more or less.

...- We must all go through suffering to show us that the world is not ...it seems to be, i.e., a pleasureable place.

*...r-* Pray for guidance and help.

...You must work on yourself to make yourself better.

*Rest-* Now the balance is turned and you have reached the middle point, the end of the long path and the beginning of the short. You rest from your efforts on the long path (the disciplines). Sum up what you have gained. Now you can rest from those efforts, this gives peace. You're now on the short path.

*Death-* The death of the ego is revealed on the short path. The life that is developed in the Overself is causing the ego to die without your effort.

*Life-* The stage where you get the conscious union with the life, mind, and power—the conscious being behind the universe (Isvara). There is harmony with Isvara and His will.

*Pity-* After the harmony and oneness with Isvara you have the insight and inner peace. Now comes the feeling that you are all right but what about the others who are not finding or looking. Compassion or pity awakens. This is the last step because you then have to retrace your steps and place yourself in other's shoes and lift them to that which they can do next. This is done in various ways—publicly, secretly, through lectures, writing, institutions. Some remain unknown, others known.

7 Lessons:

*Pleasure-* Is the easiest to learn; there is temporary joy but is always followed by pain. Having expanded from pleasure there follows the contraction by pain.

*Pain-* Gives valuable counterpart to the lessons of pleasure.

*Hate-* Hatred breeds only more hatred, it never ends. We must learn about karma and that hate boomerangs. Must learn to take the opposite of hate which is compassion or love. The effects of hate afflict others as well as yourself. Nations also suffer in this way.

*Illusion-* Wake up to the illusory nature of the world and your personal life, this is the short path. We have metaphysics to understand it intellectually and enough experience to see it in life and to begin to see through it. Now you are moving into the consciousness of the Overself. You see how the illusion is so little in comparison with the real.

*Truth-* This is the hardest to bear. It needs to be faced for oneself a oneself, the truth that the personal life has in the end to go (for there immortality for the personality). This has to be faced and accepted a the truth of the whole universe—all is doomed to disintegrate. But it by merger, by being lost in the great ocean of Being, so it is not a loss.

*Love-* The great harmony, the music of the spheres, the cosmic harm The tremendous meaning in the intent of God which may not al appeal to man. This is the loving relation between men and between and God.

*Peace-* Here no further demands or desires are made and you are satis with the being that you are within you. There is no more fo reincarnation (for we bring ourselves back through our desires). V freed from these you have the peace. This is not appreciated unti experience is had. Older souls have had it all and therefore appreciate peace—it is a matter of the age or maturity of the soul.

At the end of the Epilogue the 'Governor' is Isvara; corresponds wit insight—i.e., to see the world as the work of His hands.